DETROIT
RED WINGS

A Curated History of Hockeytown

HELENE ST. JAMES

THE FRANCHISE

TRIUMPH
BOOKS

Library of Congress Cataloging-in-Publication Data
Names: St. James, Helene, author.
Title: The franchise: Detroit Red Wings: a curated history of Hockeytown / Helene St. James.
Other titles: Detroit Red Wings
Description: Chicago: Triumph Books, 2024.
Identifiers: LCCN 2024020862 | ISBN 9781637276464 (hardcover)
Subjects: LCSH: Detroit Red Wings (Hockey team)—History. | National Hockey League—History. | BISAC: SPORTS & RECREATION / Winter Sports / Hockey | TRAVEL / United States / Midwest / West North Central (IA, KS, MN, MO, ND, NE, SD)
Classification: LCC GV848.D47 S724 2024 | DDC 796.962/640977434—dc23/eng/20240509
LC record available at https://lccn.loc.gov/2024020862

This book is available in quantity at special discounts for your group or organization. For further information, contact:

Triumph Books LLC
814 North Franklin Street
Chicago, Illinois 60610
(312) 337-0747
www.triumphbooks.com

Printed in U.S.A.
ISBN: 978-1-63727-646-4
Design by Preston Pisellini
Page production by Patricia Frey

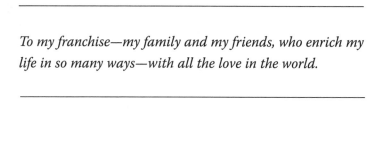

To my franchise—my family and my friends, who enrich my life in so many ways—with all the love in the world.

CONTENTS

PART 4 Russian Revolution

PART 5 Tough Guys

PART 6 How Swede It Was

PART 7 The Brain Trust

PART 8 Rivalries

PART 9 Great Lines

PART 10 Three of a Kind

Foreword

WHEN I WAS ACQUIRED BY THE RED WINGS FROM THE Winnipeg Jets on June 30, 1993, my first thought was, *How am I possibly going to make the Detroit Red Wings if I couldn't make the Winnipeg Jets?* But I was thrilled to be getting a new start, even if it was with one of the best teams in the NHL.

Training camp went well for me, and even though I started the season in the minor leagues with Adirondack, the Wings called me up in the new year. I will never forget my first game as a Detroit Red Wing, January 25, 1994, versus the Chicago Blackhawks.

Sitting in the dressing room before the game it was incredible to look around and see all these great players on the Red Wings—Steve Yzerman, Sergei Fedorov, Keith Primeau, Nick Lidström, and Paul Coffey—without feeling a bit intimated. Again, I thought, *Do I really belong here? How am I going to fit in?*

With Steve, Sergei, and Keith Primeau, I knew it was an intense competition to play center and I was willing to accept any role given to me. That's why I stuck—my desire to be in the NHL motivated me to do anything I could to stay in Detroit.

Whatever role Scotty Bowman put me in, I was going to play hard.

It certainly paid off for me. When Kirk Maltby became a Red Wing, we clicked right away, and when Joey Kocur signed, the makings of the Grind Line began to take shape. Add Darren McCarty into the mix, and we all knew what we needed to do to make the Red Wings a successful hockey club.

My playing career was more than I could have imagined. The longer I played this amazing game and the longer I was a Red Wing, the more I realized I didn't want the ride to end. I enjoyed everything about the game of hockey—the workouts, the practices, training camp, summer training, and even the injuries. I loved being an NHL player but even more so being a Detroit Red Wing.

When you're injured you realize how much you miss the game and you push your body to the limits to recover faster than the docs and trainers say you should. Professional athletes understand that you can't play forever. Father Time is undefeated: he gets all of us. I know I was fortunate to play until I was 40 years old, but at the end of it, I was like, *Now what?*

Well, I was fortunate to have built a friendship with our general manager, Ken Holland, and he offered me a position in the front office. I went from the dressing room to the front office, hanging up my jersey for a suit. It felt great to be able to stay with the Detroit Red Wings organization.

To be able to work with Holland in all areas of the game was great—I learned about the draft, free agency, and contracts. Building relationships was very beneficial.

Then Yzerman returned to the Detroit Red Wings. He gave me the opportunity to be director of amateur scouting and eventually assistant general manager. That is something I take a lot of pride in.

I was able to play more than 1,100 games with the Red Wings and be a part of four Stanley Cup championships. Now my goal is to be a part of building a Stanley Cup team next to many of my former teammates: Yzerman, Lidström, Dan Cleary, Nik Kronwall, Maltby, and Jiří Fischer.

With my job, I have the opportunity to travel the world. I realize that the Red Wings brand is a global brand, known to hockey fans all over the world.

I appreciate the opportunity from Helene St. James to contribute this foreword, and the reason I wanted to write it is because of how much the Red Wings organization means to me.

—Kris Draper
NHL forward, 1990–2011
Red Wings forward, 1993–2011
Red Wings hockey operations, 2011–present

Acknowledgments

THIS IS MY THIRD BOOK ON THE DETROIT RED WINGS, AND every one has been a joy to write. I greatly enjoy the research and interviews involved in completing a manuscript.

The franchise dates back nearly 100 years—2026 will be the centennial of the hockey club, then known as the Cougars, arriving in Detroit. The November 18, 1926, edition of the *Detroit Free Press* featured an article headlined "Welcome! Detroit 'Cougars'" and showed how excited the city was about the club: "Detroit's first year in the National Hockey League should be a great success...Detroit anticipates the enjoyment of many thrills and pleasures during her first hockey season, which opens tonight. We are pleased indeed to have been admitted to the National Hockey League and...we are confident of your ability to carry the Detroit banner to victory, and we give you our assurance of loyal and constant support."

There is never a shortage of people to interview for these books. Scotty Bowman was a treat to cover in person, and I'm deeply appreciative that even as he turned 90 in September 2023, he was as quick as ever to respond when I reached out to see if he had time to chat (he always does). Never have I met anyone with such an expansive knowledge of hockey. His insights were invaluable.

Steve Yzerman is one of the most thoughtful people I've interviewed, as a player and a general manager.

I always enjoy talking to Tomas Holmström, because I know I will come away laughing. We chatted the day after he had just returned to his home in Sweden from a trip to Detroit—or as he put it, he was finally back at the North Pole.

Nicklas Lidström is always gracious with his time, as is Henrik Zetterberg. Jimmy Devellano is fascinating to talk to, so full of details, especially about what those first years were like after Mike and Marian Ilitch bought the team. Kirk Maltby and Kris Draper I could talk to for hours about the Wings.

Draper said yes as soon as I brought up writing the foreword, which delighted me. He takes such pride in his long association with the Wings, and I knew he was an excellent choice to contribute.

My sounding board for all three books has been Gene Myers, whose encouragement and help is invaluable. A fellow winter and water sports enthusiast, we spent many hours going over details right down to the order of the table of contents. Jeff Fedotin, my editor at Triumph Books, helped guide the book from manuscript to publication.

I wrote most of the manuscript in the spring and summer of 2023, finishing up the last chapters as the 2023–24 season began to take shape. I worked everywhere, including on the flights to and from Stockholm for the 2023 Global Series. This franchise has such an immense history, I kept thinking of more stories I wanted to tell.

I dedicate this book to my family and my friends. Writing a book above all takes discipline, and it makes all the difference to have so much support and encouragement.

PART 1

THE FRANCHISE

1

In the Beginning

THE DETROIT RED WINGS ARE THE FRANCHISE OF GORDIE
Howe and Steve Yzerman, of Ted Lindsay and Nicklas Lidström,
the Production Line and the Grind Line and the Russian Five.
The team has a fan base that spans the globe and generations,
with more Stanley Cups than any other U.S.-based National
Hockey League franchise.

NHL hockey came to Detroit in 1926, when rival
businessmen put in bids for an expansion team. A clipping
from the *Detroit Free Press* of April 18, 1926, was headlined,
"Detroit Gets Pro Franchise. National Hockey League Decides
to Place Team Here." The story said, "Interest in today's meeting
centered in the fight being waged by five Detroit interests for a
berth in hockey's major league."

On May 15 the league picked the Townsend group. A group
of investors spent $100,000 to buy the Victoria Cougars, which
became the foundation for Detroit's hockey club.

In a letter dated October 8, 1926, Basil O'Meara, the sports editor of the *Ottawa Journal*, advised John Townsend to be careful of what he named the team: "When Boston came in, they selected the very unappealing name of Bruins, which did not register very well with their following...The advent of Detroit into hockey is going to be a big thing for the game, and also for Detroit in an amusement way. Once they get going with a team that is well sustained by a 'ballyhoo' there is no telling just what a splendid proposition it will turn out to be."

The Victoria Cougars were a talented lot, and players with nicknames like Hurricane Howie, Slim, Gizzy, and Hap got their names on the Stanley Cup in 1925. A report in the *Victoria Daily Times* extolled their skill: "They skated like fiends, passed the puck like masters, shot like machine guns, and their defence was as hard to penetrate as the side of a battleship."

The following season, the Victoria Cougars traveled to Montreal to battle the Maroons for the Stanley Cup but failed to defend the silver chalice. Around the same time what had been known as the Western Hockey League disbanded and the teams folded, taking their colorful sobriquets with them: The Calgary Tigers, the Edmonton Eskimos, the Saskatoon Crescents, the Vancouver Maroons (formerly Millionaires), the Portland Rosebuds, and the Cougars were no more.

Among the Cougars who moved east were Harry "Hap" Holmes. Also known as Happy, he wore a baseball cap in net to protect his bald head from spectators spitting tobacco or food at him during games. He fell sick two hours before the Cougars' first game in Detroit, ceding the net for the night to Herb Stuart. Wilfred Harold "Gizzy" Hart was a stocky, little-used forward known for his speed. Clem Loughlin had been captain of the Cougars when they won the Cup in 1925. Henry Arthur "Hurricane Howie" Meeking only played three games with the Detroit Cougars before being traded to the Boston Bruins. Frank Foyston was a skilled, offensive player.

Harold "Slim" Halderson and Frank Fredrickson, both born in Canada to Icelandic immigrants, were the first players to win an Olympic gold medal and a Stanley Cup. Halderson scored the first goal in franchise history on November 20, 1926, in a 4–1 loss to the Pittsburgh Pirates. Fredrickson scored the goal that gave the franchise its first victory, a 1–0 shutout at Chicago on November 24.

Fredrickson—anglicized from the Icelandic Friðriksson— was a particularly remarkable man. Born in Winnipeg, Manitoba, he didn't learn English until he started school. When World War I erupted, he enlisted in the Canadian Expeditionary Force and then switched to the 223rd Scandinavian Battalion and was posted in Europe. He transferred to the Royal Flying Corps and was posted to Egypt for training. While sailing to Italy for his next assignment, his ship was torpedoed by the Germans. After the war Frederickson returned home and helped form the Winnipeg Falcons hockey club. The Falcons won the 1920 Allan Cup, which qualified them to represent Canada in the 1920 Winter Olympics in Antwerp, Belgium. It was the first time ice hockey was included in the Olympics, so it was a much-heralded accomplishment when Frederickson and his teammates won the gold medal.

Frederickson had turned to a career as a pilot, but that all changed when he received a letter from Lester Patrick, who managed and played for the Victoria Aristocrats (they changed their name to Cougars in 1922). Lester offered Fredrickson $2,400 to play the 24 games that composed a season in the early 1920s, a generous offer at a time most players made less than $1,000. Fredrickson made his debut on New Year's Day 1921, scoring a goal and recording two assists to help his team beat the Vancouver Millionaires 5–3. The *Victoria Daily Times* hailed Fredrickson as "the Babe Ruth of hockey." Fredrickson began and finished his NHL career in Detroit.

The Cougars were winners in Victoria, but losers upon relocation. Fredrickson was traded to the Boston Bruins after 17 games and also played for the Pittsburgh Pirates before returning to Detroit in 1930, by which time the Cougars had been renamed the Falcons. Fredrickson would go on to be elected to the Hockey Hall of Fame in 1958.

The man in charge of the group in 1926–27 was Art Duncan, who served as the Detroit Cougars' first captain, coach, and general manager.

In the off-season, the players held various jobs to supplement their incomes: as a taxi driver (Meeking), a Chrysler salesperson (Holmes), a railroad worker (Hart), an automaker (Halderson), a concession stand owner (Jack Walker), a butcher (Foyston), and a farmer (Loughlin).

The Cougars were supposed to have their own arena in Detroit, but it wasn't finished so they played their home games across the Detroit River in Windsor, Ontario, at the Border Cities Arena. Their first game, which took place on November 18, 1926, was a 2–0 loss against the Boston Bruins. They had their first win on November 24, when Holmes shut out the Black Hawks in Chicago 1–0. The Cougars won only 12 games their first season, lost $84,000, and finished with the worst record (12–28–4) in the league.

It was a tough start for the expansion franchise, but during the second season, the Cougars gained traction. They moved into Detroit Olympia, better known as Olympia Stadium and, affectionately, as the Old Red Barn.

In addition to moving to the place they would call home for five decades, 1927 was the year Jack Adams was hired as coach and general manager. "Trader Jack," as he later became known, would shape the Wings for four decades.

The Cougars did better in Adams' first year, finishing 19–19–6, and in 1928–29 they made the playoffs, though they were quickly knocked out by the Toronto Maple Leafs. In 1929 Ebbie Goodfellow—born Ebenezer Robertson Goodfellow—signed with the Cougars for what would turn out to be 14 brilliant seasons. The future Hall of Famer played as both forward and defenseman, helped the franchise win three Stanley Cups, was captain for five seasons, and in 1939–40 became the first Wings player to win the Hart Trophy.

Goodfellow scored 17 goals his first season, but the Cougars missed the playoffs again. It had only been three years since the franchise arrived in Detroit, but it was the height of the Great Depression, and it was a challenge to keep the club operating successfully. Changing the name to the Falcons in 1930 proved futile. The team went into receivership and was taken over by the Detroit Guardian Trust Co.

James E. Norris, a successful businessman from Montreal, bought the team in 1932, renamed them the Red Wings, and instituted the winged wheel logo.

Finally, Detroit had a professional team worth attention. The Red Wings won their first Stanley Cup in 1936. In the first game of the first round, the Wings set a record for longest overtime game in NHL history, going all the way to a sixth period before Mud Bruneteau delivered a 1–0 victory.

Success begat success. The Wings won the Stanley Cup again in 1937. Then came the era of Howe, Lindsay, Sid Abel, Alex Delvecchio, Terry Sawchuk, and many more. The Old Red Barn rocked as the Wings reaped. When dark days came in the 1970s, the Wings had built a fan base that endured.

In 1982, after years of stunning mismanagement, James' son Bruce Norris gave up on the franchise and sold it to Mike Ilitch, a Detroit-born pizza baron and sports aficionado. The Wings revived, using the draft to bring in the next wave of players who would become synonymous with the franchise: Yzerman, Lidström, Sergei Fedorov, and many more.

The NHL had expanded in 1967, and kept expanding, but the Wings had something only the other Original Six teams offered: a bloodline dating back to the early 20th century. The Wings came into existence because a group of businessmen wanted a hockey team, because one Canadian transplant wanted to own his own team, and that same man understood how important it was to create a product that stirred fans. Children who grew up watching their parents celebrate Howe and Lindsay became adults who celebrated Yzerman and Lidström. From dissolution and despair on the west coast of Canada came resolution and prosperity on the banks of the Detroit River.

2

James Norris

Under the ownership of James E. Norris, the Red Wings took flight—and soared.

He was the patriarch of a family whose last name would become synonymous with the National Hockey League in the first half of the 20th century and the man who baptized Detroit's hockey club into the name by which it gained fame and glory.

Norris was born December 10, 1879, in Montreal, to a family with a history rich in seafarers and shipbuilders. His father was a grain merchant who grew inherited wealth into a fortune. Norris played collegiate hockey at McGill University and later with the Montreal Hockey Club, a men's amateur club with a winged wheel logo that Norris used for inspiration when he bought the Wings.

When he was 18, his family moved to Chicago, where Norris settled. At 28 he was named president of the Norris Grain Company and set about increasing his family's wealth by going on a spending spree focused primarily on grain and cattle. In 1926 he sought to expand his empire and made a bid to put a hockey team in Chicago. It made sense from Norris' standpoint, as he already was one of the financial backers of Chicago Stadium, but he lost the bid. Norris next dabbled with putting an NHL team in St. Louis, but at the time, the city was considered too far away to from the nexus of the league, leading to fears of unreasonable travel costs (this was in the days before commercial flying).

An attempt to buy the Ottawa Senators and relocate the club either to Chicago or Toronto was undermined by the refusals of the owners of the Chicago Black Hawks and Toronto Maple Leafs, neither of whom wanted a second team in their respective cities.

It was the struggling Detroit Falcons, only recently renamed from the Cougars franchise that germinated as a hockey club in Detroit in 1926, that finally made Norris the owner of an NHL team. Taking advantage of the team being in receivership and managed by creditors, he presented himself as a rich and resourceful rescuer. Norris renamed the franchise and gave it a logo—a wing protruding from a wheel—that resonated with a team that made its home in the center of the auto industry.

Norris used his wealth to pay off the team's creditors and give the club the freedom needed to engender success. One of the employees he inherited was Jack Adams, the coach and general manager. Norris tore up the contract Adams had with the former ownership group and gave him a one-year trial on a handshake. That process would repeat itself annually: Adams famously worked without a contract, even as he built the Wings into a superpower.

Four years after he bought the Wings, Norris bought Chicago Stadium, making him the Black Hawks' landlord. He largely engineered the syndicate—which would include his oldest son James D. Norris—that bought the Black Hawks in 1944 and was understood to be the one who silently called the shots for the team. Norris' wealth also enabled him to become the largest stockholder of Madison Square Garden, which gave him a measure of control over the New York Rangers. He was, moreover, a chief creditor for the Boston Bruins. In all, Norris parlayed his power into ownership of the Detroit Red Wings, and to varying degrees, a say in the operations of the Chicago Black Hawks, New York Rangers, and Boston Bruins. It was a stunning level of conflict of interest, but Norris' wealth and the parlance of the good ole boys' network enabled his immense reach.

Norris continued to live in Chicago after buying the Wings, and rarely saw them in person. Adams would call him after games and tell him how the team was doing. Under Norris' ownership the franchise enjoyed immense success, winning the Stanley Cup five times from 1936 until his death in on December 4, 1952. Norris was posthumously inducted into the Hockey Hall of Fame in 1958, three years after the Wings won the Stanley Cup for the seventh time in franchise history.

The James Norris Memorial Trophy, awarded annually since 1954 to the NHL's best defenseman, is named after Norris, who started his hockey career as a college and amateur defenseman in Montreal. Nicklas Lidström, the best defensemen ever to play for the Wings, won it seven times between 2001 and 2011. From 1974 to 1993, the Wings played in the Norris Division, also named after Norris.

In addition to James D. Norris, who followed his father into the Hockey Hall of Fame in 1962, James E. Norris had a daughter, Marguerite, who he selected before his death to be the next president of the Wings, and another son, Bruce Norris.

It was the latter who took what his dad had built and his sister strengthened and drove the franchise into the ground.

It is not the easiest thing in the world to take a successful product and tarnish it beyond all recognition, to turn a powerhouse into a pretender, but Bruce Norris managed. He was a rich kid from Chicago who inherited his father's hockey team when it was the best in the league, and under his guidance, the franchise descended into a joke.

"It was a deplorable situation," Jimmy Devellano said in 1984, two years after being named general manager by Mike Ilitch. "It was disgraceful. I think one more year under that type of administration, and they might have been right out of the business."

When Bruce took over the Wings in 1955 from his sister, Marguerite, the Stanley Cup was theirs to defend for the fourth time in six seasons. During Bruce's reign the Wings never touched the Cup and grew more and more distanced from it. In spring of 1982, when Ilitch bought the team, they were out of the playoff race for the 10th time in 11 years.

It was a disgrace. The Wings played in a division named after their founder, Norris. But Bruce's mismanagement, from the top level to the most minute, had left the Wings a shell of their successful past. Bruce let Adams run rampant. The result was that core players from the nucleus that had made the Wings such a dynasty in the 1950s were tossed away, to the point it created acrimony with Howe, the greatest player the franchise had known. He retired from the Wings in 1971. It was Bruce's ineptitude that led fans in the 1970s to refer to the team by a sullen sobriquet: the Dead Wings.

At an event at Joe Louis Arena held to celebrate half a century of Norris family ownership, Bruce was so soundly booed by fans, he finally went through with selling the team.

"We have been pressured by the media for two or three years," Norris said in March 1982. "We have decided to sell. We're tired of listening to this all the time."

(The 50-year anniversary was heralded by some, though. President Ronald Reagan sent a letter to the Norris family that read, in part, "Nancy and I are delighted to send our warm congratulations to the Norris family on the fiftieth anniversary of their ownership of the Detroit Red Wings. For a half a century the stewardship of this family has brought the thrills, excitement, and enjoyment of hockey to sports fans of Detroit and the National Hockey League.")

In all his years owning the Wings, Bruce, like his father, never lived in Detroit. His absence was a source of regular criticism as the team degenerated under his proprietorship. He wasn't a stranger at Joe Louis Arena, but after games, he would usually stand in the middle of the locker room, talking quietly with a coach or trainer while the players changed. His boisterous side came out at parties, such as the "command appearance" annual team dinners he hosted.

As the Wings faltered in the 1970s, so did Bruce's personal fortune—and it only worsened after he jettisoned the hockey team that had meant so much to his family. In 1984 an investment company won a jury verdict worth more than $3 million from Bruce in a suit charging that during his ownership of the Wings, the team reneged on a 1977 deal to move to Oakland County. In April 1977 Bruce announced the Wings were moving from Detroit's Olympia Stadium to a new arena that would be built across the road from the Pontiac Silverdome, then home to the National Football League Detroit Lions. Four months later Bruce abandoned the deal and announced the Wings would move into Joe Louis Arena, which was already under construction on Detroit's riverfront. Opdyke

Investment Co. attorney William Hampton accused Bruce Norris of reneging on the deal because then-Detroit mayor Coleman Young "gave Norris a sweetheart contract that gave him everything but city hall."

Three years after he sold the Wings, Bruce filed a bankruptcy claim in the summer of 1985 for his family-owned company. Norris Grain had once held interests that included a railroad, a Florida hunting and fishing resort, a South Africa cattle business, and the studio that produced the TV show *Flipper*.

Bruce died from a liver ailment on January 1, 1986, at age 61. Although the Wings never won the Stanley Cup under his ownership, he was inducted into the Hockey Hall of Fame in 1969.

3

Mike Ilitch

WHEN STEVE YZERMAN SUFFERED A NASTY KNEE INJURY ON March 1, 1988, stoking fear he might miss as much as a year, Mike Ilitch was so troubled he called Russ Thomas, the general manager of the National Football League's Detroit Lions. Thomas' playing career with the Lions had ended decades earlier, in 1949, because of a knee injury. Ilitch sought out Thomas' advice because knee injuries were considered more frequent in the NFL than the NHL. Only four years earlier, Lions running back Billy Sims had suffered a severe right-knee injury that derailed his career.

Thomas suggested to Ilitch that the Wings get a second opinion on Yzerman, recommending Dr. William Clancy, a nationally recognized orthopedic specialist at the University of Wisconsin. Ilitch sent Yzerman to Wisconsin the next day.

That was the kind of man Ilitch was. Committed. Passionate. Generous. Caring. Owning the Red Wings was a childhood dream that he made a reality because of his business sense, but he ran his hockey club with emotional intelligence.

"When I bought the team, an official with the New York Islanders said, 'You know, you're going to lose at least $2 million a year,'" Ilitch said in 1988. "I said, 'Well, okay,' but I kind of gulped. I heard it, but I didn't want to hear it. So, I figured he says $2 million, maybe I'll lose a million. Instead, I lost $3 million. When I came in, all I said was money is insignificant, not even a factor. I didn't need the money. All I was thinking about was building a team."

Ilitch was the American dream in triplicate: a boy who made himself a pizza baron, an entertainment magnate, and an owner of two high-profile professional sports teams.

He was born July 20, 1929, in Detroit to Macedonian immigrants. After four years serving in the Marines following his graduation from Cooley High School, Ilitch signed a minor league contract to play for the Tigers. He argued constantly with his father, Sotir, a machine maintenance worker at Chrysler, who called his son a bum for wanting to be a professional shortstop. Ilitch's baseball aspirations ended when he suffered a knee injury.

In 1954 he met Marian Bayoff, herself born to Macedonian immigrants, and they soon married; together they would have seven children and start a pizza empire. Little Caesars stemmed from Marian's nickname for Mike. When they opened their first restaurant in 1959, in a strip mall in Garden City, Michigan, they sold pizzas for $2.39.

Ilitch was an astute businessman (Little Caesars introduced the catchphrase, "Pizza! Pizza!" in 1979 to advertise two pizzas being sold for the price of one; it went over well in a city going through hard economic times) and a passionate sportsman. In the early 1970s, he had started a local pro softball team. He lost money—$500,000 the first three years—but he brought in good players and took home two league titles.

That was Ilitch as a sports owner: willing to spend in order to be rewarded.

He had wooed Marian by taking her to hockey games at Olympia Stadium, and as they grew richer, he set his sights on owning the Wings. The franchise that had been home to Gordie Howe, that had thrilled fans in the 1950s with one Stanley Cup championship after another, had become so devoid of talent fans called them "the Dead Wings." James E. Norris, who bought the franchise in 1932 and named it the Red Wings, had known how to run a team, and so had his daughter, Marguerite, who James bequeathed control of the team upon his death in 1952. But Bruce, James' son, ousted Marguerite in 1955 and let general manager Jack Adams make petty trades that tore apart the nucleus and sent the team on a long demise.

Ilitch first tried to buy the Wings in 1981, but his offer was rejected. The following year the Wings held a ceremony to celebrate 50 years of Norris ownership, but when fans booed Norris, that was it. He was ready to sell. A year after offering $11 million, Ilitch bought the Wings for $8 million; the sale went through in June 1982. In first interviews with local newspaper reporters, Ilitch repeatedly referred to the Wings as "the ball club." Not that anyone doubted his hockey acumen: in addition to being a fan, he was the sort of dad who would take his children to hockey practices in the pre-dawn darkness of winter mornings, carrying them across parking lots so the blades on their skates wouldn't dull.

Two years after Ilitch bought the Wings, the franchise made the playoffs.

"Ilitch has done a great job," fellow pizza magnate Tom Monaghan said at the time. "He hired the best people available to run things and it's worked."

Missing the playoffs in 1983 had grated on Ilitch. "I took it personally," he said. "I felt I had let the fans down.

"I didn't realize what a bad team I had inherited."

In a 1988 interview with the *Detroit Free Press* editorial board, Ilitch showed his lighthearted side—and his business side—as he discussed how quickly the Wings had achieved success under his ownership.

"Well, I carried a rabbit's foot around with me," he said. "You have to be a little lucky, and you have to have a plan that you have to stick to. Those are the two main ingredients. Our plan was to rebuild through the draft and not trade away any draft choices and build for the future. That was a difficult task because they lowered the age for drafting youngsters from 20 to 18, which made it much more difficult to anticipate what their development would be at age 22.

"Selecting somebody who had a lot of experience in being able to assess talent was the best decision I made. Jim Devellano had a track record of being very successful in assessing talent and drafting properly. Then, where luck comes into play along with ability was [with] the selection of Steve Yzerman as our first draft choice. Devellano's assessment, that he was the cornerstone of the franchise, was correct. So that's given us a wonderful base to build from."

Ilitch was 29 when he opened his first pizza place and 52 when he bought the Wings. By then, Little Caesars operated 300 stores across nine states.

Ilitch relied on Devellano, but at the 1983 draft—their first together—Ilitch's passion showed when it became clear he wasn't going to get what he wanted. Devellano had talked up Pat LaFontaine, a star player from Waterford, Michigan, so much that when the Islanders selected LaFontaine at No. 3, Ilitch tried to persuade Devellano to offer Islanders GM Bill Torrey $1 million to swap picks. Marian intervened, convincing her husband to trust the man he had employed for his drafting acumen.

Devellano told the Ilitches he would win them a Stanley Cup in eight years, but in 1990 the Wings missed the playoffs. (It would be the last time for a long time; in 1991 the franchise began what would be a record-setting 25-season streak of making the playoffs.) Ilitch knew the Wings were on the rise, though: in 1989 they had drafted two players out of what was then the Soviet Union, and he again showed his commitment to their success by helping to spirit Sergei Fedorov and Vladimir Konstantinov away from the Red Army.

Though their dreams of a Stanley Cup took longer than hoped, the Ilitches were having a grand time. In the late 1980s they bought and refurbished the spectacular Fox Theatre. They further showed their commitment to the city by moving their headquarters from the suburb of Farmington Hills to Detroit, into the 10-story building that housed the Fox. In 1992 Ilitch realized another sports dream when he purchased the Tigers from Monaghan. The Tigers made it to the World Series in 2006 and again in 2012 but weren't able to bring Ilitch the World Series trophy he so desired.

Ilitch was good at making money and willing to spend it. He made that clear to everyone.

"I'll do whatever I have to do to have a winner," Ilitch said shortly after buying the Wings. "I'm going to spend the money and do whatever it takes to get myself a winner."

Ilitch was a generous man. Yzerman had a clause in his contract that would pay him a $25,000 bonus if he was named rookie of the year—but he wasn't. That honor, in 1984, went to Buffalo Sabres goaltender Tom Barrasso. But Ilitch didn't care about the voting; the night the awards were announced, he handed Yzerman a $25,000 check in an envelope that said, "You're my rookie of the year." In 1987 Ilitch doubled his players' $13,000 playoff shares, and then did the same in 1988. He told players that if they played hard and did their best, they would be rewarded. They were.

Ilitch had made his fortune understanding how to take a well-known product, pizza, and make it more appealing. Ten years into his ownership of the Wings, the Wings were incredibly appealing, boasting a cast that was growing in future Hockey Hall of Fame players, but they still needed something more. Ilitch took care of that: in 1993 he went to see legendary coach Scotty Bowman personally to persuade him to come to Detroit.

Four years later, the Wings ended a 42-year drought and brought the Stanley Cup back to Detroit. Fifteen years had passed since Ilitch bought the team. In that time he had done everything in his power to restore the franchise to glory: hired the right people, who drafted the right players; thought up promotions to bring fans back to the stands; and spent $400,000 to spiffy up Joe Louis Arena. He would start each season shaking players' hands and wishing them good luck. "It really felt like he cared about everybody," Niklas Kronwall said in 2017. "You felt he could be your neighbor."

The NHL did not have a salary cap when Ilitch purchased the Wings. That would be instituted in 2005, by which point Ilitch already had won three Stanley Cups. The 1997 and 1998 teams were built on drafting and taking chances—Ilitch green-lit drafting players from behind the Iron Curtain and helped stage the subterfuge needed to lift the Curtain long enough to let player after play slip past Communist authorities.

The 2002 team was built from Ilitch's fortune. The roster—which included Yzerman, Nicklas Lidström, Sergei Fedorov, Dominik Hašek, Brett Hull, Luc Robitaille, Igor Larionov, Slava Fetisov, Brendan Shanahan, and Chris Chelios—came with a payroll around $66 million. (The first season there was a salary cap, the upper limit was $39 million. It wasn't until seven years later, in 2011–12, that the cap approached what had been the Wings' payroll a decade earlier.) Ilitch had spent thousands of dollars to bring in good players for the softball team he owned back in the 1970s; three decades later he was spending millions, showing what a good and generous owner looked like.

By 2002 he and Marian had owned the Wings for two decades, and they had three titles to show for it. Twenty years after they bought the franchise for $8 million, *Forbes* valued the Red Wings at $266 million. In 2022 the franchise was valued at $1.03 billion.

When he bought the Wings, Ilitch wanted fans to fall back in love with the team. "It's my job as leader of the franchise to produce the proper environment," he said at the time. "This is my way of doing things. I talked it over with my wife, and I said, 'Hey, Marian, I can't lay back. I know that we should do this, or we shouldn't do that,' but I said, 'that's me. I've got to go out and aggressively do things the way I do them.' I want to do things that are going to stimulate fans along with the team members and staff."

Ilitch passed away February 10, 2017, at age 87. He left behind a legacy of what hard work could accomplish. He grew up poor and died a billionaire. He opened one pizza store, and out of that assembled a food, sports, and entertainment empire. His own sports career ended with a knee injury when he was in his 20s, but he died having won four Stanley Cups as owner. He rescued the Wings from sullied indifference in 1982 and instilled a passionate commitment to success.

"You knew how you stood with him," Bowman said. "No gray area. Black or white. He wanted to win at any cost. He wanted to be informed. He always stressed if you needed something, he was just a phone call away. That was the fact of it. You just made a phone call and said, 'this is what I think we should do, this is what it's going to take,' and he was 100 percent backing of the people that worked for him."

PART 2

THE ICONS

4

Gordie Howe

When the Red Wings played in Montreal on November 12, 2016, the Canadiens paid tribute to Gordie Howe with a video that flashed back over his immense career, showing his progression from young man on down through the decades that he played. Fans at Bell Centre responded with a standing ovation.

Howe had died June 10, 2016. It was his son Murray Howe who confirmed the news to media outlets, messaging, "Mr. Hockey left this morning peacefully, beautifully, and with no regrets." At the Stanley Cup Final game two days later, there was a tribute during the first intermission.

How Howe was treated in death reflected the immense, enduring popularity he fostered through a quarter of a century with the Red Wings. He was a big, affable lumberjack of a man, shy in his early years, amenable through them all. Everyone who saw him or met him had a story about Howe: the time he held off two Canadiens with one hand and scored with the other, the time he rearranged Lou Fontinato's face, the time he stopped on the Lodge freeway in Detroit and pushed a stranded car out of the snow.

Gordon Howe was born March 31, 1928, in the rural community of Floral, Saskatchewan, one of nine children born to Ab and Katherine Howe. The Great Depression had a stranglehold, and Howe learned to skate on frozen potato patches and learned to love oatmeal, which sometimes was all the family had to eat for days at a time. He loved hockey from a young age and would recall in later years that he "used to go through every garbage can in Saskatoon looking for labels off BeeHive Corn Syrup. You'd send in the label, and they'd send you a picture of an NHL player."

Had Howe been Catholic, he would have accepted an offer from the New York Rangers in 1943, when he was 15 years old, to play junior hockey at Notre Dame Cathedral in his home state, Saskatchewan; blessedly for the Wings, Howe wasn't.

He was 16 when he first caught Jack Adams' eye while auditioning at Wings camp in the fall of 1944, invited by a scout named Fred Pinkney. Adams signed Howe to a contract—a deal that included a leather jacket that Howe, with his trademark perseverance, made sure he got—and in 1945, Howe started playing with the Omaha Knights in the United States Hockey League under coach Tommy Ivan, whose guidance helped Howe flourish. It was Ivan who, in 1946, told Adams that Howe was ready for the Red Wings.

It was a relationship unmatched in franchise history. Howe played 25 seasons with the Wings from 1946 to 1971. Steve Yzerman played 22 seasons for the Wings, logging 1,514 games. Nicklas Lidström played 20 seasons, staying mostly injury free and he still only ranks second in franchise history with 1,564 games. Howe played 1,687.

Howe was the reason Wayne Gretzky wore No. 99. Gretzky wanted to wear No. 9, like his idol, but it was taken and so instead, Gretzky doubled up. When Howe died, Gretzky was among the mourners in Detroit.

"I was really lucky," Gretzky said then. "Not everybody gets to meet their hero or their idol. And sometimes when you meet them, it wasn't as good as you thought it would be. I got so lucky that the guy I chose happened to be so special. He was very humble."

Gretzky, more than three decades Howe's junior, was a teenager the first time he played against Howe, in the late 1970s. During the warmups before the game, Gretzky thought Howe was winking at him. During a shift halfway through the first period, Gretzky took the puck off Howe, only to immediately feel Howe's stick whack Gretzky's glove, like an errant child disciplined for stealing a cookie. Gretzky feared he had broken a thumb. Howe smiled and told him, "Don't ever take the puck from me." Later, one of his teammates let Gretzky know that Howe had a blinking problem from a long-ago head injury.

That was Howe at 50. At 51 he played at Joe Louis Arena as a member of the Wales Conference team in the All-Star Game. Fans loved it, cheering Howe on with a standing ovation. He had retired from the Wings in 1971 at age 43, segueing into a front-office job that ill suited a man of Howe's energy. Sure enough, Howe's attempt to live a sedentary life was short-lived. When the Houston Aeros of the new World Hockey Association offered him a chance to play again, Howe pounced. He was 45 then and relished the chance to play with his sons Marty and Mark. But by the end of the decade, the WHA had folded, and the team Howe was playing for then, the Whalers, was absorbed by the NHL, leading Howe to suit up one last season in the league in 1979–80. The highlight of that was being able to play at the Joe on March 12, 1980, where 21,002 fans greeted his appearance with chants of "Gor-die, Gor-die."

Howe was a 23-time NHL All-Star, won the Art Ross Trophy as the league's leading scorer six times, led the league in goal scoring five times, and won six Hart Trophies as the league's most value valuable player.

His toughness befitted the legend he told of his birth. His mother was chopping wood when she went into labor on March 31, 1928, went inside their farmhouse and had Gordie, and then tied the umbilical cord herself.

Howe grew up poor during the Great Depression and hockey was his way out, his way to a more prosperous life. He was big—six feet, and in his prime, 205 pounds. It was his dexterity that caught Adams' eye in 1944, and two years later, Howe, at age 18, made his debut wearing the winged wheel on October 16, 1946, scoring a goal against the Toronto Maple Leafs. His only fear, according to the Red Wings' own promotional material, was "of the opposite sex."

Luckily for Howe, he met Colleen Joffa in April 1951 at the Lucky Strike Lanes bowling alley near Olympia, when she was 18 and he was 23. Two years later, on April 15, 1953, they married and together they had three sons, Marty, Mark, and Murray, and a daughter, Cathy. It was Colleen Howe who realized her husband's immense marketing value, who demanded the wives of the Wings players be treated with respect. "I am not a sports Barbie doll," she once said. "It's hard for me to accept things like the players having to be so subservient. I am not a subservient person." Colleen understood sports marketing at a time when few others gave it much thought, cutting deals and generating promotional ideas. At one point their business empire encompassed a restaurant, an arena, Amway distributorships, and herds of cattle and llamas. In a stroke of genius, Colleen trademarked Gordie as "Mr. Hockey" and herself as "Mrs. Hockey," creating nicknames that would last past their deaths. Howe had practiced signing his name as a teenager back in his family's farmhouse. His ambidexterity led to rumors he could sign his name 1,000 times an hour. It was Colleen who urged her husband to never leave a fan disappointed, who understood that his availability and generosity would expand his popularity and with that his value to the Wings.

It wasn't that Adams didn't value Howe (although Howe did have to remind Adams about that leather jacket he was owed: it's now part of the family's memorabilia collection, showing the signs of having been worn for years by Howe, and after that, Marty). Later on, there would be conflict, but in those early years, Adams looked after Howe and made sure he didn't feel homesick or unhappy.

Howe's rookie season was two years after Maurice "Rocket" Richard had become the first player to score 50 goals in the NHL. Richard—5'10" and 180 pounds in his prime—was an intense player whose style at times veered toward violence, but Howe's physicality was all encompassing. He was a powerful skater with a hard, accurate shot and a smart playmaker. His hands were soft with the puck, but his elbows were like granite, punishing opponents who dared to challenge Howe. He was the most complete player in the league.

The Wings were good before him, but great with him, finishing first in the regular season seven straight years from 1949 to 1955 and winning the Stanley Cup four times from 1950 to 1955.

Howe only played one game in the 1950 playoffs. In the first game of the first-round series against the Maple Leafs, Howe attempted to check Toronto's Ted Kennedy. (In 1954 Howe and Kennedy fought during a game on March 21; it's noteworthy because it's one of only two games where Howe actually had a goal, an assist, and a fight—or what became known as a Gordie Howe hat trick.) Howe crashed headfirst into the boards instead, losing consciousness. The Wings feared Howe might not survive and told his family back in Saskatoon to make travel plans for Detroit. A month later, Howe stepped onto the ice to touch the Cup, his head wrapped in bandages. Fans gave him a standing ovation.

Howe finished in the top five in NHL scoring for 20 straight seasons. He played right wing on the famed Production Line, alongside Ted Lindsay and Sid Abel. In 1950–51 Howe's 43 goals and 43 assists added up to his first Art Ross Trophy as the NHL's top point producer. His 86 points were 20 better than the guy who finished second, Maurice Richard. The following season brought another Art Ross Trophy, and Howe's first Hart Trophy as the league's most valuable player. Richard, seven years older than Howe, retired in 1960 with 544 goals, a league record. At the time Howe was second in the NHL with 446 goals. Howe broke the record on November 10, 1963, and by the end of that season had 566 goals, already 22 up on Richard.

Howe was beloved in Detroit and legendary around the NHL. By 1968–69 the league had doubled to 12 teams and the schedule expanded to 76 games. Howe recorded his only century-mark season, reaching 99 points in the third-to-last game. He had two goals and two assists in the season finale to finish with 103 points, the day before his 41st birthday. It was a momentous season for another reason: Howe convinced Adams to more than double Howe's salary from $45,000 annually to $100,000. (To put that in perspective, $100,000 in 1969 would be roughly $823,000 in 2023 when adjusted for inflation, just a touch above the $750,000 minimum salary for the 2022–23 season.)

Howe won the last of his six Art Ross Trophies in 1963. He won his last Stanley Cup in 1955 and reflected with bitterness years later that he should have had more of those. When the Wings celebrated the franchise's seventh Stanley Cup with a 3–1 victory over the Montreal Canadiens on April 14, 1955, the roster included Howe, Lindsay, Alex Delvecchio, Red Kelly, and Terry Sawchuk. But tumultuous change during the offseason destroyed that beautiful roster. Marguerite Norris, to whom James E. Norris had bequeathed control of the Wings after he died in December of 1952, lost a power struggle with her brother, Bruce. The old man knew what he was doing when he handpicked Marguerite, who had the backbone and business acumen to stand up to Adams. Bruce had none of that. He let Adams tear apart the Wings, trading away Sawchuk, whose goaltending led the Wings to the Cup in 1952, '54, and '55, and Lindsay, along with Tony Leswick, who had scored the Game 7 overtime goal in the '54 Finals. In his book *Mr. Hockey: My Story,* first published in 2014, Howe excoriated Adams' moves, writing that, "to this day, his reasons for blowing up our championship squad defy explanation."

Forty-two years passed before the Wings won the Cup again; Howe made his own history in 1997 when he took a spin for one game with the International Hockey League Detroit Vipers—at age 69.

Howe retired as a player from the Wings in 1971; 50 years later his 786 goals still stood as a record for most goals scored with one franchise. (He scored 801 total in his NHL career, which culminated with 80 games for the Hartford Whalers.) In 1972 the team flew in Vice President Spiro Agnew's plane to attend the ceremony when Howe's No. 9 was retired.

By the following year, Howe was playing in the WHL. He retired from the NHL for good in 1980. His 1,850 points would eventually be eclipsed by Gretzky (2,857), Jaromír Jágr (1,921), and Mark Messier (1,887), but Howe played longer than any of those superstars. His career spanned seven U.S. presidents, Sinatra to the Sex Pistols, and lasted long enough for him to be able to play professionally with his sons.

"Gordie was exceptional," Lindsay said in 1990. "Some people are just born strong; Gordie was one of those. Nick Londes, who managed the old Olympia when Gordie first came to the Red Wings, used to call him 'The Power.' Londes had been a wrestler, and he'd tell Gordie, 'I could make you champion wrestler of the world.'

"Continuing a career for so many years as he did takes more than talent. It takes inspiration and desire, and Gordie had all of that. He wanted to continue so he could play someday alongside his two sons and he did."

There had been chatter in 1977 of Howe returning to the Wings, with Colleen spearheading the talks. But Bruce Norris was still in charge, and ultimately nothing came of it. It wasn't until Norris sold the Wings in 1982, angered at having been booed during what was supposed to be a ceremony celebrating 50 years of Norris ownership, that Howe returned to where he belonged. When Mike and Marian Ilitch bought the team and hired Jimmy Devellano to be the general manager, the group realized the importance of reestablishing a connection with Howe. It wasn't just a smart emotional decision; it made sense from a business standpoint, too: the Wings had just 2,100 season ticket holders when the Ilitches bought the team and getting Howe back in the fold helped rebuild fan excitement.

In 1983 an 18-year-old Yzerman encountered Howe in the hallways of Joe Louis Arena. Yzerman had just been drafted by the franchise at No. 4 a few months earlier. In typical Howe fashion, he introduced himself, as humble as when he was an 18-year-old rookie with the team nearly four decades earlier. Howe regularly milled about the locker room at the Joe; players learned that even in his older age, they had to beware those famous elbows: Howe was an animated storyteller.

Howe took to the ice at the Joe in 1990 when he was part of a charity game pitting Red Wings legends against a collection of Hollywood celebrity hockey players that included St. Clair Shores native Dave Coulier of *Full House* fame and *Jeopardy!* host Alex Trebek. It was Howe who got the warmest welcome: a gathering of 12,348 saluted him with a standing ovation.

The Howes enjoyed life in the metro Detroit area again, living in a house in Bloomfield Hills. It was there that Colleen Howe passed away on March 6, 2009, at age 76. She had been diagnosed with Pick's disease, a neurological disorder resembling Alzheimer's, in 2002.

Howe battled dementia in his 80s, and in October 2014, he suffered a stroke that further debilitated him. He lived for a while with Cathy, their daughter, in Lubbock, Texas, where the mild climate allowed Howe to spend time outdoors daily. He still wasn't one to be sedentary, replacing a hockey stick with a rake. His connection to the Wings remained as strong as ever. When the Wings held a pair of alumni games preceding the 2014 Winter Classic, Howe dropped the ceremonial puck before the second game. On March 28, 2016, three days before his 88th birthday, he attended what would be his last game at the Joe, where fans sang "Happy Birthday."

A little more than two months later, Howe passed away.

Four days after he died, Howe lay in repose at Joe Louis Arena. The banners, heralding the Stanley Cups he won, framed two to each side the No. 9 banner that was lowered to hang above Howe's closed casket, which was adorned with red and white flowers. Thousands waited in line to pay their respects, to offer condolences to his family. Among them was Willie Norris, who decades earlier had tried to play for a youth team at Olympia Stadium only to be told, he said, that "Negroes weren't allowed." Norris was there that June day because Howe had welcomed Norris when he saw him waiting for an autograph near the locker room at the old arena, stopping to sign and say hello. It was typical of Howe and evocative of how his family has described him: he was as tough as they come on the ice, his skill exacerbated by his immense strength, and as great a player as Howe was, he was an even better person.

5

Steve Yzerman

TOOTSIE? TOOTSIE.

It was the night of June 7, 1997, and in a few minutes, the Red Wings would take the ice for the biggest game of the season. They had a three-games-to-none lead in the Stanley Cup Final, they were at home, and for two days, the city of Detroit had been buzzing about when the parade would be.

Yzerman was the Wings. He was "The Captain," the soft-spoken, big-game performer who had been expected to bring the Cup back to Detroit ever since he was drafted 14 years earlier, when he was part of the rebirth of the franchise a year after it had been bought by Mike and Marian Ilitch.

Yzerman already had addressed his teammates earlier, urging them to do their job as a team, extolling them to not squander this opportunity to clinch. But he also recognized that the last thing the team needed was to be uptight. So, just before players rose from their stools and grabbed their sticks, he began a game of movie trivia with fellow film buff Brendan Shanahan. Yzerman threw out some names, and his teammates looked at him a bit oddly, and then they understood what was going on. They needed to relax.

"He threw *Tootsie* at me," Shanahan said later. "I was like, *Come on,* Tootsie? It was on TV that afternoon. I caught the last 10 minutes of it. I told him, '*Tootsie*, come on, don't waste my time.'"

It was typical Yzerman, understanding what his team needed for him and when. "Steve was a quiet leader for the most part," Kirk Maltby said in 2023. "When everything is going great, it's easy to be a good leader. But he knew what to say when we had a crisis, and he knew what to say when we needed to loosen up. He is a relatively quiet guy, but what he did on the ice said everything. We all saw how incredibly driven he was, how much it meant for him for the Red Wings to be successful."

When Yzerman returned to the Wings after a nine-year absence, even the stars aligned. It was the 19th of April and the year, 2019. What more perfect day could there be to welcome back the most beloved living Red Wing, whose No. 19 had been hung from the rafters after he retired in 2006. Yzerman played 22 seasons for the Wings, rising from consolation draftee to youngest captain in franchise history to Stanley Cup champion.

Yzerman's arrival in Detroit in 1983 spurred a pronunciation guide for his last name in local newspapers. After an attempt by new owner Mike Ilitch to use his fortune to rewrite history at the NHL draft that June, the Wings selected Yzerman at No. 4. Jimmy Devellano, the general manager who was Ilitch's first hire, knew Yzerman was a good selection, but Ilitch had his heart set on Pat LaFontaine, a personable, superbly skilled forward whose provenance from the suburbs of Detroit made him a marketable dream for a formerly great hockey club that had endured a decade of misery. Ilitch was prepared to offer Bill Torrey, the general manager of the New York Islanders who had taken LaFontaine at No. 3, $1 million to swap picks. It was Ilitch's wife, Marian, who convinced her husband to trust Devellano, to trust that they got a good pick in Yzerman.

What the Ilitches and the Wings got in Yzerman was a player who transformed the franchise. It wasn't long before his last name flowed from fans' lips, though soon they just called him Stevie, and eventually, The Captain.

Yzerman was to Wings fans in the 1980s what Gordie Howe had been to fans nearly half a century earlier: a hockey hero. They played different styles of hockey, in vastly different eras, but they carried themselves with humility and hard work.

Like Howe, Yzerman scored in his debut, on October 5, 1983. Management had brought Yzerman, then 18, to training camp that September already having publicly committed to giving him a spot on the roster. Devellano had scouted Yzerman since he was 16 and knew him to be a very good skater with a gifted level of hockey sense. Going into the draft, Devellano's biggest worry was that one of the three players he liked would not be available: LaFontaine, Yzerman, or Sylvain Turgeon. The Wings had finished the 1982–83 season 18th out of 21 teams, giving them the fourth pick, behind the Minnesota North Stars, the Hartford Whalers, and the Islanders.

Devellano's worry was assuaged as soon as the North Stars selected Brian Lawton. When that happened, Devellano knew he would get one of the three players he viewed as potential difference-makers.

The draft back then wasn't the TV event it became; choices were made quickly. One: Lawton. Two: Turgeon. Three:

LaFontaine. Selections came quickly from the draft floor at the Forum in Montreal.

Four: Yzerman.

He was there that night, in a suit and red tie, and when he heard his name, he was relieved. Yzerman had two years left of junior eligibility, but as he eyed the Wings, he hoped those days were in his past.

"They're rebuilding," he said. "I think I have a chance."

The Wings were prepared to give Yzerman his chance that fall. He was scouted as a superb puck handler, a good passer, and a fine skater. But he was 5'10", 177 pounds, and still looked like he had a bit of baby fat on him.

Yzerman would be on the team—but in what role?

After seeing his first shift during camp, Devellano and coach Nick Polano recognized Yzerman was the best player on the ice.

After the draft Yzerman had returned home to Nepean, Ottawa, (he grew up there, though he was born in Cranbrook, British Columbia) to his parents' house. When he made the Wings, he moved to a two-bedroom apartment on Detroit's riverfront, rooming with fellow 1983 draft pick Lane Lambert.

"Steve and I became very close early on," Lambert said in 2020. "A lot of the guys were married back then, so we struck up that relationship at the draft. It just kind of fell into place. I think Jimmy D. probably would have preferred we lived with family, but we decided to go out on our own and see what that was all about. We were pretty raw and pretty green, and both came from sort of smaller towns in Canada, and, all of a sudden, our eyes are wide open in Detroit, Michigan."

Devellano would take the teenagers out to dinner to make sure they were eating well.

The Wings had 2,100 season ticket holders when the 1982–83 season ended. By November 1983 attendance at Joe Louis Arena improved by nearly 6,000 compared to the previous autumn. In December, Yzerman was named the NHL rookie of the month. (The reward was a video cassette recorder.) In January he was the only rookie named to the NHL All-Star Game. In typical Yzerman fashion, he craved team success more than individual success.

"I'd just as soon be in the playoffs," he said. "Really, my only goal at the beginning of the season was to make the playoffs."

Yzerman got the other thing he wanted as the Wings advanced to the playoffs for the first time since 1977–78. There wasn't much pedigree to the squad—Polano described the roster as having "nine not-wanted guys and four finesse guys," the latter group numbering Yzerman, John Ogrodnick, Brad Park, and Ivan Boldirev. (Boldirev fit in both categories, as the Wings had, in Polano's words, "gotten him for nothing.") The Wings lost the best-of-five series, three-games-to-one to the St. Louis Blues. Yzerman was a beast in the playoffs, leading his team with four goals and six points, but they ended on a scare for him when he was carried from the ice with 11 seconds left in the second period of the fourth game having suffered a severe knee sprain.

"I played my hardest," he said afterward. Blues defenseman Rob Ramage, the guy whose blindside hit had sent Yzerman reeling, complimented Yzerman's toughness. "He's the rookie of the year in my book," Ramage said.

Yzerman led all rookies with 48 assists and 87 points. (His 39 goals were one behind No. 2 pick Turgeon. LaFontaine had delayed his NHL career until after the 1984 Winter Olympic Games in Sarajevo, Yugoslavia, and did not play for the Islanders until February 29. LaFontaine finished with 19 points in 15 games, with a 1.27 points-per-game average that topped Yzerman's 1.06 average.)

As superlative as Yzerman was, Professional Hockey Writers Association voters favored Buffalo Sabres goaltender Tom Barrasso, who got 242 votes to Yzerman's runner-up 203 votes, for the 1984 Calder Trophy. But Ramage was not alone in his feelings: the night of the NHL awards banquet, Ilitch gave Yzerman an envelope with a $25,000 check and told him, "You're my rookie of the year."

The Wings were delighted with their draftee and a year later signed Yzerman to a seven-year contract, longer than any other deal in franchise history at that time. It was estimated to be worth $350,000 a year. That was in October 1985. Two days before the start of the 1986–87 season, coach Jacques Demers presented Yzerman with a sweater bearing a "C" at a news conference, making him the youngest captain in franchise history, at 21 years. Yzerman finished that season with a team-leading 90 points. The next season Yzerman became just the fourth player in franchise history to score 50 goals in one season. (For that, Ilitch gave Yzerman a $50,000 bonus.) Yzerman reached the milestone when he scored a goal on March 1, 1988. Nowadays the puck would be dug out of the net and preserved as memorabilia, but back then Yzerman tossed the puck into the stands on his way back to the bench because he thought someone else would appreciate the memento more than he would.

"I have the memory of it and I'll never forget it," he said. "I don't need a puck." He did have the puck from his first goal, which was presented to him on a plaque by Devellano and at the time hung in his parents' home in Nepean. Yzerman also ended up with the one from that March night in 1988 because the fan who caught the puck gave it to Demers, who in return gifted the fan a different puck and a stick.

But the lasting memory of that game was a painful one: with 1:59 left in the second period of the game against the Buffalo Sabres, Yzerman crashed into a goal post and suffered a severed posterior cruciate ligament in his right knee. The injury was deemed so serious that after a first opinion from the head of orthopedic surgery at Hutzel Hospital in Detroit, the Wings flew Yzerman to Wisconsin on a private plane for a second consultation with the head of Wisconsin's Department of Sports Medicine.

Yzerman underwent arthroscopic surgery, returned to Detroit, and set about waiting. His teammates marched on into the playoffs, beating the Toronto Maple Leafs in round two and then the St. Louis Blues to set up a meeting with the Edmonton Oilers in the Campbell Conference Final. On May 5 Yzerman took part in warmups before Game 2 of the series, but Demers said no when Yzerman asked if he could play. Finally, after nine weeks, he was back in uniform on May 7 for Game 3. On his first shift, Yzerman dove to block a shot. He earned an assist on the Wings' first goal. The Wings lost in five games to the Oilers, but in the three games Yzerman played, he contributed four points.

The following season, in 1988–89, Yzerman recorded a career-high 155 points (65 goals, 90 assists), finishing third in regular-season scoring behind Mario Lemieux (189 points) and Wayne Gretzky (168 points). Yzerman was voted the MVP by his fellow players (the award changed names from Lester B. Pearson to Ted Lindsay in 2010) and was a finalist for the Hart Memorial Trophy, the MVP award voted on by NHL writers.

Yzerman was doing well professionally and personally (marriage, fatherhood), and the Wings were a much-improved team as the 1990s began, benefiting from the amazing 1989 draft that saw the Wings select Nicklas Lidström, Sergei Fedorov, and Vladimir Konstantinov. But the ultimate playoff success remained elusive.

In 1993 Yzerman began playing under his sixth Wings head coach. The Wings had elite centers in Yzerman and Fedorov and elite defensemen in Lidström and Konstantinov, and the only aspect the Ilitches had left to address was bringing in an elite coach. Bowman was considered quirky, but he got the best out of his players, and he had won the Cup six times by the time the Wings hired him.

Bowman set to work familiarizing himself with his new team and its captain.

"I didn't know that much about Steve because I was in another division, but I did know he had had a terrible injury," Bowman said in 2023. "The knee was not that great. But he was the captain and had been there nine, 10 years. I had a good relationship with Mike Ilitch. He told me with Steve I hadn't seen anything yet. He said the guy had been in the league for a decade and that he hadn't even reached his full potential. And sure enough, he hadn't."

Bowman set about getting the Wings to play a style of hockey conducive to playoff success, starting with Yzerman.

"I explained to him that we were trying to get better in the playoffs, and to do that, you just can't try to score goals," Bowman said. "Teams can get shut down in the playoffs. The refereeing is a little different, and teams play each other maybe up to seven games. I said to Steve, 'We can't worry about trying to outscore teams all the time; we have to play some defense.' And he had had 160 points and I don't know how many goals. I said, 'You're probably going to lose some of your own production.' But he didn't care. He wanted to win a Cup. I just told him the whole team has to play a different style, and usually it starts with you. And then he was blocking shots and he was killing penalties. He didn't care that he wasn't going to get the same point total. He told me, 'I don't care about that at all.' Sure enough, that's the way he transferred his skills.

"Steve took it and ran with it, and it had a big influence on the way the team played a different style. They had a good team before I went there. They could score goals, but the playoffs were a different story."

The playoffs were a different story, eventually. The Wings lost in the first round in 1994, just as they had in 1993, but in 1995 they advanced to the Stanley Cup Final—only to be swept by the New Jersey Devils.

It wasn't just coming up short so close to the Cup that challenged Yzerman in 1995; he also was the subject of trade speculation for the second time in his career. In 1992 it had been 10 years since Ilitch bought the team, and Bryan Murray had taken over as general manager after Jimmy Devellano moved into an executive position. The Wings had missed the playoffs in 1990, lost in the first round in 1991, and been swept in the second round in 1992.

In 1991 LaFontaine, the local hockey star who Ilitch had coveted at the draft, forced the Islanders to trade him, landing with the Buffalo Sabres. The Wings and Sabres discussed trading Yzerman and LaFontaine straight up but ultimately Ilitch nixed the idea.

Yzerman's name came up in trade talks again three years later. Again, it was tied around the appeal of being a hometown player, only this time, Yzerman was the one who was a local. The Ottawa Senators had joined the NHL in 1992 and they were terrible and struggling to draw fans. Yzerman had grown up around Ottawa, in Nepean, and held the exact same appeal LaFontaine did for the Wings in 1983. Randy Sexton, the Senators general manager, reached out to Bowman, who was also the Wings director of player personnel, to discuss an Yzerman trade.

Any such deal would have needed Ilitch's approval to go through, but it never got to that point. The Senators didn't have anyone who the Wings wanted more than Yzerman, and more importantly, they couldn't afford Yzerman's salary. What Bowman did get out of it was letting Yzerman know he wasn't untouchable.

The 1995 trade rumors percolated in October, just before the season. Yzerman was mad enough about seeing his name involved in such discussions that he criticized the organization in local newspapers, saying that he thought management owed it to him to tell him in person. He also said he wasn't upset at the possibility. Yzerman could give as good as he took.

The fact that it was mostly Bowman playing games with Yzerman didn't matter to fans. They greeted Yzerman's introduction at the home opener with cheers and chants, letting management know just how beloved Yzerman was. Bowman? He got booed almost as loudly as Yzerman was cheered.

That was the last time Yzerman's name was sullied by trade talks.

Yzerman was 18 when the Wings drafted him and 32 when he finally hoisted the Stanley Cup. His resume by then already impressed. On February 19, 1997, he played in his 1,000th NHL game (and assisted on three of the goals in a 4–0 shutout of the Calgary Flames), joining Howe and Alex Delvecchio as Wings with 1,000 regular-season games. "It's all been with Detroit," Yzerman said, "but I feel like I've been on four or five different teams here." The year before, he had scored his 500th career goal. Then there was the highlight goal of his career, when he scored in double overtime in Game 7 against St. Louis in the 1996 Western Conference Finals. He was named to his seventh NHL All-Star Game in 1997.

The one NHL item missing was the Cup, and that changed on June 7, 1997. Two nights earlier, before the first of that Final's games in Detroit, the crowd at Joe Louis Arena lost all composure when Yzerman was introduced, rattling the roof with deafening noise. It was 14 years of watching Yzerman work so hard and deal with every disappointment with dignity. And finally, finally it was over, and Yzerman accepted the Cup, hoisted it over his head, and smiled, his grin gap toothed because a toothache that flared during the playoffs led to a crown in his front teeth being removed, and he hadn't had time to get a new one.

Tomas Holmström had only joined the team that season, and he got emotional watching Yzerman that night. "I almost started crying," he said.

Yzerman had become a complete player under Bowman, and with that came the reward that completed his NHL dream.

"Steve was a determined player," Bowman said in 2023. "When the game started, he seemed to be in a zone. A lot of times, people had to quiet him down because he was so competitive, like about the referees calling penalties or not calling penalties. He wasn't a crybaby, but he was determined. He was in a zone when the game started, it looked like he was somewhere else for two-and-a-half hours.

"What he had going for him, more than most people, was that he was ultracompetitive. He really wanted to win and he wanted to do more. He wasn't a big man, but it didn't bother him. He got a lot of attention, but he always wanted to do more."

Yzerman did do more, much more: He won a second Cup in 1998, leading a group raw with emotion from having dealt with a devastating limousine accident six days after the 1997 Cup championship that ended the careers of Vladimir Konstantinov and team masseur Sergei Mnatsakanov. The night he hoisted the Cup, again, Yzerman was also awarded the Conn Smythe Trophy, given to the playoff MVP.

On November 26, 1999, Yzerman became the 11th player in NHL history to score 600 goals. On June 15, 2000, he also was awarded the Frank J. Selke Trophy as the NHL's best defensive forward. On February 24, 2002, Yzerman won an Olympic gold medal with Team Canada.

What he did in 2002 added to Yzerman's legend. His right knee by then was in such bad shape that he only played one game for the Wings after the Olympics, but he was there for them in the playoffs, all 23 games it took to win another Stanley Cup.

"Steve on multiple occasions came back from some horrendous injuries," Kirk Maltby said in 2023. "Like, sometimes he didn't need to say anything because all you had to do was look at him. When you watched Steve play, there were times you felt the pain for him. When you watched him fall down, getting back up, it was a battle for him. To be able to do it, I don't think there are too many people in the league who would have played through what he played through. And he didn't complain about it once. Not before, not after. He just did what he had to do to prepare himself.

"I remember when he took the puck in the face, and he got that awful eye injury, he wanted to keep playing. It's like, *you can't*. We're like, *if you get hit in the face again, like just a shove, the bones are broken, they could go into your eye socket*. But Steve—he wanted to be there. That's Steve. He just wanted to play. And Steve Yzerman at 60–70 percent is better than most players, and I think that's probably the percentage he was at in those '02 playoffs."

Yzerman had 23 points in the '02 playoffs, including two goals in the Game 5 finale against the Carolina Hurricanes. But what his teammates remember is what he did after they lost the first two games of the first-round series against the Vancouver Canucks. It was an unbelievably bad look because the 2001–02 team was the one that 20 years later boasted nine players who had been inducted into the Hockey Hall of Fame, plus Bowman.

"When you're a team like we were and you lose the first two games, we had a crisis," Maltby said. "Steve handled it. And all he really said was that we all had to play better. He said, 'Let's not doubt ourselves.' It wasn't a big speech, like, *come on, boys.* And he started by pointing at himself. He just basically said that we have to stay the course, that we have to believe in ourselves."

His right knee had bothered Yzerman since 1988, when he scored the goal that gave him his first 50-goal season but also crashed into a goal post. He underwent an osteotomy, a realignment procedure that at the time was considered radical. There were questions about whether he would be able to play again. He missed 66 games, but again he showed that indefatigable side of him that was so admired: Yzerman returned to play on February 24, 2003, greeted, again, by a standing ovation.

Yzerman played on through 2003–04, which ended with a second-round loss to the Calgary Flames and another scary injury for Yzerman. In Game 5 Yzerman was hit in the head when teammate Mathieu Schneider's shot deflected off a defender and slammed into Yzerman. Yzerman was down for a couple minutes before being helped off, clutching a towel to his left eye.

Yzerman had time to recover, waiting through the labor dispute that wiped out the 2004–05 season. He suited up for 61 games in 2005–06. The Wings finished with 124 points, the second-highest total in franchise history, and cruised into the playoffs having won the Presidents' Trophy. Yzerman endured a torn oblique muscle that sidelined him for Games 4 and 5 in the first-round series against the Oilers but returned to play in Game 6, earning an assist. The 4–3 loss ended up being the last time Yzerman suited up to play an NHL game for the Red Wings.

He was eight days shy of his 41st birthday and had pushed his body beyond all reasonable limit. He announced his retirement in July, and three years later, when he was inducted into the Hall of Fame, admitted he should have retired after the '02 season. "I was so relieved to retire," he said. "I was falling apart."

Yzerman almost called it a career during the season. He had toughened it out through so many injuries that it was almost impossible to tell the degree to which he was in pain. He had missed the November 26 game because of what he said at the time was a sore knee. But Yzerman had also suffered a head injury, and that seemed a sign to hang up his skates. Tentative plans were for Yzerman to play his last game on December 1, when the Wings were back home. Yzerman suited up November 28, and, as fortune would have it, Robert Lang suffered a groin injury that forced him to leave the game in the second period. The Wings needed Yzerman, and he responded with a goal and an assist. The performance convinced Yzerman to change his mind.

"I had planned to retire," he said. "I had some injuries there; I felt terrible, and our team was doing well. We were in California, and I had been thinking about it for a little bit and debated it just by myself. I wasn't happy with how I felt, and my team was doing well. There wasn't going to be any announcements before the game about a 'final game.' But I would have liked to play one more game in Joe Louis Arena and go from there. I was hoping to do it quietly, with one more game, then go."

Yzerman and general manager Ken Holland talked again after Yzerman's performance in Los Angeles. With the prospect of getting more minutes, Yzerman postponed his decision till Christmas. And then he postponed it for the rest of the season.

"I was like, *well, we've got to make the best of this*," Yzerman said.

He finally made his announcement July 3, at a news conference at the Joe, nine weeks to the day he played his last game.

By the time he retired, Yzerman already was a trusted sounding board for the Wings hockey operations department, someone whose input on decisions big and small mattered. "We know he can be a help to our organization in many, many, many ways," Devellano said. "He's smart. He knows what it takes to win.

"He is a Red Wing."

Yzerman spent four years working in the front office under the title vice president of hockey operations, winning his fourth Stanley Cup in 2008 as a member of management. By 2010 Yzerman's services were in demand—the Minnesota Wild interviewed him to be general manager in 2009, ultimately selecting Chuck Fletcher instead—and the Ilitches didn't want to see Yzerman be anything but a Red Wing. Mike Ilitch approached Ken Holland about shifting positions from GM to team president, but Holland wasn't ready to relinquish the role he had been promoted to in 1997.

That was in early May 2010. By the end of the month, the unthinkable had happened: Yzerman would work for another NHL team. Yzerman broke the news that he had accepted the

GM job with the Tampa Bay Lightning by going over to the Ilitches house and telling them in person.

His time with the Lightning was rewarding, as Yzerman built an up-and-coming team into a contender. But his family life remained in Detroit, where he and his wife had built their home. In September 2018, Yzerman announced he was stepping back to serve as an advisor, in what was the last year of his contract with the Lightning.

This time, it was Holland who preemptively cleared the path for Yzerman's return, discussing the subject with Chris Ilitch, the son whose ownership role expanded after Mike Ilitch's death in February 2017. This time, everybody wanted Yzerman to manage the Wings.

It would happen as soon as the Lightning's season ended—and as it happened, that came quickly, swept out in the first round. The Lightning were ousted on April 16, and three days later, The Captain was the general manager where he belonged. Marian Ilitch attended the news conference. As Yzerman and Chris Ilitch posed for pictures, Marian Ilitch called Yzerman's return "the best thing that has happened to me lately."

Her words could have been spoken by Wings fans everywhere. Gordie Howe defined the Wings during the Original Six era; Steve Yzerman did so during the Ilitch era, representing the franchise's rebirth. He played 1,514 games, producing 692 goals and 1,063 assists, and 196 playoff games with 70 goals and 115 assists. His leadership was legendary. So was his lack of pretension.

"I remember the first time I met him," Kris Draper said in 2023. "It was January 24, 1994, and it was my first game with the Detroit Red Wings. I walked in for the pregame skate and Steve came over and introduced himself and said, 'Hi, I'm Steve Yzerman.' He said, 'Welcome to the Red Wings and good luck, let me know if you need anything.' The way he carried himself then, he still does it. I watch him interact with our prospects and he introduces himself. He wants these guys to feel comfortable here in Detroit and understand the expectations. I don't know if he realizes how many careers he impacted just by leading by example, not even having to say anything."

Draper, Maltby, and Lidström became part of Yzerman's inner circle in his role as GM. They all say the same thing: that relentless drive to win that he showed as a player is still there, still defines Yzerman as he works out of his corner office at Little Caesars Arena with a view of Woodward Avenue and downtown Detroit. "You always see it with him," Maltby said. "He loves the Red Wings."

6

Nicklas Lidström

AMONG THE LEGENDS ASCRIBED TO NICKLAS LIDSTRÖM IS the time he saved the Red Wings in the 1997 playoffs.

It was Game 2 of the Western Conference Finals. Joe Sakic won a faceoff against Steve Yzerman and the puck squirted out to Scott Young, who fired a shot from the top of the right circle that Mike Vernon came out of his net to stop. Vernon wasn't able to corral the puck and while he was still far away from his crease, Eric Lacroix directed a point-blank shot at the net. With an effortless grace, Lidström glided through the blue paint and used his stick to deflect the puck as it headed for the open net. Had it gone in, it would have been 3–3. Instead, Darren McCarty scored on a breakaway a minute later for a 4–2 victory to tie the series at one game apiece.

"They would have been right back in the game," Yzerman said afterward. "Nick saved it for us."

Yzerman was as effusive 15 years later when Lidström called it a career after 20 seasons of perfection: "He's going to go down as one of the all-time best defensemen to ever play. Having played with him, you have to watch him closely to appreciate how good he is because he makes the position look so easy. He was special."

The story of how Lidström came to be drafted by the Wings demonstrates the power of connections. A player named Jörgen Holmberg saw Lidström in practice a few times while they were playing for Västerås and was so impressed with what the teenager could do that he recommended Lidström to his friend Christer Rockström, who was a scout for the Wings. Rockström in turn brought in Neil Smith, one of the Wings' top scouts, and he saw the same thing Holmberg and Rockström did: a fluid skater who made everything look easy. Never was Lidström caught out of position, even against wily older players who were bigger and stronger.

"I saw him play 13 or 14 times and I never saw him make a mistake," Rockström said in 1989. "He's a defensive defenseman who can move the puck and pass well. He's not flashy, but he has the perfect attitude."

Back then, there wasn't much vetting of a player's background—all that mattered was if he looked good on the ice. But had the Wings dug into Lidström's tender past, they would have found nothing more incriminating than that he used to steal apples from a neighbor's trees.

Smith and Rockström, who answered to general manager Jimmy Devellano, wanted to draft Lidström. They knew he didn't have the cachet to be a first-round pick because he did not stand out statistically in his draft year: two points in 20 games in the top league and five points in 15 games in the lower-level Allsvenskan. Most of the NHL scouts who came to Sweden leading up to the 1989 draft were there to see Patrik Juhlin, a forward who ended up being selected 34th by the Philadelphia Flyers. Still, in order to keep their interest a secret,

Smith forbade anyone in the Wings organization from talking about Lidström—even to each other.

What couldn't be heard, couldn't be overheard.

On the other side of the Atlantic Ocean, Rockström tried to detract attention away from Lidström when other scouts—or player agents—were at games. Don Meehan, who would go on to represent Lidström for part of his pro career, had to ask multiple times who that player was wearing No. 9 for Västerås before Rockström relented and told him. Rockström entreated Meehan to keep things quiet. When Meehan got back to North America, he called Smith, who at first pretended not to know who Lidström was—and then resorted to an expletive-filled plea not to talk about him with anyone else.

The Wings were so desperate to keep Lidström a secret that they were willing to disappoint him: a week before the draft, Rockström called Lidström and told him not to come to Minnesota, site of the draft. Smith was worried a scout from another team might see Lidström and decide to draft him before the Wings could get to him.

The draft fell on June 17 at the Met Center in Bloomington. (The arena was demolished in 1994 and the site is now home to Swedish superstore IKEA.) Mats Sundin became the first European-born player to be drafted first overall when the Quebec Nordiques selected the 6'5" Swede. Sundin was an exceptional talent, for the general perception at the time was that European players weren't as tough as Canadian ones, and that the Stanley Cup didn't mean as much to them. Of the 42 players selected in the first two rounds in 1989, only five were from outside North America.

The Wings followed that pattern and used their first picks on Canadians: Mike Sillinger at 11th and Bob Boughner at 32nd.

Then Smith and Rockström set to work on Devellano, urging him to draft Lidström. They only had one shot left, because back then, there was a rule that teenagers had to be drafted in the first three rounds. Smith was certain that if the Wings didn't take Lidström then and there, when their pick came up at 53rd, he would either be taken by another team before the round was over—or go in the first round in 1990; either way, Smith was certain this was their only chance at Lidström.

Rockström highlighted everything he liked about Lidström as Devellano listened: Smooth skater. High-end hockey sense. Impossible to rattle. Incredibly sound positionally. Adept in all situations.

Devellano wanted to know how big he was: 6'1", 178 pounds. Smith was blunt: Lidström needed to get stronger and needed to spend another year or two playing in Sweden, but he would be worth the wait. He was absolutely worth taking in the third round over any Canadian player. Devellano trusted his scouts, telling them, "Okay, he's your pick."

Lidström found out about it when the Wings called him at his parents' house. His mom and dad had asked him to answer the phone that day, reluctant to chance hearing someone speaking English on the other end.

Smith's urgency was valid: Lidström went on to be a star for Västerås the following season; he made the national team and played for the World Championship team that brought home the gold medal from Finland.

Lidström signed a three-year contract with the Wings in May 1991. His arrival in Detroit that autumn coincided with that of another of the Wings' 1989 draft picks: Vladimir Konstantinov, selected in the 11th round. Together they were the young star defensemen whom the Wings depended on to carry them to the Stanley Cup.

Lidström finished his rookie season with 60 points, tying Pavel Bure, but it was the Russian star who won the Calder Trophy as the NHL's top rookie. (In the overall voting tally, Bure topped Lidström 222–183, but Bure's lead in first-place votes was only 26–23.)

Known by the nickname "Lidas" in his native Sweden, Wings teammates started out calling Lidström "Super Swede," but between his flawless performances on ice and his flawless English, he soon became known as "The Perfect Human."

By the mid-1990s, Lidström's perfection was pushing the Wings toward longer playoff runs. It was Lidström who scored 1:01 into overtime in Game 1 of the Western Conference Finals against the Chicago Blackhawks, sending jubilant fans at Joe Louis Arena to their feet. His blast from near the blue line cemented a 2–1 victory and caused an outpouring of appreciation from his teammates.

"Nick's got one of the best shots in the league," defense partner Paul Coffey said. "People don't realize how good he is." Slava Fetisov, himself one of the best defensemen ever, said Lidström, "represents well the European school of hockey. He is very skillful, a good skater, and he has an unbelievable shot. He is not easy to hit, and he's tough enough, for sure. That's a pretty good combination, I think."

The following year, 1996, Lidström was selected to the first of his 12 NHL All-Star Games. (When he told his sister, she replied, "Now you get to play with Wayne Gretzky.") There were teammates who naturally garnered more attention— Yzerman, Coffey, Sergei Fedorov—because they were flashier and scored more, but nobody played more: Lidström was the team's workhorse, averaging around 25 minutes a game. His intelligence, his positioning, his skating, his shot—it was what Rockström and Smith had seen nearly a decade earlier, only even better than they had anticipated. Lidström didn't deliver the sort of crunching hits that drew highlight-reel clips, like Konstantinov, because Lidström didn't need to—by playing so positionally perfect, he eliminated his opponent, rendering him ineffective.

It wasn't just Lidström's flawless play that begat his being called "The Perfect Human," it was also that he came across that way in all aspects: he said little, never complained, worked hard, did what was asked, hung up his own equipment, kept himself as neat and efficient as his performances. Bob Rouse, a fellow defenseman, would later tell the story of how Lidström reacted when Rouse called to tell him the $90,000 Mercedes Rouse had borrowed from Lidström had a dented bumper from a restaurant valet service: "I didn't hear him swear," Rouse said, "but I think there was a little smoke coming out of his ears." Lidström's soon-to-be wife, Annika, bore witness that it was a rarity to see him upset: "He's always so calm."

The only penalty Lidström took during the 20 games it took the Wings to win the Cup in 1997 was in Game 3 of the conference semifinals against the Anaheim Ducks. It was a rare sight: Teemu Selanne managed to annoy Lidström enough to draw him into a high-sticking violation that left the Wings short-handed with their best penalty killer serving two minutes in the box.

When the Wings faced the Philadelphia Flyers in the '97 Stanley Cup Final, it was Lidström and partner Larry Murphy who Scotty Bowman decided to match up against Eric Lindros and his Legion of Doom linemates John LeClair and Mikael Renberg, so nicknamed because each of the three was 6'2" or taller and weighed over 230 pounds. Lidström never let Lindros have any room. Of the 12 goals Lindros scored in the '97 playoffs, only one came against the Wings.

"Nick played a basic game," Bowman said in 2023. "There was nothing fancy about it, but he was airtight defensively. He had nuances—he knew how to play with his feet, he could use his stick to hold guys off, he didn't get very many penalties. There have been some great defensemen, but a lot of them have been great offensively, but they didn't have the defense like Nick. I think all the coaches that ever had him always played Nick against the other team's best players. When you have a Nick Lidström on your team, his job is to play against the other team's best players."

In the '98 playoffs, St. Louis Blues star Brett Hull—a future teammate with the Wings—wasn't heard from in the second round after a Game 1 goal, and his frustration percolated to the surface once the Wings had clinched the victory in Game 6. "Pretty much every time I stepped onto the ice, he and Murphy were out there, and I rarely saw any room to operate," Hull said. "Both are tremendous position defensemen. I wish Lidström was bigger and more inclined to go after you. That way it would be easier to make a move on him or to get him to bite. You just can't rattle him into making mistakes."

Lidström had an effortlessness about his performances that belied how hard he worked. "He controls the game," Fetisov said in April 1997. "I think he is the most valuable defenseman in the league. His skill level is incredible. Some great defensemen are very good at offense, but he is so good in both ends of the rink. He is very quiet, but he has so much presence."

Teammates took it as a personal victory if they could outperform him.

"Scotty Bowman, he wanted to see hard work in practice, he wanted you to execute drills," Kirk Maltby said. "We would do drills two-on-one, and I would commonly go with Kris [Draper]. And we would get halfway down the ice making a few passes and Nick's gap was perfect, and he'd get the puck from us. The few times we did get the puck across, we would finish the drill and it was like you had scored on Nick Lidström. He was perfect. He should have been a dual-sport athlete in hockey and baseball because his hand-eye coordination was incredible, the way he batted the puck out of the air. Right at the blue line he would bat it away. He really was perfect at it."

In the 1997 playoffs, Lidström averaged nearly 30 minutes a game, garnering chatter as a candidate for the Conn Smythe Trophy. "Mike Vernon will probably win it, but to me Nick has been as valuable as anybody on our team," Wings scout Mark Howe said the day before the clinching game. (Howe was right: Vernon did win it.) Lidström scored the first goal in the 2–1 victory that sealed the Cup championship on June 7, 1997.

A second Stanley Cup followed in 1998. Lidström carried a heavy workload that season because of the tragedy that had befallen the Wings six days after they won the Cup, when Konstantinov, Fetisov, and team masseur Sergei Mnatsakanov were involved in a limousine crash. The accident robbed Konstantinov of his career. Now the defense numbered Lidström, who was 27—and an aging corps consisting of Fetisov (39), Murphy (37), and Rouse (33), plus inexperienced youngsters in Jamie Pushor and Aaron Ward (both 24), Anders Eriksson (22), and Mathieu Dandenault (21). Lidström responded as would be expected: for the first time in his career, he finished atop the scoring race among league defensemen, with 59 points in 80 games. Game after game, Lidström delivered. The Wings used him against opposing top lines, on the power play and penalty kill, when they needed to protect a narrow lead, and when they needed to overcome a deficit. He never got caught up ice. He never needlessly gave up the puck. If he had possession of the puck, the Wings knew they would keep it until a scoring play could be made.

Lidström was consistent, he was durable; he was the very definition of a consummate pro. He was 31 years old when he won his first James Norris Memorial Trophy as the NHL's top defenseman in 2001—but then he won it again five of the next six seasons, and a seventh time in 2011, the year before he retired. Lidström has the most Norris trophies after the NHL expanded from the 18 teams that were in the NHL when Bobby Orr finished his reign of eight straight Norris trophies from 1968 to 1975.

Lidström scored a memorable playoff goal in '97 when he found the back of Philadelphia's net in the Cup-clinching game, but it was in 2002 that he scored his most improbable one. It was 1–1 in Game 3 of the first-round series against the Vancouver Canucks, with the Wings having lost the first two games. There were 24.6 seconds left in the second period when Lidström carried the puck up the middle of the ice and ripped a slap shot from center ice that eluded goaltender Dan Cloutier.

Lidström scored five goals in the '02 playoffs. His fifth one was noteworthy, too: the Carolina Hurricanes had won Game 1 in overtime, at the Joe, and it was 1–1 as the third period wore on in Game 2. Lidström averted another overtime when he scored during a power play at 14:52.

"Some of the guys were teasing me in the locker room when we watched the replay," Lidström said. "They said, 'Hey, Nick, you actually showed some emotion there. You raised your arms and had a little leg kick, too.'"

The Wings were used to Lidström plowing away, playing monster minutes, doing everything perfectly, while never drawing attention to himself or showing up on highlight reels.

"I always say, watch Nick carefully and you'll appreciate him even more," Yzerman said. "He plays a smart game. He knows what spots to be in, so I think he doesn't exhaust himself."

As in 1997, Lidström only took one penalty, a minor, in the 2002 playoffs.

When the Wings' run in '02 ended after 23 games, there were teammates with more points than Lidström's 16, but there was no one more deserving of the Conn Smythe. On June 13, 2002, he became the first European to be awarded the trophy.

Few were happier to see the members of the Professional Hockey Writers Association vote in favor of Lidström than associate coach Dave Lewis, who ran the defense and had helped nurture Lidström's excellence. "It's about time he got some recognition. What a player. He is probably, if not one of the best defensemen in hockey history, he is side by side with anybody."

In the triple-overtime third game of the series, Lidström was on the ice for 52 minutes and three seconds, the only skater to top the 50-minute mark on both teams. Two nights earlier, he had logged 34:38 in a regulation game.

"Look what Nick Lidström did all the way through the playoffs, the minutes he logged," Bowman said. "He's just about a perfect player on the ice. Very few mistakes. He scored some big goals for us. It's a wonderful tribute to him."

More accolades followed. In 2006 Lidström scored the gold medal-clinching goal for Sweden at the Winter Olympics, which earned him a place in the Triple Gold Club (players who have won gold at the Olympics and World Championship and a Stanley Cup). Lidström finished as the tournament's top-scoring defenseman with two goals and four assists in eight games.

"When things got tight, we went down to some key players, and of course he is one of them," Swedish coach Bengt-Åke Gustafsson said. "He played a great, great tournament for us."

When Yzerman retired that offseason, Lidström was named the team's next captain. "The fact that he's generally the best player on the ice I think is the biggest reason," Yzerman said. "He's always there, so guys just know what to expect. He sets the tone for the professionalism for the players, and I think that's really important and that may be his strongest asset as a leader. He's a great representative for the organization."

In 2008 Lidström became the first European born-and-bred player to captain a team to the Stanley Cup. "It felt great to be the first guy to touch the Cup," he said.

Lidström was 41 when he won his seventh Norris trophy in 2011. In January of 2012—Lidström's 20th NHL season— Toronto Maple Leafs coach Ron Wilson asked, "Why doesn't he retire, anyway, and give us all a break?" Wilson laughed as he said it; it was an acknowledgment of Lidström's greatness.

"I know when I've coached along the way here, we've used him as an example to show, in terms of video—if you don't have good things to show about your own team, you always show Nick Lidström highlights," Wilson said. "This is how he moves the puck, this is how he defends...And he's not a physical player at all and yet he defends as well as anybody. Even at his age, to be able to put points up on the boards—just his shooting from the point, he rarely gets his shot blocked. The little subtle things that he has in his game are great teaching tools for younger players to use him as a model."

As it turned out, Lidström did retire that year. His NHL hardware included four Stanley Cups, seven Norris Trophies, and a Conn Smythe. Mark Howe, son of Gordie Howe and himself a Hockey Hall of Fame member, recalled the time in 2011 when he was asked to put together a six-man team of the best players he had seen. Mark Howe named his dad, Terry Sawchuk, Mario Lemieux, Wayne Gretzky, Bobby Orr, and Lidström.

To Bowman, whose list of players he coached was a who's-who of hockey, Lidström was as low-maintenance as they come.

"You didn't try to coach him because he had a unique amount of hockey sense," Bowman said in 2023. "I think what he did more than anything—he was always a guy that didn't want to make mistakes. He didn't take very many chances. He didn't really grab the puck and try to carry it all the time. Yet if you look at his offensive production, it was amazing."

Lidström retired having played 1,564 regular-season games, second in team history behind Gordie Howe's 1,657, during which Lidström had 264 goals and 878 assists, a plus-540 rating and just 514 penalty minutes. He played 263 playoff games, posting 54 goals and 129 assists, a plus-61 rating and 76 penalty minutes. (While Lidström never won the Lady Byng Trophy for gentlemanly play, he was a six-time finalist.) During Lidström's tenure, the Wings never missed the playoffs.

"He made it look so easy," Maltby said. "He was so effortless. He was a guy you thought really could have played a full 60-minute game and not broken a sweat. His hockey sense was ridiculous. He made life easier for us."

PART 3

THE STANLEY CUPS

7

The First Cups

THE YEAR 1932 MARKED A TURNING POINT FOR THE FRANCHISE. The club, then known as the Detroit Falcons, made the Stanley Cup playoffs for the first time, finishing third in the NHL American Division with a record of 18–20–10. They didn't go far, losing in the opening round to the Montreal Maroons in a two-game series decided by the most goals scored. It was the same year James E. Norris purchased the club and renamed it the Red Wings.

In 1933–34 the Wings won their first division title with a 24–14–10 record and advanced to the Stanley Cup Final for the first time. They defeated the Canadian division-leading Toronto Maple Leafs in the semifinals before losing to the Chicago Black Hawks in the Final, three games to one. Mush March scored at 10:05 of double overtime to give the Black Hawks the championship.

"We will win it all next year," coach and general manager of the Wings Jack Adams said afterward.

He was close: they won it all two years later. It began with the longest game in NHL history.

The 1935–36 Wings began the playoffs by facing the Montreal Maroons in the semifinals. The series began on March 24, at the Forum in Montreal. Game 1 began at 8:30 PM and ended at 2:25 AM. Mud Bruneteau, a rookie who had been called up two weeks earlier, scored at 16:30 of the sixth overtime, beating Maroons goaltender Lorne Chabot to win the game 1–0. Detroit goaltender Normie Smith earned the shutout with more than 90 saves.

"I can't remember everything that happened 50 years ago," Smith said in a 1986 interview in the *Detroit Free Press*. "But I do remember I had a pretty good club in front of me. We were real good."

Smith, who was only 5'7" and 165 pounds, played a huge part in the lore created by the '35–36 team. He led the NHL that season in minutes played (3,030) and victories (24) and he played all of the Wings' seven games in the two rounds of the best-of-five playoffs (the Wings won their second straight regular-season title, drawing a bye in the first round).

Shots on goal weren't recorded then, but Smith is generally considered to have made either 91 or 92 saves.

"When I went into the game, I had some butterflies," Smith said. "Of course, I had no idea how long the game would eventually last. But as it got longer and longer into the game, I seemed to settle down."

Smith began to feel the strain after the first couple overtime periods. "Near the end, the pads and equipment were getting heavy from being soaked with sweat and water," he said. "When I saw the red light go on to end the game, I thought, 'School's out!' I was very happy it finally ended. I really found out how tired I was afterward, when we went to the Lumberjacks Club in Montreal, and I had one bottle of ale. That set me right back on my heels."

Pete Kelly, a right wing on the team, described his memories of Bruneteau's goal.

"I remember in those days, they didn't make ice in between periods like they do now with the Zamboni," Kelly said. "They only swept the ice, so it was quite rough with a lot of skate marks. The longer the game went, the more difficult the puck was to control.

"Hec [Kilrea] carried the play to the goal area and had made a play on the goal. A rebound resulted, and Bruneteau banged it in on a scramble. There was a fair crowd in front of the net. I was supposed to get half the puck as a memento. But Jim Norris [owner James E. Norris' son] got it."

The Wings swept the Maroons in three games, setting up the championship series against the Maple Leafs. The Wings won the first two games at Olympia Stadium but lost the next game at Maple Leaf Gardens 4–3 in overtime after squandering a 3–0 lead.

In Game 4, also at Maple Leaf Garden, the Wings led 2–1 after the second period on goals from Ebbie Goodfellow and Marty Barry. Kelly scored what would be the Cup-clinching goal at 9:45 of the third period. His shot hit the support bar at the back of the net and came out so quickly the goal judge didn't turn on the light.

Kelly almost panicked.

"I thought they weren't going to count it since the light didn't go on," Kelly said. "I started to complain to the goal judge, then I saw referee Bill Stewart come over and say, 'Yes, yes, yes, I saw it go in.'"

Ten minutes later, the Red Wings celebrated their first Stanley Cup championship in franchise history.

In 1937 the Wings became the first American team to repeat as Stanley Cup champions. Led by Vezina Trophy winning Smith, they finished first in the American Division. (Smith played in the era of maskless goalies and tried wearing a baseball cap for a while to shade his eyes from the glare of the stadium lights. It didn't help.) Both the semifinal series against the Montreal Canadiens and the Final against the New York Rangers went the full five games. The Wings and Rangers played the first game at Madison Square Garden, but the rink was unavailable after that because the circus was in town, so the remaining four games all took place in Detroit, at Olympia Stadium.

The Wings finished last in their division the next season and missed the playoffs. Instead, they ventured overseas to play a pair of exhibition matches against the Montreal Canadiens on May 5 and 11, 1938, at Earls Court Stadium in London. The Wings qualified for the playoffs in 1938–39 and defeated the Canadiens in a best-of-three quarterfinal series but lost in the semifinals to the Maple Leafs. The Wings lost in the second round again in 1940 and were swept by the Boston Bruins after advancing to the Stanley Cup Final in 1941. Another trip to the Final followed in 1942, and it went down in history because the Leafs overcame a 3–0 deficit against the Wings to win the series in seven games. Game 7, at Maple Leaf Gardens, drew 16,218 fans, setting a record for largest crowd to see a hockey game in Canada at that time. Wings forward Syd Howe scored at 1:45 of the second period, and the Wings took that lead into the third period. The Leafs scored three goals less than nine minutes apart to complete the unprecedented comeback.

Vengeance for the Wings came the following spring, when they eliminated the Leafs in six games in the semifinals and then swept the Bruins in the Final. Goalie Johnny Mowers blanked the Bruins in the final two games, and Joe Carveth scored the Cup-winning goal.

It was the franchise's 17th season, 11th as the Red Wings, and their third Stanley Cup championship.

8

The First Dynasty

FOLLOWING WORLD WAR II, THE RED WINGS EMBARKED on a winning binge that brought glory and fame, enshrining the franchise as a spectacular success. From 1948–49 through 1954–55, they won seven consecutive NHL regular-season titles and four Stanley Cup championships. The men who populated those teams grew into legends whose accomplishments were enshrined in the Hockey Hall of Fame.

The Stanley Cup first made its home in Detroit in 1936 and 1937, when the likes of Marty Barry, Syd Howe, Mud Bruneteau, Ebbie Goodfellow, and Larry Aurie turned a nascent hockey club into a treasured champion.

A third Cup followed in 1943. As the 1940s rolled on, the Wings began to resemble a juggernaut.

After being knocked out early in 1946 and 1947, the Wings rose to the top of the league standings and advanced to the Stanley Cup Final in 1948 and 1949 only to lose both years to the Toronto Maple Leafs. In 1949–50 Ted Lindsay, Sid Abel, and Gordie Howe—Detroit's efficient, powerful Production Line members—finished first, second, and third, respectively, in the NHL in points, leading the Wings to the league title with a 37–19–14 record and 88 points. Howe only played one game in the playoffs because of a near-catastrophic injury suffered when an attempt to finish a check ended with Howe crashing head-first into the boards. While Howe recovered, his teammates defeated the Leafs in seven games in the semifinals and bested the New York Rangers in the Final, also in seven games. After Pete Babando scored at 8:31 of double overtime in Game 7 at Olympia Stadium, fans chanted Howe's name and greeted him with a standing ovation when he came onto the ice to be a part of the Cup celebration.

The dynasty was underway.

The Wings' defense of the Cup was strengthened by arrivals of Metro Prystai, Bob Goldham, and Gaye Stewart from the Chicago Black Hawks, the promotion of defenseman Marcel Pronovost, and with Terry Sawchuk in net. They appeared poised to repeat, but were foiled by the Montreal Canadiens, who won a six-game semifinal series.

In 1951–52 the Wings won a fourth straight league title, finishing 44–14–12, and outdistanced their nearest rival, the Canadiens, by 22 points. Sawchuk won the Vezina Trophy on the strength of a 44–14–12 record that included 12 shutouts and came with a 1.90 goals-against average. Howe won the league scoring title with 86 points, 17 points ahead of runner-up Lindsay.

Sawchuk matched his regular-season brilliance in the playoffs, shutting out the Leafs twice in the opening round and the Canadiens twice in the Final to finish with a .63 goals-against average. The Wings won both series in four games.

Prystai scored twice in the fourth game of the Final, in the first and third periods, to secure the Wings' second Cup in three years and fifth in franchise history.

Sawchuk matched his regular-season brilliance in the playoffs, shutting out the Leafs twice in the opening round and the Canadiens twice in the Final to finish with a .63 goals-against average. The Wings won both series in four games, becoming the first team to post a perfect record in pursuit of the Cup.

It was that spring, in April 1952, that saw the start of a tradition that came to define the franchise. Pete Cusimano and his brother, Jerry, sold fish at Detroit's Eastern Market. As it happened, they were hockey fans. Pete Cusimano carried an octopus with him to Olympia Stadium, choosing the eight-limbed mollusk because at that time, it took eight victories to win the Cup.

"We were putting out a display of fish," Pete Cusimano said in a 1987 interview in the *Detroit Free Press*. "My brother, Jerry, picked up one of the octopus and said, 'Pete, here's this thing with eight legs. Why don't we throw it on the ice, and maybe the Wings will win eight straight?' I said, *it's too flimsy; it'd be hard to throw. Why don't we cook it first?*"

At the game, Pete Cusimano, seated just behind one of the nets, hurled the mollusk.

"We threw one. That was it," he said. "We never threw it to disrupt play."

At first, there was confusion.

"The linesman reached down to pick it up," Cusimano said. "Then one of the Wings hit it with his stick, and it kind of moved, and the guy jumped. He thought it was still alive."

Once fans realized what the octopus symbolized, the transition took off. It faded as the Wings' fortunes waned but was revived in the 1980s and cheered as the Wings returned to Cup glory in the 1990s.

Abel was 34 when the Wings won the Cup in 1952 and figured he would play one more season before retiring. But another plan was brewing in Chicago, where a number of Black Hawks players knew Abel from playing with him in Detroit: Babando, Roy Conacher, George Gee, Bep Guidolin, and Rags Raglan. (Clarence Eldon Raglan played 100 games in the NHL between 1950 and 1953. He went by "Rags," sharing a nickname with an American burlesque performer who drank with Orson Welles, acted with Red Skelton, and was friends with Frank Sinatra.)

The ex-Wings recommended to Black Hawks management that Abel would be an excellent choice to coach in Chicago. Jack Adams, Detroit's general manager, gave his permission, and Abel agreed to coach the Black Hawks—and also to play, if needed.

It was an exciting opportunity for Abel, a way to extend his career in hockey. But it meant the end of the original "Production Line" in Detroit, where Abel had been the wise, veteran middleman between hotshot wingers Howe and Lindsay. Alex Delvecchio was a second-year center when he slotted into Abel's old spot, but as good as Delvecchio was, the chemistry wasn't the same.

In December of 1952, James E. Norris, who two decades earlier had rescued the franchise from receivership and rechristened it the Red Wings, passed away. Per his orders, his daughter, Marguerite, was named president of the team. It was a smooth transition, and the Wings turned in another fine regular season with a 36–16–18 record, finishing atop the standings for a fifth straight time in the spring of 1953.

Howe led the league with 49 goals and 95 points—24 ahead of second-place Lindsay and 34 ahead of Montreal's Maurice

THE FRANCHISE: DETROIT RED WINGS

Richard—and was named to the Hart Trophy for a **second** consecutive time. Repeating as champions once again **eluded** the Wings, however, as they were knocked out in six **games** in the first round by the Boston Bruins. The Wings **had not** successfully defended the Stanley Cup since 1937.

It was the Canadiens who entered the 1953–54 season as Cup champions. Howe managed to secure the league **scoring** title again with 81 points, 14 ahead of Richard, but **it was** Richard who led in goals with 37 to Howe's 33. The Wings and Habs dominated the scoring race: Lindsay was in third **place,** Canadiens Bernie Geoffrion and Bert Olmstead in fourth and fifth, respectively, and Detroit's Kelly and Dutch Reibel **in sixth** and seventh, respectively. The Wings took the league **title** again with a 37–19–14 record to Montreal's 35–24–11, **but the** Canadiens scored 195 goals to the Wings' 191 and finished only seven points behind in the standings.

In the first round of the playoffs, the Wings dispatched the Maple Leafs in five games and the Canadiens swept the **Bruins,** setting up a Stanley Cup Final between the top teams **in the** NHL.

The Wings and Canadiens split the first two games, **each** winning 3–1. Delvecchio scored in the opening minute of **Game** 3, and by the end of the first period, Lindsay added **another** goal to quiet the crowd at the Montreal Forum. The Wings led by as much as four goals before the final score settled in their favor 5–2.

Sawchuk bested Jacques Plante in Game 4, delivering **a 2–0** shutout that put the Wings up three games to one **going into** Game 5 back at Olympia Stadium. It was an incredibly **tight** game, scoreless until Ken Mosdell beat Sawchuk at **5:45 of** overtime. Back to Montreal the teams went. This time **it was** the Canadiens who ran up a 3–0 lead en route to a 4–1 **victory.**

Game 7 was at Olympia Stadium. Floyd Curry gave Montreal a lead midway through the first period, but Kelly converted on a power play in the second period to make it 1–1. It remained that way until 4:29 of overtime, when Tony Leswick scored, and once again the Stanley Cup belonged to the Wings. The rivalry by then was so bitter that the Montreal players refused to shake the Wings' players hands after the game.

The Wings had won three Stanley Cups in five years. They were a powerhouse, boasting star power at every position. Howe, Kelly, and Sawchuk would go on to be considered among the best ever at their positions.

A new coach led the defending champions into the 1954–55 season. Tommy Ivan had guided the Wings to the Stanley Cup in 1950, '52, and '54. He was a popular coach in Detroit and beloved by his players, but he had tired of Adams' interference and left to manage the Black Hawks. Adams, who had coached the Wings to the Cup in 1936, '37, and '43, promoted Jimmy Skinner, a 37-year-old minor league coach with no NHL experience.

"They said I had an easy job taking over that club, but it was tough," Skinner said in an interview with Bill Dow in the *Detroit Free Press* in 2005. "People said I couldn't go anywhere but down, and I had to prove the team would play for me."

The Wings trailed Montreal for much of the season, but a winning streak that began with three weeks to go set up a close race for the league title.

"When we started winning, there was just no way we were going to lose," Howe said in 2005. "The attitude was, 'How much are we going to win by tonight?' Either we adjusted to Jimmy Skinner or maybe he adjusted to us, but he got us going in the right direction."

One of the most infamous—and violent—events in NHL history ended up impacting the battle for first place.

On March 16, NHL president Clarence Campbell suspended Richard for the remainder of the season—including the playoffs—as a result of an ugly altercation three days earlier. During a game in Boston, Richard attacked Bruins defenseman Hal Laycoe in retaliation for Laycoe using his stick to hit Richard in the head. When officials tried to break apart the two, Richard punched linesman Cliff Thompson so severely he lost consciousness. After the game Boston police attempted to arrest Richard but were blocked by Richard's teammates and assuaged by a promise that the league would discipline Richard.

When the Wings and Habs took the ice at the Forum the night after the suspension was announced, the crowd seethed with resentment over the punishment. It didn't help when the Wings, at that time an archival, had their way with the home team: Kelly scored on a power play five minutes in, Dutch Reibel made it 2–0, and Kelly followed up with another goal while the Canadiens were on a power play. That was all before the game was 13 minutes old. Right around that time was when Campbell—flouting advice to stay away—showed up, accompanied by three secretaries from the NHL office. If he hoped being surrounded by women would serve as a shield, he erred: fans pelted him with anything they had in their hands or could find.

Detroit Free Press hockey writer Marshall Dann described the scene in the paper the next day: "From the time Clarence Campbell came into the arena after 11:50 of the first period had been played, debris of every kind was thrown in his direction. I could see spectators throwing eggs, tomatoes, rubber overshoes, bags of peanuts and programs at Campbell as he made his way to his box seat. One fan slugged him, and police unloosed a tear gas bomb about 50 feet from Campbell and people ran for the exits."

It got so ugly that the city's fire marshal called off the game after the first period, and the Wings were awarded a 4–1 victory.

"It was forfeited, but even if we had played shorthanded all night, they wouldn't have beaten us because we were a very hot, hot hockey club at that time," Howe said.

Riots continued on the streets until Richard made a plea in French and English on radio and television.

The Canadiens regained a share of first place two nights later when they beat the Rangers. Three days after the forfeited game, the Wings and Habs were tied for first place and met at Olympia Stadium for the last game, which would determine the Prince of Wales Trophy winner.

Seventy Detroit police officers attended the game. Lindsay, who had missed the recent trip because of a shoulder injury, scored a hat trick and rocked the Old Red Barn in a 6–0 thumping for the league championship. Sawchuk's 12th shutout of the season helped him clinch his third Vezina Trophy as the league's top goalie.

"It was kind of nice skating by their bench and smiling," Howe recalled in 2005.

After the game Adams told reporters, "They said we couldn't do it a month ago. They also said the only champs left in Detroit were the Lions. Well, here it is, seven in a row."

(It was indeed a glorious time for the Detroit Lions, who won the National Football League Championship three times that decade: in 1952, '53, and '57.)

The final standings show how close the teams were: the Wings, 42–17–11 and the Habs, 41–18–11. For a seventh straight time, the Wings owned the league title.

Their defense of the Cup began well with a sweep of the Leafs in the semifinals. The Canadiens bumped the Bruins in five games, setting up a rematch of the '54 Final.

The Wings won the first two games at Olympia Stadium, including a 7–1 victory in Game 2 that featured a four-goal, natural-hat trick performance by Lindsay. The series saw both teams protect home ice, sending it to a Game 7 back in Detroit. Before 15,541 fans at Olympia, two goals from Delvecchio and one from Howe gave the Wings a lead they turned into a 3–1 victory. Howe recorded the Cup-clinching goal with 11 seconds to go in the second period. His 20 playoff points set an NHL record. The line of Howe, Lindsay, and Dutch Reibel combined for 51 points, which also set an NHL record.

For the first time in nearly 20 years, the Wings successfully defended their Stanley Cup championship—but the absence of Richard did not go unnoticed.

"We had defeated Montreal with Richard and they beat us with him, but to be fair, if you have a player with that talent in a seventh game, he can score one or two goals without any difficulty," Lindsay said in 2005. "He was so explosive and a real goal scorer."

The lack of Richard was Montreal's misfortune; the Wings had a championship to celebrate. The Cup was presented at center ice, and the Wings toasted with bottles of Coca-Cola.

"Our parade took place from center ice to the dressing room," Marcel Pronovost said. "We had a bash that night at the Sheraton Cadillac Hotel, and then it was goodbye."

Pronovost was one of six Hall of Famers on the '55 team, along with Howe, Lindsay, Sawchuk, Delvecchio, and Kelly.

Howe would later write in his biography that the Wings should have kept repeating as champions, but something happened that would change the team's fortunes for decades, leading them on a long demise. Bruce Norris, James E. Norris' youngest son, managed to oust his sister. Marguerite Norris was the first female executive in the NHL and her professionalism and perceptiveness earned her the respect of Howe, Lindsay, Kelly, and many others. But where Marguerite excelled, Bruce blundered. His biggest failure was to unshackle Adams from the accountability Marguerite had demanded.

Six weeks after the Wings won their fourth Cup in six years, Adams torpedoed his championship roster. He traded Leswick, Johnny Wilson, Glen Skov, and Benny Woit to Chicago, and Sawchuk, Vic Stasiuk, Marcel Bonin, and Lorne Davis to Boston.

"A lot of us wondered if Jack had been checked up lately," Howe said when he looked back 40 years later.

Of the nine players received in the deals, only two, Warren Godfrey and Bucky Hollingworth, were still around after the following season.

Two years later, Adams traded Lindsay and Glenn Hall, the reigning Vezina Trophy winner as the NHL's best goaltender, to Chicago.

"We had five more Cups in us," Lindsay told the *Detroit Free Press'* George Puscas in 1994. "We had good chemistry and got along well. We were really a close-knit outfit. With one or two moves by management, we could have kept on winning into the 1960s. What happened was that Adams destroyed the team. When we won the Stanley Cup in 1955, Jimmy Skinner was the coach and Adams was the general manager. We needed only to make our defense stronger and we could have kept winning. But Adams didn't want to do it. It's too bad. I feel we would have won the Cup at least five more times."

Instead, it was the Canadiens who went on a celebratory spree. In 1955–56, the Habs stripped the Wings of their two titles, breaking their seven-year hold on the regular-season championship by finishing 24 points ahead in the standings, and then beating them in the Stanley Cup Final in five games. It looked like the Wings might recover the following season when

Howe won his fifth scoring title with 44 goals and 89 points and the team finished back atop the standings, but they were eliminated by the Bruins in five games in the semifinals.

Adams continued to raze the roster. He reacquired Sawchuk from the Bruins before the 1957–58 season, but parted ways with Johnny Bucyk, who became a star in Boston. Lindsay and goaltender Glenn Hall were dealt to Chicago for Johnny Wilson, Bill Preston, Hank Bassen, and Forbes Kennedy, which turned out to be a bust trade for the Wings.

"I was traded to Chicago, and Glenn Hall, who had just won the Vezina Trophy, joined me there, and for the next 15 years, he was the best goalie in hockey," Lindsay said. "Two years after Hall, Red Kelly joined us in Chicago."

The revelry that marked the first half of the 1950s unraveled in the latter half. Skinner resigned during the 1957–58 season and was replaced by Abel. Howe was the Hart Trophy recipient for a second consecutive year, but the Wings went nowhere in the playoffs, swept away by their rivals in the first round. The Canadiens were in the midst of winning five straight Stanley Cups, ending one of the Wings' most successful stretches in franchise history, their dynasty undone at a time it could have lasted the decade.

9

The Cup Returns

On a Saturday night in June 1997, 42 years of frustration mixed with anticipation erupted in an explosion of joy. In Detroit, its suburbs, throughout Michigan, and around the world, fans of the Detroit Red Wings celebrated the franchise's eighth Stanley Cup championship. Detroit police took an oversized jersey off the Spirit of Detroit statue to avoid temptation for vandals but put it back on the city's hardest goaltender in time for the parade.

The Wings finally took off their champagne-soaked uniforms in the early hours of Sunday morning, peeling off their gear for the final time that season. It was a gratifying, exultant celebration after more than seven weeks of playoff hockey that began on April 16 at Joe Louis Arena.

The 1996–97 Wings stumbled into the playoffs, winning only two of their last seven regular-season games. They matched up with the St. Louis Blues in the first round in what would prove to be the toughest series of the playoffs. They outscored the Blues by one goal—13–12—in six games. They were shut out twice by future Hall of Game goaltender Grant Fuhr.

From a short-handed goal in Game 2, Game 3 turned on Steve Yzerman's power play goal late in the second period, but what followed in Game 4 was an embarrassing, 4–0 loss.

The Captain commanded his team's attention, speaking for 10 minutes in the visitor's dressing room at Kiel Center.

"We've just got to play harder," Yzerman said. "Our top players have got to play harder. We've got to produce and lead the team. Everybody has a certain expectation and responsibility, and you've got to play up to them."

Yzerman answered his own call. His 95-foot slap shot, taken one stride in from the red line, found its way into the net early in the first period of Game 5, sending fans at the Joe to their feet.

Sergei Fedorov began to look like the superstar he was, asserting himself to set up Vyacheslav Kozlov's goal that gave the Wings a lead they never lost.

"I thought that was the best game Sergei Fedorov has played," Brendan Shanahan said. "I think he's the next player to really break out."

Fedorov went on to lead the Wings in playoff scoring.

The Wings went on to win Game 5 with a final score of 5–2. For the first time in the playoffs, the Russian Five—Fedorov, Kozlov, Igor Larionov, Slava Fetisov, and Vladimir Konstantinov—played together for an entire game.

"We know each other really well," Larionov. "We play the same hockey."

The Wings were up 3–2 in the series with Game 6 back in St. Louis. Brett Hull, who five years later would star with the Wings, scored less than three minutes into the first period to give the Blues a lead. It lasted only a few minutes with Kozlov scoring before the period was at the halfway point. They took a 2–1 lead when Shanahan scored in the second period. Kirk Maltby ensured the series would end in six games with a goal in the third period, sending the Wings on to Round 2.

In the Eastern Conference, one semifinal series pitted the New Jersey Devils against the New York Rangers, a matchup that wouldn't even require going to the airport. In the Western Conference, the semifinal for the Wings—at home in the Eastern time zone—meant they had to haul to southern California.

The quicker they could dispatch the Anaheim Ducks, the better.

Time to sweep.

Martin Lapointe was the hero in Game 1, scoring 59 seconds into overtime before a jubilant crowd at the Joe. Lapointe won a battle for the puck along the boards and hit a streaking Shanahan with a pass. Everyone at the game figured Shanahan would shoot—but instead he passed to Lapointe.

"I didn't even think, I just one-timed it," Lapointe said. "There's nothing like overtime, especially when you score the goal. You always want to be the hero."

Game 2 was epic. It was May 4, a Sunday. What began as a matinee ended as a marathon, lasting five hours and 40 minutes. The Wings won 3–2 after 91 seconds of the third overtime when Kozlov scored on a power play. His shot was the game's 122nd, the Wings' 71st. Detroit had been 0-for-9 in the series with the man advantage. After the Ducks cleared the puck from their zone, Fetisov skated the puck from his blue line, behind his goal and back to center ice, where he hit a streaking Kozlov coming down the right boards. Closing in on Anaheim's net, Kozlov pulled up and passed to Konstantinov at the point. Konstantinov immediately passed the puck back to Kozlov, who fired a slap shot from the face-off dot and beat backup goaltender Mikhail Shtalenkov, who replaced starter

Guy Hebert after he left the game with a groin injury in the third period.

"I didn't see the net," Kozlov said. "I just snapped it."

On to Anaheim.

Game 3 was the highest scoring of the series, but at least it ended in regulation. It was 3–3 going into the third period. The Russian Five struck again. Fedorov made it 4–3 at 3:34, and Kozlov added his fifth goal of the playoffs 21 seconds later.

The Wings were doing what they wanted: dispatching the Ducks. Only one more victory needed to earn a bit of rest.

Game 4 fell on May 8, at the Arrowhead Pond. Only two teams in NHL history had rallied from 3–0 deficits: the New York Islanders in 1975 (against the Penguins) and the Toronto Maple Leafs in 1942 (against the Wings in the Stanley Cup Final).

The Ducks had been tenacious, annoying opponents with their trapping, dumping, and stalling tactics. The Wings had won the first three games—in overtime, triple overtime, and rallying from a two-goal deficit, but the Ducks had held leads longer than the Wings in the series. They led 1–0 and 2–1 in Game 4, but goals from Doug Brown and Nicklas Lidström rallied the Wings and forced overtime.

Lapointe addressed his teammates during intermission.

"Marty stood up and said a few words," associate coach Dave Lewis said. "Marty went through it in Game 1, and he knew from experience how it felt. He was saying, 'It's a great feeling, guys. Somebody's going to get it. It's in here. Somebody's going to get it.'"

It was 3:27 AM in Detroit when the Wings completed their sweep. Shanahan scored 17:03 into double overtime, giving the Wings a 3–2 victory.

"We felt we deserved to win," he said. "We didn't want to be flying across the country anymore. If we win it now, we knew we could relax and take a couple of days off."

The first round had challenged the Wings, forcing them to find the gear that put them into playoff hockey mode. The second round required them to buckle down.

The third round was personal.

The Western Conference Final had the Wings and Colorado Avalanche meeting one another for a second straight year. But the rematch was a mismatch. The Wings outworked and outclassed the defending champions, shutting their mouths and shutting down their season.

When he wasn't facing shots in his net, Avalanche goaltender Patrick Roy was taking them at the Wings. He taunted Scotty Bowman, saying, "He's coached a lot of good teams, and it's a lot easier when you coach all those good teams. I mean, all those years in Montreal, they were unreal teams with a lot of talent. In Pittsburgh he was with Mario Lemieux and all those guys. And in Detroit he still has a very good team. But it's a little different—in Detroit he has to coach, and maybe that's why he didn't have that much success." Before the series began on May 16 at McNichols Sports Arena in Denver, Roy practically guaranteed his team would advance. "We know what it takes to win," he said. "We also know that last year, we went to Detroit, and they were the favorites. We're not going to sit on it. We're going to make sure we don't make the same mistake they did and lose the first two games at home."

The first game was the night the lights went out at the arena. Half an hour before the scheduled opening faceoff, a generator failure on a stormy night knocked out power. Backup generators supplied power to parts of the arena—but the concession area, restrooms, and the press area were in the dark. The Wings' radio broadcasting team of Ken Kal and Paul Woods improvised by broadcasting over a landline in the dark, passing the phone back and forth the entire game.

They could make do in the dark. But the ice was another matter. Two failed compressors left it so mushy that puddles formed. There was, however, enough power for the TV feeds, and that led the NHL to decide the game must go on.

The Wings dominated Game 1 for all but a five-minute span in the third period, when the Avs took command and scored twice to take a 2–1 victory. A similar scenario threatened to unfold in Game 2 until the Wings scored three unanswered goals and won 4–2, all the sweeter to undermine Roy's brash talk of the Avs winning the first two games at their home.

Mike Vernon stole Game 3. Before a joyous, expectant crowd at Joe Louis Arena, he made 27 acrobatic, sprawling saves, and Slava Kozlov scored both goals for the Wings in a 2–1 victory.

Roy spent most of the next two days talking, all but guaranteeing the Avs would win the next game. Claude Lemieux, the man who a year earlier rearranged Kris Draper's face with a cheap shot into the boards and with that became the most hated man in Detroit, suggested a need for mayhem.

The Wings said little until the game got underway. Then their sticks talked and talked.

Igor Larionov scored 1:52 into the first period, converting on a power play. Five minutes later, he scored again. Kozlov and Fedorov followed up in the second period. The third period dissolved into the mayhem Lemieux had talked about, but not to the Avs' advantage. They racked up 100 minutes in penalties, and their coach, Marc Crawford, made a fool of himself trying to storm the Wings' bench, yelling and cursing profusely.

Yzerman looked on in disbelief. Bowman told Crawford he knew his father before the Avalanche coach did and said his father would be embarrassed by his son's actions. Crawford was fined $10,000 for the performance and apologized repeatedly at a press conference. "Things got out of hand," Crawford said. "Nobody is proud of it."

The Wings took Game 4 with a convincing 6–0 victory, taking a 3–1 lead in the series. After the game ended at the Joe, the song "Happy Trails" emanated from the Wings' locker room. The song's catchy, hummable lyrics were not matched by the Wings: they were terse, their own soundtrack focused on needing to win one more game to advance.

"There's no reason to celebrate," defenseman Larry Murphy said. "This game doesn't mean anything. We've got nothing. We have to remember that."

The serious approach looked like a farce as the Wings were so ineffective in Game 5 that they were the ones trying to explain a 6–0 loss. The one upside was the possibility to clinch the series at home. Bowman's message the day before Game 6 was simple: don't blow it.

"I told the team that they would rue the day if they didn't show up and play the games of their lives," he said. "You always want to remember the game that put you into the Stanley Cup Finals, not the one that you didn't win to get there."

The Wings listened. The 3–1 final score in Game 6 did not reflect how soundly they dominated, outshooting and outworking the Avs from the opening faceoff. A 14–3 edge in shots in the first period finally led to a goal in the second period from Lapointe. Fedorov made it 2–0 early in the third period, scoring what would be the series-clinching goal. Shanahan's empty-netter with 30 seconds to go left the rafters shaking.

The victory sealed the Wings' trip to the Stanley Cup Final, avenged the previous spring's loss to Colorado in the conference Finals, avenged Lemieux's gutless, goon-ish behavior. (Lemieux went out meekly, turning away in the handshake lane to avoid shaking the hand of McCarty, who he had pummeled before a jubilant crowd at the Joe on March 26. Draper had, naturally, refused to shake Lemieux's hand.)

"The Detroit Red Wings were the better team in this series," Crawford said. "Ultimately, they wore our team down."

It was May 26, 1997, Memorial Day, and the Wings were four victories from ending a four-decade drought.

"Joey Kocur said it best when we were huddled around," McCarty said. "He said, 'Don't worry, boys, the next one feels even better.' This is not the end. There's still a lot of hockey to be played."

Over in the Eastern Conference, the Philadelphia Flyers had dispatched the Pittsburgh Penguins, Buffalo Sabres, and New York Rangers, winning every series in five games. The Final began May 31, in Philadelphia. It was the first playoff meeting between the two franchises.

Since winning the Cup in 1955 with the game's best player, Gordie Howe, on the roster, the Wings had failed in the Stanley Cup Final in 1956, 1961, 1963, 1964, 1966, and 1995. The Wings entered the 1997 Final portrayed as the underdog against the big, fearsome Flyers. Eric Lindros, at the time considered the next great player on a plateau with Mario Lemieux and Wayne Gretzky, was the centerpiece of the Legion of Doom line, between left winger John LeClair and right wing Mikael Renberg (each of the three was 6'2" or taller and weighed over 230 pounds).

Hockey pundits projected the Wings would use the defense pairing of Vladimir Konstantinov—the very definition of tough—and Slava Fetisov—the very definition of savvy—against the Legion of Doom. But Bowman outsmarted everyone and countered with the finesse pairing of Nicklas Lidström and Larry Murphy, two superb positional defenders, and the Grind Line—Maltby, Kris Draper, and Darren McCarty.

A thunderous crowd at CoreStates Center chanted "U-S-A! U-S-A! U-S-A!" The Wings silenced them with a 4–2 victory in Game 1. Maltby, a recent *Sports Illustrated* cover boy, scored the first goal while killing a penalty in the first period. The Wings took a 3–1 lead on goals from Kocur and Fedorov, but LeClair scored with less than three minutes to play in the second period.

The Wings weren't about to let the Flyers rally. Yzerman wheeled through the neutral zone, got one skate across the blue line and aimed the puck on net, 60 feet from the goal line. The puck slipped between Ron Hextall's legs, and Flyers fans turned their voices to jeering their own goaltender. Lindros—who had been caught on TV mikes yelling an ethnic slur at Fetisov—called it "an unfortunate night."

There would be three more such nights for the Flyers. The Wings were unstoppable. The tests in the earlier rounds, the emotions that had been carefully contained for fear of being unleashed too early, were near bursting point. The Wings took Game 2 by the same score 4–2, taking a 2–0 series lead home to Detroit.

It had only been two years since the Wings last hosted a Stanley Cup Final game at the Joe. They lost both home games to the New Jersey Devils in 1995, building on what was a bad trend dating back decades: the Wings had lost seven straight Stanley Cup Final games on home ice, dating to two in 1964, three in 1966, and the pair from 1995.

Fans in the Detroit area had no worries: little red flags flew from the roofs of cars. An inflatable King Kong with a Wings jersey was added to the Fisher Building.

The Flyers did have worries going into Game 3. They switched goaltenders again, from Hextall back to Garth Snow. Paul Coffey, the former Wings defenseman who had been part of the trade that brought Shanahan to Detroit, was concussed.

The atmosphere at the Joe was almost indescribable. Fans saluted Yzerman by chanting "Ste-vie! Ste-vie! Ste-vie!"

"It really gets your heart pumping," Yzerman said afterward. "It gave me the chills."

The Flyers scored the first goal, converting on a power play at 7:03 of the first period. Yzerman quelled any hope the Flyers had of staging an upset by scoring his own power play goal two minutes later. By the end of the period, the Wings had a 3–1 lead. By the end of the game, it was 6–1. With two goals and two assists, Fedorov alone had more points than the entire Flyers bench.

The Wings had a three-games-to-none hold on the series. When the playoffs began, the talk centered on *if* the Wings could win the Stanley Cup. Now *if* had become *when*.

Game 4 fell on June 7. The Stanley Cup was in Detroit, on display for fans at the Renaissance Center, roped off and guarded, ready to be awarded. Corn-broom sweepers were a hot item—fans drove with them sticking out of their car windows. Scalpers were asking as much as $1,500 for a ticket to the game. Official attendance was listed as 19,983.

At the Joe, two of the legends from the Wings' dynasty from the 1950s, Howe and Ted Lindsay, were among the spectators. "Got to bury 'em tonight," Howe said before the game. "When you've got a team down like that, you can't give 'em any air."

The game marked the first time the Wings could win the Cup on home ice since April 23, 1964 (they were thwarted that year by Bobby Baun, who crumpled in pain after taking Howe's slap shot on an ankle during regulation but returned for overtime and scored the winning goal for the Toronto Maple Leafs).

Just before the game began, Yzerman addressed his teammates. Martin Lapointe remembered the message afterward: "He said, 'Let's make sure we come out hard and we do our job. We're professionals. It doesn't matter what we did in the past, it only matters what we do tonight. We've got to play the game of our lives.'"

The first period was relatively uneventful until the last minute, when Lidström scored with 33 seconds left and gave fans something to cheer going into the intermission.

At 13:02 of the second period, McCarty scored a goal for the ages. Yzerman won a battle along the boards, and Tomas Sandström collected the puck and passed it to McCarty near the red line. McCarty skated toward the Flyers' net, dropped defenseman Janne Niinimaa to the ice with an outside-inside move, and drove to the net. The puck on his backhand, McCarty waited until Hextall was out of his crease before pulling the puck to his forehand and depositing it into the net.

Mike Vernon, who had been such a rock for the Wings in the playoffs, came within 14.8 seconds of a shutout, allowing Lindros' only goal of the series as fans counted down the third period.

When the horn blew around 10:50 PM, sounding the end of the game, confetti fell from the rafters. Helmets, gloves, and sticks went skyward, landing on ice that grew more crowded by the seconds. Players on the bench erupted onto the ice, piling on top of Vernon and knocking the net off its mooring. "Oh, What a Night" blared from the loudspeakers, background music to the joyous roar of the fans.

A red carpet was rolled out at center ice. Yzerman hopped over it, skated to the bench, and embraced owners Mike and Marian Ilitch. Bowman disappeared for a few seconds while he donned his practice gear and skates. Vernon was awarded the Conn Smythe Trophy for his efforts in the playoffs, but the night it became his, he only held it about 10 seconds. "I wanted to get rid of it," he said. "I wanted to get Lord Stanley out there because that's what we're all here for. The Stanley Cup was what we all wanted to hold up."

At 11:00 PM the Cup was presented to The Captain. It was almost exactly 14 years to the day Yzerman had been drafted by the Wings. He hoisted the Cup and took it for a lap, his gap-toothed smile the perfect summation of his joy.

Yzerman skated back to the Wings' bench, holding the Cup out for Ilitch, who held it high for a brief moment before handing it back to Yzerman.

Yzerman skated back to his teammates and handed hockey's most famous trophy to Fetisov and Larionov. It was a poignant moment, a show of camaraderie with two comrades who had taken on the mighty Soviet Red Army for the right to play in the NHL.

"I was surprised," Larionov said. "I [played] with Slava for many, many years, and we [waited] for this long time. It was an honor to carry the Cup after Steve Yzerman. It was great feeling in front of 20,000 people in Joe Louis Arena and people all over the world."

The two veterans took the Cup for a lap together, speaking in their native Russian.

"I [had] a lot to say to him," Fetisov said. "I [said] to Igor, 'We have to get the Cup together.' I have been through so many years and lots of hockey games. I can't describe it. I [will] never forget this moment the rest of my life."

It was an unforgettable moment for the 63-year-old coach, too, even as it was his sixth time celebrating.

"I always wanted to be a player in the NHL and skate with the Cup," he said. "How many chances do you get to do that? I said if we win, I'll go for it. I have always dreamt about doing that."

The Cup made its way to Shanahan, to Fedorov, to Murphy, handed off by one player to the elation of another. After everyone had gotten their turn, the Wings skated a victory lap as a team, Yzerman leading the conga line with the Cup held aloft. It took two minutes for them to circle the ice. Then they sprawled at center ice for a picture that would be a centerpiece in memorializing the special evening.

The party on the ice lasted nearly half an hour before shifting to the dressing room, which was packed with family and friends, numbering in the hundreds.

"We just came in here, and mayhem pretty much broke out," Maltby said.

Champagne, sweat, and cigar smoke mixed into a potent, pungent smell. Soon, everyone was soaked from the showers of champagne bottles opened and emptied into the Cup. A few fans managed to get by security and joined the party.

"You see all the people around here; they give us so much support," Fedorov said. He paced his teammates with 20 points in the playoffs and finished the run playing with broken ribs. "I never thought we have so many friends and so many fans that can support us. It's great."

One of the messages pinned to the bulletin board in the dressing room since the playoffs began urged the team to "win the battles."

It read, in part: "We are here once again. We are here to win the battle. This battle requires character. Your reputation will be judged. This battle requires commitment. You will be challenged to go deeper into your soul than you have ever gone before. This battle requires unyielding confidence, and it will be tested. This battle is what we all dream for. It is the greatest experience of your life. You will never forget the reward. This battle begins today. Enjoy the ride."

The battle had begun in the middle of April. Seven weeks later, the Wings took what would be their last drive to the Joe for a game that season, arriving around 5:00 PM. The streets and parking lots already lined with fans.

Maltby described the scene as crazy: "I've never seen anything like that before. I've never seen that kind of traffic and people in the streets. I've never seen so many jerseys. It's just awesome. This city deserves this, we deserve this, and it's just a great feeling all around."

BRENDAN SHANAHAN

"I remember the day he arrived. He flew in and was running late and he got into the locker room with two minutes to warmups, so we said, 'Hey, we'll wait,' and we all went on the ice together. It was awesome."

That was Kirk Maltby in 2023, looking back on October 9, 1996, the day the Red Wings acquired a key player in their quest to win the Stanley Cup. Brendan Shanahan had an outsize shot and personality; he was as willing to fight as he was to spin a yarn; he was powerful and personable and perfect for a team that had reached for the Cup the last two seasons but was unable to grasp it.

"He was a heck of a player," Maltby said. "He put us over the hump. He brought an element of a style that we didn't have. We had Marty Lapointe, and we had Darren McCarty, but Shanny was a 40–50 goal scorer. When you bring a guy like that in, it also made the team physically tougher. You feel better when you are on the ice when you've got guys like that as your teammate."

It was the Wings' good fortune that Shanahan, 27 years old at the time, had requested the Hartford

Whalers trade him because of the uncertainty hanging over the franchise (it would relocate to Raleigh, North Carolina, to become the Carolina Hurricanes in 1997). Scotty Bowman, the Wings' coach and director of player personnel, spent days working on the trade, which eventually came down to the Wings sending forward Keith Primeau, a first-round pick from 1990 embroiled in a contract holdout; elite offensive defenseman Paul Coffey; and a first-round pick.

"It was after my third year, and Keith Primeau was really coming into his own as a big center," Bowman said in 2023. "He was younger than any of the other ones. He wanted a big contract. Mr. Ilitch thought he was going to be the next franchise player, but he wanted too much money. I remember talking to the Ilitches, and they said, 'We're not trading him. He can sit out as long as he wants. He can sit out a whole year. But he will eventually want to play.'"

Even with Shanahan as the target return, the trade was difficult to pull off.

"That was the year it was made public by somebody that Brendan wanted to get traded," Bowman said. "I knew it was going to be tough because Primeau was going to be a good player for a long time. But Brendan had that knack for scoring goals and was a stand-up guy. He could play any way you wanted—if you got in a scrap, he could scrap. It wasn't an easy trade because Paul Coffey had signed a long contract with us, but we felt Shanahan had something we wanted."

Once Ilitch understood how much the Wings stood to gain, he was all in. He sent his private jet to pick up Shanahan in Hartford and fly him to Detroit, where a car waited to take him to Joe Louis Arena.

Shanahan arrived at 6:44 PM and, at 6:55 PM, he was on the ice with his new teammates. In his first game wearing the winged wheel, Shanahan started a fight with Edmonton's Greg de Vries less than four minutes into the first period. He scored his first goal for them on October 21 and by the end of the season had 46 goals and 87 points, spending time on a line next to Steve Yzerman.

"They mix well together because it takes a lot of focus off Yzerman," Bowman said at the time. "You can't leave a guy like Shanahan alone because he gets a lot of shots. We were looking for somebody that would take the focus off Stevie, because he took a lot of checks. We needed a shooting winger; we had a good center."

Not just a shooting winger, but a big one: Shanahan was 6'3" and 220 pounds, adding bulk as well as skill. The Wings had been pushed over by the New Jersey Devils in the 1995 Stanley Cup Finals and pushed around by the Colorado Avalanche in the 1996 Western Conference Final, but in the 1997 playoffs there was Shanahan, there was McCarty (6'1", 210 pounds), there was Lapointe (5'11", 215 pounds), there was Joe Kocur (6', 222 pounds), and there was Tomas Sandström (6'2", 205 pounds).

"We were much tougher," Nicklas Lidström said in 2023. "We could put a big winger on each line, if not two of them, and it made a difference."

Playoff hockey was the reason the Wings traded for Shanahan, and he delivered. By the end of the first-round series against the St. Louis Blues, he had three goals and three assists, including a three-point performance in Game 5, and a goal in the decisive Game 6. On May 8, teammates celebrated his goal in the second overtime of Game 4 against the Mighty Ducks of Anaheim, which completed the second-round series in a sweep, in Anaheim, California. It was 3:27 AM in Detroit when the game ended.

"I hope people stayed up to watch it," Shanahan said. "The way I saw it was just a scramble in front. I just tried to get loose and I pushed myself away from some guy, and the puck just popped out. I just found myself open, and it was a nice gift as the result of the hard work of Marty and Stevie."

Shanahan had four points in the next round, scoring in the sixth and decisive game that ended with the Wings eliminating the Colorado Avalanche from the Western Conference Finals. He had been baptized into the rivalry March 26, when his response to seeing Patrick Roy leave his crease and stride toward Darren McCarty was to leap into Roy's path, where Shanahan was intercepted by Adam Foote.

Shanahan delivered his seventh goal of the playoffs in Game 2 of the Stanley Cup Finals against the Philadelphia Flyers, scoring unassisted 1:37 when his shot banked off a Flyers defender—off all players, it was Coffey, who had held up the Shanahan trade eight months earlier and had lasted just 20 games with Hartford before being traded to Philadelphia. Shanahan scored again midway through the third period.

Shanahan came through with another multipoint performance in Game 3, setting up a power play goal by Sergei Fedorov and scoring shortly afterward. When the Wings clinched the Cup in Game 4, Shanahan had nine goals and eight assists.

"He was one of the players that is the reason why we won," Maltby said in 2023. "He scored a lot of big goals in that first Cup. He was just a heck of a player that had the respect of his teammates and of the league. You had to be careful if he was taking a one-timer, or if you gave him a little nudge, he was ready to punch you in the face. He didn't back down from anything. And he loved to tell stories. You weren't always sure how much of his story was true. He loved to talk and putting his own twist on things."

The trade had worked out so well, Shanahan ended up playing nine seasons with the Wings, winning the Stanley Cup again in 1998 and in 2002. It was in a Wings jersey that Shanahan scored the 500th goal of his career, on March 23, 2002. Shanahan produced his third 40-goal season for the Wings in 2005–06, but after Yzerman retired that summer, Shanahan took it as a sign it was time for him to move on, too. He played two seasons with the New York Rangers and wrapped up his career in 2008–09 with the New Jersey Devils, finishing his NHL career with 1,354 points in 1,524 games. Shanahan parlayed being the second overall selection in the 1987 draft into a Hockey Hall of Fame career, achieving his greatest glory after one of the best trades in Wings history.

10

The Second Dynasty

THE 1997 STANLEY CUP CHAMPIONSHIP HOLDS A SPECIAL place in Red Wings history, separated by 42 years from the dynastic 1950s. When the Cup finally returned to Detroit, it was as if a time warp had occurred, with some fans old enough to remember the days of Gordie Howe and Ted Lindsay and a new generation of fans idolizing Steve Yzerman and Nicklas Lidström.

When the players and coaches and other personnel gathered for training camp in the fall of 1997, it was with Vladimir Konstantinov and Sergei Mnatsakanov at the forefront of everything that mattered. The 1997–98 season became about the two men whose lives and careers were devastatingly altered in a limousine accident on June 13, 1997. Slava Fetisov was also in the vehicle that a chauffeur crashed into a tree on Woodward Avenue, but Fetisov recovered and played another season.

"The car accident changed us," Kirk Maltby said in 2023. "It's hard to repeat, and then to repeat with what happened to

Vladdie, Sergei, and Slava—I think the accident maybe brought us closer together. We were mostly the same team that went into the '97–98 season. Scotty made a point when we were in Florida, we got to go see Vladdie—he was adamant we meet with him, and guys wanted to. It was strange playing without Vladdie. He was such a competitor. He was dominant. He would hit guys who were 30 pounds heavier than him and three inches taller. We wanted to win for him and for Sergei. Fortunately, Slava healed and was able to play again."

It was Vyacheslav Kozlov who brought a pet rock a fan had given him to the Joe in the fall of 1998; the original inscription on the rock read, "I believe," but it was changed to "we," as in "we believe."

"It helped me win the Stanley Cup," Kozlov said that September. "But I give it now to Vladdie, and hopefully it can bring him luck, too." Eventually, it was shortened to "believe."

Konstantinov was one of the game's best defenseman; he had just turned 30 that March, and together with Lidström, those two were expected to anchor the team's defense corps for years to come. His absence from the lineup on opening night was emotional; the absences of Sergei Fedorov and Mike Vernon were professional. Fedorov staged a lengthy holdout; Vernon had been traded to the San Jose Sharks during the offseason.

The 1997–98 squad was formidable even without Konstantinov, Vernon, and, for many months, Fedorov, still boasting a lineup that included forwards in Kozlov, Steve Yzerman, Brendan Shanahan, and Igor Larionov, along with the Grind Line—Kris Draper, Kirk Maltby, and either of Darren McCarty or Joe Kocur; a defense headlined by Lidström, Fetisov, and Larry Murphy; and young Chris Osgood holding his own as the lead goaltender.

"We were presented with a lot of adversity before the puck was even dropped," Shanahan said on New Year's Eve 1997. "It's been a team effort. It's something we learned last year in the playoffs. Everyone gets similar shifts. The ice time is spread around pretty evenly. That brought us success in the playoffs, and it seems to have brought us success in the first 41 games."

It certainly helped when Fedorov joined the team at the end of February; he played only 21 games but crammed 17 points into that span—and most importantly, they had him for the playoffs. Fedorov led the Wings with 10 goals in the 22 games it took to repeat as champions, trailing Yzerman's team-leading 24 points by four.

The two men whose lives were altered a week after the 1997 Cup championship were never far from the hearts and minds of the players tasked with moving forward. When the 1997 champions were honored by President Bill Clinton at the White House at the end of January 1998, Konstantinov was there, flashing a smile and a thumbs-up sign. (Mnatsakanov, partially paralyzed, was not able to travel.)

In the week before the 1998 playoffs began, Kozlov, he of the pet rock, hung a picture of Konstantinov and Mnatsakanov in his locker, the two of them standing side by side with the Stanley Cup. Kozlov spoke for his teammates when he said that the two "are still on our team. They are still with us. If we help each other, we can win another Stanley Cup—for ourselves and for Vladdie and for Sergei."

The Wings entered the playoffs as the third seed in the Western Conference, pitting them against the Phoenix Coyotes in round one. The Wings took care of that series in six games, ditto a second-round series against the St. Louis Blues, and a six-game engagement with the Dallas Stars in the conference finals.

It was the Wings' third trip to the Stanley Cup Finals since they left disappointed in 1995.

The Washington Capitals had fought their way through Eastern Conference opponents while the Wings were busy in the west, setting up the 1998 Stanley Cup Final. Lidström and Kocur scored a little more than two minutes apart in the first period of Game 1, leading the Wings to a 2–1 victory at Joe Louis Arena. Two nights later, on June 11, Martin Lapointe and Doug Brown scored in the third period as the Wings rallied from a two-goal deficit to force overtime. Draper provided the heroics with four minutes left in the first overtime, finishing a play set up by Lapointe and Shanahan, and the Wings left Detroit with a two-games-to-none lead.

Game 3 was June 13 at MCI Center. The Capitals tied it midway through the third period, but Fedorov scored less than five minutes later, and the Wings claimed a third straight game.

That set in motion a plan that had been underway back in Detroit: get Konstantinov to Washington. He and his wife, Irina, were part of the group that flew on a charter on June 15, the day before Game 4, surrounded by the families of the players and other team personnel.

Konstantinov watched the Final from section 116 (Konstantinov had worn No. 16); it was Capitals territory, but as fans caught on to his presence as the game went on, it led to a standing ovation for Konstantinov in the third period, complete with stick taps from both teams.

The Wings had a 3–1 lead after the second period, and shortly after Brown scored early in the third period, Irina Konstantinov helped wheel her husband to ice level. He was there on the ice to celebrate the Wings winning the Stanley Cup in 1998, just as he had been in 1997.

"I still remember Steve giving him the Cup when we won again and putting the Cup in his lap," Maltby said in 2023. "In the dressing room afterward, we gave him a drink from the Cup, and we had to pull him away from it and joke, *enough, Vladdie.* He was in our minds and in our hearts moving forward into the season and all through the playoffs. With the whole situation, it was unbelievable to have him down on the ice and be in the team picture. Unfortunately, it was a special year because of that. It cut short the celebration of our first Cup, and the next year we were able to take the Cup to our local areas, schools, parks, places like that, and that is special to players—to see how people light up when they see the Cup."

Two days later, the Wings celebrated the ninth Cup in franchise history with an estimated 1.2 million people crammed into downtown Detroit. The Wings believed and had set in motion the start of a second dynasty.

There were disappointments, too: the Wings bowed out of the 1999 playoffs in the second round, eliminated by their archival, the Colorado Avalanche, after sweeping a first-round series against the Anaheim Ducks and winning the first two games against the Avs.

It would take a couple more years, and enduring being ousted by the Avalanche again in the second round in the 2000 playoffs, and the embarrassment of lasting only one round in the 2001 playoffs, but then the Wings got so strong, they could once again call themselves champions. The 2001–02 Wings cruised through the regular season, winning the Presidents' Trophy by 15 points. The team is considered one of the best in NHL history, producing, within 20 years, nine players elected to the Hockey Hall of Fame in Yzerman, Lidström, Fedorov, Shanahan, Larionov, Brett Hull, Chris Chelios, Luc Robitaille, and Dominik Hašek; Bowman already was in the Hall of Fame when he came to Detroit in 1993.

Bowman announced his retirement from coaching the night of June 13, 2002, minutes after the Wings had clinched the Cup. He had done what he had been hired to do and coached the Wings into a championship team.

Dave Lewis, who had been an assistant coach under Bowman, was promoted to head coach, but when the Wings were upset in the first round of the 2003 playoffs and lost in the second round in 2004, the organization pivoted to finding someone more demanding. Mike Babcock was named head coach on July 15, 2005.

By that time Fedorov was gone, as were Hull and Robitaille. Yzerman retired after the 2005–06 season—which ended with a first-round loss to the Edmonton Oilers—and Shanahan took that as a cue to move on to a different NHL team.

The Wings appeared on a downward arc, but their dynasty was saved by two amazing draft picks: Pavel Datsyuk in the sixth round in 1998 and Henrik Zetterberg in the seventh round in 1999. Datsyuk had been a rookie on the 2001–02 team, and Zetterberg joined the Wings the following season. By the mid-to-late aughts, the two had ascended as leaders, regarded as two of the best two-way centers in the game. They were formidable on separate lines and unstoppable together.

The Wings advanced to the Western Conference Finals in 2007. The collective bargaining agreement that was forged after the 2004–05 season was lost to a bitter labor dispute instituted a salary cap; no longer could management garland the team with prize free agents bought with owners Mike and Marian Ilitch's millions.

The 2007–08 roster didn't shine like the one in 2001–02, but it still boasted Lidström, along with three other skaters who had been part of the three recent Stanley Cup championships in Tomas Holmström, Kris Draper, and Kirk Maltby. The Wings had bought out Darren McCarty's contract to help get them compliant with the salary cap, but he made a comeback and was with them by the spring of 2008. There was another player, too, making a homecoming: Dallas Drake, who had been drafted by the Wings in 1989 and but played most of his career elsewhere. He ended up serving as something of a rallying point, with teammates knowing it was Drake's last chance to win the Cup.

Hašek made a return appearance, too, after a confusing absence that saw him deal with what had seemed an injury that would end his career, then a reversal and a return to the NHL via the Ottawa Senators. When that didn't work out, Hašek rejoined the Wings, at age 41. Chris Osgood, who the Wings had lost on waivers after acquiring Hašek in 2001, was also back in Wings uniform.

Among the faces who had come in after the 2002 Cup were Niklas Kronwall, a defenseman kind in person but ferocious on the ice. When general manager Ken Holland acquired Brad Stuart at the 2008 trade deadline, a fearsome partnership was formed. Kronwall and Stuart were the open-ice heavy hitters, a perfect complement to the finesse pairing formed by Lidström and Brian Rafalski, the latter an undersized defenseman with outsize skill.

It was a good mix on the roster, and the Wings finished the season with 115 points, earning another Presidents' Trophy and setting up a first-round meeting with the Nashville Predators. When Hašek looked like age had caught up to him (he had turned 43 in January 2008), he was pulled in Game 4 and replaced by Osgood. The Wings won in overtime on a goal by Johan Franzén, and Osgood made 20 saves in Game 6 to deliver a 3–0 shutout and series victory.

The road to the Cup once again went through the Colorado Avalanche, but the Wings' old nemesis had no bite left; all the principals from the storied rivalry the previous decade were gone. Franzén had a hat trick in Game 2, and the Wings scored seven unanswered goals in Game 4 to win 8–2 and clinch the series.

Datsyuk showed off his skills with a hat trick in Game 3 of the Western Conference Final against the Dallas Stars, and the Wings would go on to win the series in six games.

The Pittsburgh Penguins were making their first appearance in the Final since winning consecutive Cup championships in 1991 and 1992, back when Mario Lemieux and Jaromír Jágr graced the roster. Now it was budding superstars Sidney Crosby and Evgeni Malkin who were in charge.

The series began at Joe Louis Arena, where, in a nod to each franchise's history, Game 1 included a ceremonial puck drop featuring Yzerman and Lemieux. The Wings won the game 4–0 on two goals from Mikael Samuelsson and one each from Daniel Cleary and Zetterberg. Osgood recorded a second consecutive shutout in Game 2, won 3–0 by the Wings.

The Penguins protected home ice and won Game 3, but the Wings prevailed in Game 4, creating the possibility of winning the Cup at home. The Penguins ruined that when Maxime Talbot scored with 34.3 seconds to go in regulation, and Petr Sýkora scored the winning goal on a power play midway through the third overtime.

Rafalski gave the Wings an early lead in Game 6, back in Pittsburgh, and Valtteri Filppula and Zetterberg also scored as the Wings won 3–2, clinching the Cup on the road. Zetterberg finished the playoffs with 13 goals and 27 points, including six points in the six games it took to best the Penguins. But there was more than offense to Zetterberg's playoffs highlights: he had done such an outstanding job defensively that Crosby only scored two goals the entire series, in Game 3. Zetterberg also helped (along with Lidström and Kronwall) deny the Penguins on two lengthy two-man power plays, one lasting a minute 26 seconds in Game 4 and the other lasting a minute 33 seconds early in Game 6.

The Cup belonged to the Wings, the Conn Smythe Trophy to Zetterberg. As captain, Lidström was the first to hoist the Cup; he handed it to Drake, for whom it was the first. Before the night ended at Mellon Arena, Holmström, Draper, and Maltby, who had been with the Wings for the duration of the dynasty, had their turns with the Cup, too.

When it was put to Holmström in 2023 that he had had a remarkable career in the NHL, reaching 1,000 games played and winning four Stanley Cups, his response was immediate.

"It should have been five Cups," he said.

To the bitter and lasting memory of those who were around for the second dynasty in the franchise's history, the legacy includes the utter disappointment of the 2009 Stanley Cup Finals. The Wings swept the Columbus Blue Jackets in the first round, won a seven-game series against the Ducks in the second round, and dispatched the Chicago Blackhawks in the conference Finals to advance to the Stanley Cup Final for the 24th time in franchise history and sixth time since 1995. The Penguins were once again the opponent. The Wings won the first two games, were up 3–2 in the series, and had home-ice advantage in Game 7. For all of that, they lost the Final.

"I remember to this day how disappointed we were," Maltby said in 2023. "We were so close, we were up 2–0 and 3–2 but couldn't find a way in the end, even though we were at home. We really thought we were going to be able to repeat."

The first dynasty, in the 1950s, was remarkable for what a winning binge the Wings went on during the era of the Original Six. When they won the Cup again in 1997, there were 21 teams; by 2009 there were 30.

From 1996–97 through 2008–09, the Wings won 110 playoff games, 31 more than the next-closest team, the Colorado Avalanche. Featuring some of the best players in the game, they were a perennial Cup favorite in the late '90s and into the early aughts, and, just when it seemed they would trend downward, they were able to again rise to playoff glory.

11

A Cup for the Ages

FEW THINGS EVOKE MEMORIES AND LAUGHTER FOR THOSE who were there quite like the fabled, fantastic, full-of-future-Hockey-Hall-of-Famers 2001–02 Red Wings.

"The fourth line was me, Igor Larionov, and Luc Robitaille," Tomas Holmström said in 2023. "You almost felt sorry for Igor, playing with two bad skaters. Before us he played with Sergei Makarov and Vladimir Krutov. But Igor was the guy dishing out pucks, and Luc had a good shot, so we had a good thing together."

The Wings weren't short on star power when they entered the 2001 offseason with a lineup highlighted by Steve Yzerman, Nicklas Lidström, Sergei Fedorov, Brendan Shanahan, Chris Chelios, and Larionov. They were a formidable team, still, but eager to grow stronger in light of having been bounced in the first round of the playoffs. So, when Buffalo Sabres general manager Darcy Regier called Ken Holland, his counterpart with the Wings, and said the Sabres needed to shed salary and to see if the Wings were interested in Dominik Hašek, Holland's answer was a resounding yes. Never mind that the Wings had Chris Osgood, who had backstopped them to the Stanley Cup in 1998; Hašek had six Vezina Trophies and two Hart Memorial Trophies.

Holland made the deal, sending the Sabres a first-round pick in the 2002 draft and forward Vyacheslav Kozlov. Just like that, the Wings had added a superstar goaltender. It was finalized June 30, 2001.

On July 2, a little after 10:00 in the morning, Hašek was introduced at a news conference at Joe Louis Arena, donning a Red Wings sweater as Holland beamed from the side. Nine hours later, Holland was in his office, listening to Luc Robitaille say that he wanted to put on a Wings sweater, too. Before the day ended, Robitaille, who was a free agent, had been signed to a contract. (That lessened the blow of losing forward Martin Lapointe, who the Boston Bruins threw a lot of money at, in free agency.)

It was a pretty spectacular start to a week.

"To win the cup, that's my goal," Hašek said. "Nothing else. Nothing less."

Robitaille responded: "I think we will do it."

It was what fans had come to expect of Mike Ilitch, who from the moment he bought the Wings in 1982 had expended time and money to restore the franchise to its proud origins.

"Once the city gets used to it, you get used to it," Ilitch said then. "You've got to pay the price. We're going to fight like the dickens. We've got to do anything we can. The Red Wings are so much a part of the city now, you just want to keep it that way."

The Wings had the second-highest payroll in the NHL in 2000–01 at about $55 million, and while several millions had been trimmed, the payroll ballooned to around $60 million after signing Hašek for three years and $24 million and Robitaille for two years and $9 million.

"The reason we were able to make the deals is our owner, Mike Ilitch," team executive Jimmy Devellano said at the time.

When Brett Hull let it be known he would like to join the fun, too, Ilitch green-lit a two-year contract worth $9 million. In order to make room for Hull's contract, Yzerman, Shanahan, and Chelios restructured their contracts to alleviate the immediate impact on the payroll.

Hull, Robitaille, and Yzerman marked the first time one team could boast three 500-goal scorers; before the season was over, Shanahan would be the fourth.

The eight skaters who within the next decade-and-a-half would be inducted into the Hockey Hall of Fame finished one through eight in team scoring: Shanahan with 75 points, Fedorov with 68, Hull with 63, Lidström with 59, Robitaille with 50, Yzerman with 48, Larionov with 43, and Chelios with 39. (Yzerman had missed 30 games with a re-aggravated knee injury.) Hašek finished with an NHL-best 41 victories and a 2.17 goals-against average.

The Wings finished in first place in the standings, winning 51 games and earning 116 points. It was satisfying, but it wasn't why Ilitch had agreed to spend so much money.

The extravagant investment looked like it might be a fiscal disaster when the Wings lost the first two games of their first-round series against the Vancouver Canucks. Hašek looked like a beer-league goaltender, allowing eight goals on 45 shots and sporting a 3.60 goals-against average and .822 save percentage. The Wings lost the first game 4–3 in overtime, and when they lost the second 5–2, fans at Joe Louis Arena booed them off the ice.

Players later would admit they were nervous: "We knew what a bad situation we were in, how disappointed people were," Maltby said in 2023, "and we were disappointed in ourselves. This wasn't how it was supposed to go. We knew that."

It was Yzerman who served a restorative tonic. After the first practice in Vancouver, he reminded teammates of how much they had accomplished, of how much time there was still left in the series. "Nothing rah-rah," Maltby said. "He just told us to relax and to play like we could."

Yzerman went out and scored the first goal in Game 3 and assisted on the third one by Shanahan. But the goal that turned around the series was the second one: in the final minute of the second period, with the score 1–1, Lidström fired the puck from the red line, and somehow it eluded Dan Cloutier and landed in Vancouver's net, forever memorialized in video.

"It's no secret that I should have had it," Cloutier said the next day, which was his 26th birthday. "You have to put it out of your mind."

If anything, it was Yzerman's goal that upset Cloutier, who claimed the Wings' captain had bumped him. Cloutier had complained to officials but was told he was out of his crease, and fair game.

Lidström's goal was the winning goal from the third game, and the victory was just what the Wings needed. They won again in Vancouver to tie the series, went home, gave fans a 4–0 shutout to cheer, and wrapped up the series in Game 6 in Vancouver.

On to St. Louis. The nerves or malaise that had beset the Wings when the playoffs began were gone, and they took care of the Blues series in nine days, losing only once. Just as well: the Wings needed all their reserves as they once again had to go through the Colorado Avalanche to get closer to the Cup.

The old rivals took turns winning the first four games, and then the Avalanche gained the upper hand when Peter Forsberg scored at 6:24 of the first overtime in Game 5.

"We knew what our situation was, but we also were confident we could bring the series back to Detroit," Maltby said in 2023. "We knew we were good enough to win in their building again."

So the Wings did. Shanahan scored the first goal, knocking in a puck that lay loose in the crease while Patrick Roy mistakenly held his glove high, his Statue of Liberty pose rendered an embarrassment when it turned out he had not saved Steve Yzerman's shot: the puck was not in the glove, it was in the net. The Wings won 2–0 with Hašek making 24 saves at Pepsi Center.

That was all well and good, but now both teams were on the brink of advancing and elimination, and the Avs knew they could win at the Joe, too.

The buildup between the end of Game 6 and the start of Game 7 was intense with both sides acknowledging the pressure. Claude Lemieux, the villain from the late '90s, was gone from Colorado by then, but the core of the rivalry—two excellent teams facing off against one another—was as strong as ever.

All of that respect and rivalry talk is why it was so utterly unbelievable and ultimately hilarious what unfolded when Game 7 began.

Less than two minutes in, Holmström scored on a tip-in (it was knocked in by Avalanche defenseman Greg de Vries). Less than two minutes after that, Fedorov scored on a slap shot that deflected off Avalanche defenseman Rob Blake's stick and then hit Roy's right arm. Before the period ended, Robitaille and Holmström made it 4–0.

When Hull scored early in the second period, and Fredrik Olausson less than two minutes later, Roy had given up six goals on 10 shots in 26 minutes and 28 seconds of play. David Aebischer, a Swiss goaltender whose NHL career spanned 214 regular-season games and 13 in the playoffs, was in net when Pavel Datsyuk scored late in the third period.

"It's disappointing to go out like this," Roy said. "We definitely did not play our best game, and it was not my best game. I thought we battled hard all year, but we just came up a bit short."

A bit short was a bit of an understatement: it was the most lopsided game seven score in NHL history.

"You imagine and you pray for something like this," Hull said. "But you don't realistically think that it's going to happen."

Fans loved it, singing along to Neil Diamond's "Sweet Caroline" in the third period in anticipation of the final opponent. The Carolina Hurricanes had advanced to the Stanley Cup Finals on May 28, three days before the Wings.

The series began June 4 at the Joe. Ron Francis scored in overtime, but four games later, that enabled the Wings to celebrate at home. The third game was especially memorable. Larionov's first goal made him the oldest player to score in a Stanley Cup Finals game. He was several hours older when he scored his second, netting a backhand shot at 14:47 of the third overtime. The 41-year-old Larionov took a pass from Holmström and cut across the slot, causing Carolina forward Bates Battaglia to lose his balance and calmly beat goalie Artūrs Irbe in what was the third-longest Finals game in history.

"We may be old, but I was telling Igor that 'I'd rather be old and smart than young and dumb,'" 37-year-old Hull said. "Youth and enthusiasm can only take you only so far."

Larionov called it "the biggest goal of my career. Holmström made a great play, and I decided to wait a little bit. [Battaglia] committed to me, and he slid on ice, so I took my time and put it in."

Hašek made 17 saves in Game 4's 3–0 victory, sending the series back to Detroit with the Wings holding a three-games-to-one lead. Game 5 fell on June 13. Holmström, scoring his eighth goal of the playoffs, finished a setup by Larionov to make it 1–0, Shanahan made it 2–0 and then 3–1.

All the investments had paid off. Hašek and Robitaille each won their first championship, the Wings, their 10th in franchise history. It was the ninth title for 68-year-old Bowman and his last as a coach, as he announced his retirement minutes after the game was over. Yzerman handed off the Cup to Bowman in recognition of Bowman's place in history.

"It's my last game as a coach," Bowman said. "I made up my mind at the Olympic break...I just told my wife 10 minutes ago. I'm not an old man, but it's time to go. I never knew before, but I felt this year that this was it. I'm so happy that I was able to go out with a winning team."

Bowman shed his jacket and put on skates before accepting the Cup, taking it for a lap before handing it off to an equally radiant Hašek. Lidström was awarded the Conn Smythe Trophy as the most valuable player in the playoffs—the first European to win it, just as Hašek was the first European goalie to lead his team to the Cup.

Bowman already had been inducted into the Hockey Hall of Fame in 1991. Larionov was inducted in 2008; Yzerman, Hull, and Robitaille in 2009; Shanahan and Chelios in 2013; Hašek in 2014; and Lidström and Fedorov in 2015.

"It was such a special group for us back then," Holmström said in 2023. "We knew we had so much expectation on us. We had so many stars, more than any other team. We all had such a good time. It was incredible, incredible feeling when we won Game 5, and all the fans were going crazy, there was so much noise. It was just the best feeling, knowing we had done what we were supposed to do."

PART 4

RUSSIAN REVOLUTION

12

Sergei Fedorov

SERGEI FEDOROV WAS AT HIS FIRST RED ARMY CAMP WHEN he caught the attention of one of Soviet Russia's greatest players. During a scrimmage Fedorov found himself in traffic front of the net.

"He made a couple of nifty moves, then put the puck in the top shelf," Igor Larionov said in 1994. "I knew then that he would become a good hockey player—not good, a great hockey player."

It wasn't just what Fedorov could do on the ice that impressed.

"He came to the biggest team in the world, the Red Army team, when he was just 16 years old, no family, nothing," Larionov said. "His goal was to learn how to play and polish his skills. The rest of the stuff, all that other stuff the guys do, didn't interest him, and 16—that's a dangerous age. He was a serious hockey man."

Fedorov was a 19-year-old star in his homeland when the Wings chose him in the fourth round of the 1989 draft. In those Cold War days, picking a player from behind the Iron Curtain carried the risk that he may never be able to get to North America. But the men who were making the selections for the Wings at that draft knew the risk was worth it considering the potential reward if they could lure Fedorov to Detroit. Christer Rockström, the team's chief European scout, had convinced Neil Smith, the Wings' top amateur scout, and Nick Polano, the assistant general manager, to come to Sweden in 1989 to watch Fedorov at the World Championship. All three came away wowed—as did Steve Yzerman, who played against Fedorov in that tournament.

"Steve came back and told us he was a very, very good player," Smith said the night of the draft. "That made us even more interested in him."

Fedorov had been so impressive that Rockström told his colleagues that "he can do more things better" than the other hot-shot Russian available in that draft, Pavel Bure.

When the Wings' turn came up, they selected Fedorov at No. 74. It was the highest a Russian ever had been drafted in the NHL.

The adoration for Fedorov was understandable: He was as strong as an ox, as fluid as a racehorse. He was 6'2" and 195 pounds when he was drafted and topped 200-odd pounds in his prime. His explosiveness was unparalleled; he could skate forward and backward with incredible swiftness. Those who had seen him ahead of the draft said he would have been a top selection had the Iron Curtain not been a deterrent.

Decades later, then general manager Jimmy Devellano still remembered the snickers that greeted the Wings' selection of Fedorov at the 1989 draft: "People said we would never get him because of the Iron Curtain," Devellano said, "but we knew we had just drafted the best young player in the world." (There wasn't another Russian player selected until the sixth round, when Bure—who was rated as a better prospect than Fedorov—was taken at No. 113, 39 spots after Fedorov—by the Vancouver Canucks. Remarkably, of the 16 Russians that were drafted in 1989, nine went on to play in the NHL.)

"There were some who said we were wasting a pick," Devellano said, "but Neil and Christer were convinced of how good he was, and we decided to pick him. We could have taken a Canadian player, but nine times out of 10, in the fourth round, he would have ended up in the American Hockey League. We figured Fedorov was worth it."

First, though, they needed to get him into the fold.

The Wings first made contact with Fedorov in August 1989 during an exhibition game in Helsinki. Through an intermediary, they gave him a letter with an offer for $250,000 to come play for them. Fedorov was interested, but he needed to finish his military service, which ran through the end of the year.

A clandestine meeting with Jim Lites, a team executive, took place in Chicago during a Super Series stop. Lites presented Fedorov with a copy of his contract. Fedorov remained hesitant. In April he helped the Russians win the gold medal at the world championship tournament in Bern, Switzerland.

Then something happened that soured Fedorov on Russia and helped the Wings. He and a group of friends headed to Sochi to vacation at a Black Sea resort. Fedorov's passport had no address stamped in it because the Red Army was still looking for an apartment for him. (It was Red Army officials' way of pressuring Fedorov to sign a long-term contract.)

Without an address, a person was considered homeless. The receptionist at the hotel suggested Fedorov try the local police station for help. There, an officer suggested Fedorov stay the night in a jail cell, instead of his swanky hotel.

Fedorov's friends came through with a bribery of beer and cigarettes, and Fedorov got the paper he needed to stay at the hotel. But he was a star hockey player at the time, and the treatment rankled. That offer from the Wings, and the prospect of living in the United States, magnified in appeal.

At the same time in Detroit, a plan was forming to engineer Fedorov's defection. The Goodwill Games, an international sports competition created in response to the political turmoil that marked the Olympics in the 1980s, were scheduled to be held that summer. That meant that in July, Fedorov would be in Portland, Oregon, for an exhibition game ahead of the tournament.

Lites and Polano, the former head coach turned assistant general manager, traveled to Portland in Mike Ilitch's private jet and checked into the same hotel where the Soviet team stayed. Fedorov was in on what was happening: He slipped his hotel room key beneath the door to Lites' room, enabling Lites to access Fedorov's room and collect his belongings while the Soviets were at the arena.

When the team returned to the hotel, Lites was waiting in the lobby. The plan called for Fedorov to follow Lites out of the hotel. The only person Fedorov told what was happening was his roommate, who spotted Fedorov leaving the lobby.

Outside, a limousine waited to whisk them to the airport. when the chauffeur got too inquisitive, Lites tipped him $100 to stop asking questions.

The Soviets took Fedorov's defection badly: Viktor Tikhonov, the famed national team coach, said that Fedorov "betrayed me."

Fedorov's defection is part of his lore, but his legend was shaped by the impact he had on the Wings. He scored in his debut game, on October 4, 1990, giving the Wings a 3–1 lead over the New Jersey Devils on a power play when he skated between the circles and one-timed a pass from Yzerman into the Devils' net. Fedorov also drew a holding penalty while killing a penalty and played the entire first two minutes of one power play.

Fedorov was a wonder to watch, able to change the tone of a game with his skating. He was as determined to fit in in Detroit as he had been as a teenager at his first Red Army camp, right down to the camaraderie that bonds a team. He was part of a group of Wings who skated together before training camp began, and when he came in one day to find his skates taped together—and knowing the culprit was Joe Kocur—Fedorov responded by taping together Kocur's bag the next day. Kocur was delighted: "I like to see that," he said. Another teammate, Kevin McClelland, used to rile Fedorov daily by "saying something really fast in English," Shawn Burr said. "Poor Sergei has no idea what Kevin's babbling about. He just gives Kevin kind of a blank look. But Sergei has a really good sense of humor."

Fedorov also had incredibly high standards for himself: when he went two games without a point in early December, he told reporters that "for me, that is a big problem." Countered his coach, Bryan Murray: "Can you imagine a rookie in this league believing that's how good he can be?"

At the end of December, Fedorov paced all rookies with 17 goals and 39 points in 39 games, seven more goals and six more points than the No. 1 pick from 1989, Mats Sundin.

"Fedorov is probably the best defensive player to come out of Europe," Polano said a few months into Fedorov's rookie season. "I don't think there's ever been a European player who understands his defensive responsibilities like Sergei does. But I didn't think he would be this good offensively this soon."

Murray, who was coaching at the time, described Fedorov as "at his very best when we are down by a goal or the score is tied. He tries to do more things individually in the third period of a close game. He's one of the people who can take charge of a hockey game: Early in games, he played within the group. Later, if it's not working, he goes for it. What do they call it? Instant offense? I think his potential to score is unlimited."

Born December 13, 1969, in Pskov, a city in northwestern Russia roughly 10 miles east of the border with Estonia, Fedorov had grown up playing hockey on frozen soccer fields. In his bedroom he had a picture of Red Army hero Sergei Makarov, which he would look at while doing his homework and dream of one day being as good a skater, passer, and puck handler.

The Fedorov family also spent time in Apatity, a city in Russia about 70 miles north of the Arctic Circle and 100 miles east of the Finnish border. (That was where Fedorov's younger brother, Fedor, was born in 1981.) "We had big winters there," Fedorov said. He would skate in the morning and again in the evening, and in between he would play games against men. When he was a teenager, he was enrolled in a sports academy in Minsk, Belarus (then part of the Soviet Union). As part of his training, he would lie on the ice, jump up, race to the other end, lie back down flat on his back, jump up, and race back the other way. Over and over, he would push himself, hearing in his head the words of his father: *the first five steps are the most important.*

Valery Matveev, a reporter for Pravda, wrote an article at that time noting that Fedorov, Alexander Mogilny, and Pavel Bure were considered the heir apparents to form the line that would replace the greatness that was Makarov, Igor Larionov, and Vladimir Krutov. "Tikhonov paid much attention to the young guys, and when he brought Sergei to Red Army, Fedorov was the coach's favorite guy on the team," Matveev said. "He was quiet, worked hard, and he was big and strong. Tikhonov knew it was unusual to find so many good things in one person."

In 1993, when Scotty Bowman was named coach of the Wings, he marveled at Fedorov's skating ability.

"Sergei fit in very well because he was so powerful," Bowman recalled in 2023. "He was a big man. He didn't look it all the time, but he had big legs and he weighed 200 pounds. He was one of the unique players who could skate forward and backward with equal dexterity."

That "serious hockey man" that Larionov observed in Fedorov when he was 16 was in full evidence in Detroit. It was a common sight for teammates to see Fedorov peel off his sweat-soaked uniform after games and go lift weights, then ride a stationary bike. Nowadays that's not unusual to see NHL players do, but back in the 1990s, Fedorov's conditioning regimen was exemplary.

Fedorov paced all NHL rookies with 31 goals and 79 points, 20 points ahead of second-place Sundin. But as with Yzerman in 1984, Fedorov placed second in Calder Trophy balloting, losing rookie of the year honors to Chicago Blackhawks goaltender Ed Belfour. (Yzerman had placed second to Buffalo net minder Tom Barrasso.)

The NHL awards ceremony was held in early June. Fedorov had had a phenomenal first year in the NHL, but that didn't ameliorate how homesick the 21-year-old felt. "My passport is in a Moscow office," he said. "I may never get it back. I want to go home. But if I go, I'll never come back. They'll keep me.

Sometimes I miss Moscow. I talk with my parents often, and they understand what's going on."

But things were changing back home. In August communist hardliners attempted a coup to overthrow Soviet leader Mikhail Gorbachev but failed. Already the Union of Soviet Socialist Republics was dissolving with Estonia and Lithuania among the first to declare state sovereignty. The thaw extended to ice hockey: in mid-August, Fedorov was invited to rejoin the Soviet National Team for the upcoming Canada Cup tournament, a six-nation event scheduled to take place in several Canadian and American cities. Conscious of how much red tape still had to be untangled, Fedorov didn't want to talk about it in the media—but the man who led Fedorov out of the hotel lobby on July 20, 1990, shed some light on the situation.

"Through us, Sergei received an invitation from a representative of the Soviet National Ice Hockey Federation to participate in the Canada Cup," Lites said. "But it doesn't include any specifics about when or where or what, and he hasn't responded to it because he doesn't have any travel documents. He can't go to Europe, or to Canada even, on behalf of the Soviet Federation because he doesn't have international travel documents because the same people who wrote the letter are holding his passport."

(An H-1 permit enabled Fedorov to work in the U.S., and he was able to play in Canada because of a special visa issued by the Canadian government.)

Lites said Fedorov told him that he wasn't going anywhere until he had his passport. Lites wasn't sure Soviets hockey officials fully understood the situation: "It's a funny country. But I know from our point of view, we're happy that the Soviets have realized that this kid didn't do anything wrong in coming to play here."

The Soviet Union placed fifth in the tournament, its roster weakened by the political turmoil in Moscow, but at least Fedorov was able to represent his country again.

The dissolution of the USSR also enabled Fedorov to bring his mother, father, and brother to Detroit. He was happier at home, and happy at work: Fedorov topped his 31-goal rookie season by scoring 32 in his second year (and finishing as runner-up for the Selke trophy) and 34 in his third season. He gained a new coach in the summer of 1993, when Bowman replaced Murray. Bowman came to the Wings already having won six Stanley Cups and with a reputation for getting the most out of his players. It was Bowman's idea to play Fedorov and Steve Yzerman on the same line with Fedorov moving to right wing, and Bowman's idea to put Fedorov on defense.

The initial experiment with Yzerman was relatively brief because Yzerman ended up being sidelined by a herniated disk. But with that absence came greater opportunity for Fedorov, and he loved it. There were nights his playing time flirted with 30 minutes, almost unheard-of for a forward. On December 13, 1993, the day Fedorov celebrated his 24th birthday, he ranked third in the NHL with 47 points, 10 behind leader Wayne Gretzky.

"When I came to this country, I tried to learn everything I could from my partners, my teammates," Fedorov said. "This league was totally different for me. Steve was one of the greatest players in the NHL. I watched him every game, every shift. It kind of built my attitude about this job. That's really important, to have a good attitude about your job. If you're proud of yourself, you'll play so much better than if you have different emotions."

In that same interview, Fedorov touched on what everyone who watched him play noticed: "Play good defense," he said, "and the points come along. This year I've tried more offensive things, and they've been successful, but it all comes from good defensive play."

Bowman was impressed: "I always had him down as a good, two-way forward, a complete player, which is kind of unusual for a European. But now I compare him to a guy I coached in Montreal for eight seasons, Jacques Lemaire. They both always checked the other team's top guy and they always seem to lift the team when it's most needed. And they're always thinking. Fedorov's got great speed, but he doesn't just take off. There's a lot of thought in his play. And the most underrated part of his game is his goal-scoring. People tend to think of him as more of a playmaker. He's got a good demeanor, too. He's interested and he wants to really improve his game."

By the end of December, Fedorov paced the NHL with 65 points in 36 games. Gretzky trailed him by two points—but Fedorov also had a plus-25 rating to Gretzky's minus-4.

Yzerman reappeared after missing 26 games and marveled at Fedorov's play: "He's always had that one shift a game where you'd go, 'Wow.' Now he's doing it every shift. He's spectacular every time he's on the ice."

Fedorov enthralled the hockey world. In January of 1994, he was named to the NHL All-Star Game. (Fedorov played on a line with Bure and Alexander Mogilny, a reunion of their days together as young starts with the Central Red Army Club. "It's the best time I ever had, this All-Star weekend," Fedorov said afterward.)

He was featured in a two-page spread in *Sports Illustrated*. A poll in the *Hockey News* of the writers who vote on the annual NHL awards showed Fedorov as a landslide leader for league MVP. The *Toronto Star* polled 20 NHL head coaches to find that 15 named Fedorov as the best player in the league.

In March a sellout crowd at Joe Louis Arena saluted Fedorov with a standing ovation after he recorded his first career NHL hat trick; the second goal put him at 100 points. Two weeks later Fedorov became the fifth player in Wings history to reach the 50-goal plateau, joining Danny Grant, Mickey Redmond (twice), John Ogrodnick, and Steve Yzerman (five times).

Almost five years to the day that Fedorov became the highest-drafted Russian in NHL history, Fedorov became the first Russian-born player to win the Hart Memorial Trophy as the NHL's most valuable player. His haul at the awards show that June 16, 1994, also numbered the Frank J. Selke Trophy as the league's best defensive forward—30 years onward, he was still the only player in NHL history to capture both in the same year—and the Lester B. Pearson Award as the league's most outstanding player, as voted by fellow players. (The award was renamed after Wings great Ted Lindsay in 2010.)

Fedorov won the Hart in a landslide with 194 points to 86 for runner up Dominik Hašek, a future teammate who was then with the Buffalo Sabres. (Voting for the Selke was a tad closer: 175 for Fedorov to 107 for Toronto Maple Leafs center Doug Gilmour.) Echoing what he said five months earlier at the All-Star Game, Fedorov called it "the greatest time I have ever had. It's a great honor."

A great honor for a glamorous player, but Fedorov knew the NHL's biggest piece of hardware was still missing. "I have only one motivation," he said in September 1994. "I can't forget all those first rounds we lose."

A labor dispute that delayed the start of the 1994–95 season until January did have a silver lining for Fedorov: he was able to return to his motherland in November to play hockey. "It's kind of a funny feeling," Fedorov said before leaving for the five-game exhibition event. While in Moscow he met with high-ranking government officials at the Kremlin about getting a new Russian passport. They had asked him about staying and playing for the

Red Army depending on what happened in the NHL, but this time, Fedorov felt free to say *nyet*. "I'm playing in Detroit," he told them.

Fedorov had a star turn in the 1995 playoffs, setting a Wings record with 24 points in 17 games, but while the playoffs ended not in the first round but in the fourth, the Wings still exited on a loss.

Fedorov continued to make the Wings look like geniuses for drafting him: during the 1995–96 season, he delivered two five-point performances and finished with a team-leading 107 points. Another five-point outing followed the next season, when Fedorov netted all of his team's goals in a 5–4 overtime victory over the Washington Capitals on December 26, 1996. "This night was like rolling stones from the mountain coming at me," he said. "I was very excited because the overtime goal. That's the most exciting part of the game."

Only one Wings player had ever done better: Syd Howe, who on February 3, 1944, scored six goals against the New York Rangers. Fedorov's performance contrasted the one goal he scored the first 11 games of the season. Bowman pointed to playing time: "He's been better since we played him more. Tonight was like a dream game." It also helped that Bowman had reunited the Russian Five, playing Fedorov with Larionov, Vyacheslav Kozlov, Vladimir Konstantinov, and Slava Fetisov. "After we started playing together, Sergei had lots of quality chances," Konstantinov said.

The season wasn't without turmoil: in March the *New York Post* ran a headline that "Fedorov wants out," citing an unnamed source claiming the Wings had agreed to trade Fedorov if they didn't win the Stanley Cup. "Not true," said Fedorov. Later that same month, Fedorov showed what incredible talent he had when he thrived on an assignment as a defenseman.

"It really was a fluke," Bowman said in 2023. "We put him back on defense because we had injuries. But that got him more ice time. I think when I first put him back there he might have played a couple times with Nicklas Lidström, not knowing what he could do, but then we put him with other players, and he played about a month on defense. He liked it because he could play more minutes there. He was great back there. I do recall a conversation with Wayne Gretzky after I retired. He said no one player that he had ever seen could do what Sergei did, playing forward and defense. He said, 'I could not go back and play defense and I don't think Mario Lemieux or Jaromír Jágr could have done it. We just didn't have the uniqueness to skate forward and backward.' But Wayne knew what a phenomenal skater Sergei was."

Statistically, the 1996–97 regular season was a downturn for Fedorov, who had just 63 points, 44 fewer than the season before. But in the playoffs, he was magnificent, coming through with 20 points in 20 games, including a two-goal, two-assist performance in Game 3 of the Stanley Cup Finals.

"Fedorov has come up with a tremendous playoffs for us," Bowman said on June 5, 1997, two days before the Wings won the Stanley Cup.

A few days later, the Wings were feted with a parade down Woodward Avenue, riding in open cars. Seated next to Fedorov was his girlfriend, 16-year-old tennis player Anna Kournikova by his side. The glamorous couple made headlines at Wimbledon in July, while as the summer months wore on, a chill set in at home. Fedorov, whose defection in 1990 had prompted Tikhonov to say he felt betrayed, heard similar criticism from Fetisov when Fedorov was a no-show for a planned Cup parade in Moscow. "The young guys, they make money, but they do not help," Fetisov said. "Everything was too easy for them." Fetisov had staked his career and professional

THE FRANCHISE: DETROIT RED WINGS

reputation to help the younger generation of Russian players to be able to join the NHL.

Fedorov's defection from the Soviet team in 1990 certainly wasn't easy, but he didn't pay the price that Fetisov did: team officials put him in a military uniform and gave him a desk job for a year.

Fedorov pulled away from his Russian teammates in Detroit as he pulled away from the Wings. Contract talks between the team and Fedorov, a restricted free agent, had gone nowhere in the spring, when he was offered $4.5 million a season for his choice of anywhere between one to four years.

The 1997–98 season began without Fedorov in uniform. Throughout the fall, talks went nowhere. While most of his teammates received their Stanley Cup rings in a gala ceremony in November, Fedorov received his during a January visit to general manager Ken Holland's office, where a two-year offer worth $5.5 million annually was greeted with contempt.

Fedorov took to practicing with the Ontario Hockey League Plymouth Whalers. Skating with a lower-league team wasn't unheard of for holdout players, but Fedorov's appearance added to the icy relations with the Wings because the Whalers were owned by Detroit businessman and Ilitch rival Peter Karmanos Jr., who also owned the NHL's Carolina Hurricanes. Fedorov might as well have been seen in public eating a pizza that wasn't Little Caesars.

In February he hit Japan like a rock star, stepping off the bullet train in Nagano, Japan, wearing black jeans, a Planet Hollywood jacket from Sydney, Australia, a beret turned backward—and a standoffish attitude. "I have no intention to talk about my personal NHL problems," he said. He should have added, *in English.*

Fedorov had no issues talking about the Wings to the *Daily Sport Express.* When the Russian news outlet asked if he had made comments about trade demands, Fedorov said, "Yes, I said it in order to speed up the process and so that my position would be clear to management because I don't think they have believed up until now I won't be returning to the club. But I have already fallen away from them and I can't see a place for myself there. Therefore, the faster they trade me, the better for the team and for me."

Asked if he had excluded returning to Detroit, Fedorov said, "I excluded it a long time ago. I made this decision in August and still haven't changed it. They think they can break me with the help of some financial tricks, but they don't know the kind of person I am. They don't know who they are messing with."

The comments did not go over well privately with team officials, but publicly, all Holland said was that the Wings had made Fedorov fair offers.

The situation between Fedorov and the Wings—and the reason that, privately, some within the organization echoed Tikhonov and Fetisov in feeling a sense of betrayal—escalated in mid-February when Fedorov signed an offer sheet tendered by Karmanos' Hurricanes and designed to put the Wings in a noose. The contract was $38 million for six years—on average that was $6.3 million, less than $1 million more than the Wings had been offering. It was the details that stunned: it was structured to the extent that should the Wings—who, unlike the struggling Hurricanes, were projected to go on a long playoff run—have a successful spring, they could owe Fedorov $28 million by summer. There was a $14 million signing bonus, and a $12 million bonus for making the conference Finals on top of the $2 million salary. Fedorov gloated: "I'm very proud this happened," he said.

Fedorov had accused the Wings of messing with him, but it turned out he was the one who failed to grasp who he was trying to mess with. On February 26, less than 10 days after the offers sheet was tendered, the Wings matched. They knew he was a key to repeating as champions, and as daunting as the structure of the deal was, they determined that, just as in 1989 at the draft, Fedorov was worth the gamble.

On February 27, 1998, Fedorov was back in a Wings uniform for the first time since they won the Cup on June 7 the previous year. Most fans booed; some cheered. Ilitch made a rare pregame visit to the locker room to shake Fedorov's hand; Fedorov considered that to mean that "everything went away."

Once again, the Wings' investment in Fedorov proved worth it: he paced the Wings with 10 playoff goals and ranked second with 20 points. When they repeated as champions on June 16, he made light of the previous year's acrimony while soaked in champagne.

"Deep inside, I always wanted to stay here and play," he said. "To be honest, I never thought I would, but I hoped I would. I think about it, and Detroit is my second hometown. I came here from Russia only to play for the Red Wings, and I can never forget that I'm a hockey player here, and I have to produce and play well. Some people got mad because of what happened. My challenge was to win some fans back. I really had a good chance to do that, and now we're back on top. Things worked out. I wouldn't let anybody stop me."

Fedorov never again dominated with the Wings like he had earlier, only posting one more season where he averaged more than a point per game. He continued to be tabloid fodder over his relationship with Kournikova (the two would eventually marry and divorce) and seemed to crave a more glamorous life than was possible in Detroit. He won a third Stanley Cup in 2002, which segued into the last year of the deal designed by the Hurricanes.

Hoping to avoid another spectacle, Ilitch had a personal meeting with Fedorov in November 2002, offering him a five-year deal worth $50 million. When nothing happened it was reduced to four years but still at $10 million annually. It didn't help that Fedorov's father, Viktor, sounded off in *Sport Express*, complaining about Fedorov at times serving as a defenseman and suggesting his son should not re-sign with the Wings. In late June 2003, as his contract neared its final days, Fedorov threw his mother a big birthday bash and then headed to southern California, ostensibly to see friends. (The weather there was also better for driving his latest big acquisition: a $650,000 Ferrari Enzo.)

A few days into free agency, Fedorov accepted a four-year, $50 million offer to play for the Mighty Ducks of Anaheim. Ilitch had appealed to Fedorov until the very end, calling him a few days before the July 19 deal with the Ducks became official.

It was a disappointing if not entirely unexpected outcome for the team responsible for bringing him to the NHL.

"Sergei Fedorov was a great player who allowed our franchise to take it to a new level in the '90s," Devellano said. "He is a player I hoped would take the mantle over from Steve Yzerman as he is finishing up his career. He is somebody I was hopeful would play 20 years as a Red Wing, and we would hang his jersey to the rafters."

Fedorov's dream of living the southern California lifestyle lasted little more than a season. On November 15, 2005, the Mighty Ducks traded Fedorov to the Columbus Blue Jackets for Tyler Wright (who would go on to serve as the Wings' chief of amateur scouting from 2013–2019). It was an unseemly landing spot for a player of Fedorov's caliber: the Blue Jackets were only in their fifth season since joining the NHL and wouldn't make the playoffs for another four years. Fedorov did play his 1,000[th] game there on November 30, 2005.

He didn't appear in the playoffs again until he was traded to the Washington Capitals at the 2008 deadline. That was where he finished his NHL career in 2008–09 with 483 goals and 1,179 points in 1,248 games; 400 of the goals and 954 of the points had come in 908 games in a Wings uniform.

Fedorov returned to Russia to finish his playing career, spending three seasons with Metallurg Magnitogorsk in the Kontinental Hockey League.

Fedorov was booed when he played at Joe Louis Arena for several years after he left. The rift he created when he defected from the Soviet team in 1990 took less time to mend than his departure from Detroit. The sense that he had snubbed Ilitch, the harsh words to the Russian press, all the criticism leveled by his father—it did not start to dissipate until Fedorov was elected to the Hockey Hall of Fame in 2015. Then he was treated to a standing ovation at the Joe when he dropped a ceremonial puck on November 10, 2015. That night he described himself as a "Red Wing at heart."

The "serious hockey man" that Larionov had observed in Fedorov when he was a teenager at a Soviet hockey camp had grown into a man who became a millionaire in the United States. Had Fedorov stayed with the Wings—his last season in the KHL, 2011–12, was the same as fellow 1989 draft pick Nicklas Lidström's last year with the Wings—there might have been more Stanley Cup celebrations.

"Sergei was a superstar," Bowman said in 2023. "He was such an elite player. He never had the same success after he left. He was one of the very best."

13

Vladimir Konstantinov

RED WINGS SCOUTS PROCLAIMED VLADIMIR KONSTANTINOV would be their best all-around defenseman from the moment they selected him at 221st overall in the 1989 draft. They were that enamored and impressed with the young Russian, which is why they chanced choosing him at a time the Cold War loomed as a deterrent to adding players from behind the Iron Curtain. Konstantinov was 22 when the Wings drafted him and 24 when executive vice president Jim Lites undertook months-long negotiations with Soviet officials to free him while simultaneously underwriting Konstantinov's escape via an audacious adventure.

In early 1991 the Wings were told Konstantinov would be allowed to join them the following February, after the Winter Olympics. They spent the spring and summer trying to move up that timeline because they really wanted Konstantinov to come to training camp and earn a job that autumn. They had just gotten another of their 1989 draft picks, promising young defenseman Nicklas Lidström, under contract and were eager to see both of them start the 1991–92 season together. The Wings had the pair earmarked to anchor their defense for the coming decade and beyond.

It was early September by the time they got Konstantinov signed to a contract. He had cleared the Red Army and was in the process of clearing the red tape to work in the United States, and the Wings were thrilled.

"He's a world-class player, a solid defensive defenseman," then–general manager Bryan Murray said on the eve of training camp. "He's not flashy. He just gets the job done."

To say Konstantinov got the job done sounds remarkably restrained with the hindsight of what he did get done. Konstantinov did have flash to him—as in the flash of a moment it took him to size up an opponent coming his way, lower a shoulder, and send him tumbling. Konstantinov epitomized the type of player fans love if he is on their team, and otherwise complain about nonstop. Not just fans, either: Colorado Avalanche coach Marc Crawford once spent an entire press conference during the 1997 playoffs berating Konstantinov's style of play, accusing his every shift of being one long disregard for discipline. It was just what delighted Konstantinov: getting opponents to think about him, not about scoring goals.

"I know him since he was 16," fellow Russian defenseman Slava Fetisov said in March 1997. "Everybody [called] him grandpa because he was so serious when he played, even when he was so young. He is very competitive when he plays the game. He doesn't take stupid penalties. He would hit his brother. He is never soft on anyone. But everybody respects him."

Konstantinov was, in the all-too-brief time he played for the Wings, a dynamic, dedicated fireball of fun and fearlessness, born north of the Arctic Circle, raised in Russia, and freed in Detroit.

The Wings knew what they were getting when they drafted Konstantinov. Neil Smith, a top scout in the organization, had seen Konstantinov at the 1987 World Junior Championship in what was then Czechoslovakia, where the Soviet Union–Canada game deteriorated into a free-for-all. The melee was so out of control that officials tried turning out the lights for 20 minutes as a countermeasure. Among the damage inflicted was Konstantinov's head-butt that broke Greg Hawgood's nose. Both teams ultimately were disqualified—the Soviets already were out of medal contention anyway, but for Canada it cost the country a chance to play for the gold medal. Besides Konstantinov, multiple future Wings were part of the "Punch-up in Piestany," including Sergei Fedorov, Steve Chiasson, and Brendan Shanahan.

Konstantinov's performance left an impression on Smith. As the 1989 draft dragged into the later rounds, it made much more sense to select a European, even from behind the Iron Curtain because they tended to be more mature, well-rounded players.

At the time of the 1989 draft, only seven players ever drafted in the 11th round had appeared in the NHL—and the best one of them was Russian Igor Larionov, who was 28 when he made his debut in North America.

Smith and chief European scout Christer Rockström already had campaigned general manager Jimmy Devellano to take multiple Europeans that day—Lidström in the third round, Fedorov in the fourth—and decided to take a swing at Konstantinov. Rockström, remembering the World Junior Championship, suggested to Smith, "How about that nice

THE FRANCHISE: DETROIT RED WINGS

Vladimir Konstantinov?" As with Murray's comment two years later about Konstantinov getting the job done, Rockström's description was marvelously understated. The Wings wanted Konstantinov precisely because he wasn't nice on the ice.

Getting Konstantinov to Detroit came with all the headaches and headlines befitting a late 1980s exit strategy set against the backdrop of Soviet premier Mikhail Gorbachev's reformation efforts. The first hurdle to clear was making sure Konstantinov even wanted to leave. He was the captain of the Central Red Army and Soviet national teams, a high-profile player with a wife and a toddler. "When I first approached him about leaving Russia, he said it was just impossible to leave," Valery Matveev, a former *Pravda* reporter who became a facilitator for the Wings, said in a 1994 interview with the *Detroit Free Press*.

What seemed to change Konstantinov's mind was when the Red Army team visited Detroit for a Super Series game against the Wings in 1990. Konstantinov was able to chat with Fedorov, who gave him some insight into what life was like in North America: big paydays, no dictatorial bosses, and grocery stores stocked with fresh food. The Wings even slipped Konstantinov a red team sweater with his name on it.

When Matveev asked Konstantinov again in New York at the end of the series, Konstantinov was amenable. "He saw how Sergei was living in Detroit and he started thinking," Matveev said. "He said, 'Yes, I'm ready to go.' I returned to Detroit and met with Jimmy Lites, and we started thinking about a plan. The only way I thought we might be able to do it was pay lots of money to somebody in the Russian army to get his release. Jim said, 'Okay, go to Moscow and start working on it.'"

Matveev ultimately deemed that plan too risky—he would have to cast a wide net, and with every moneyed handshake came the risk of betrayal and an indefinite stay in a gulag.

Instead, over dinner with a doctor friend, Matveev hit upon a devious, brilliant idea: bribe one doctor to say Konstantinov had a rare form of cancer that required he be released from the army and allowed to go to the United States for treatment.

"I had a good connection to this clinic," Matveev said. "They told me it was possible to prepare all the papers for Vladdie so he could get his release." While Matveev worked the medical angle, Konstantinov's wife, Irina, pleaded with Konstantinov's Red Army superiors—general manager Valery Gushin and coach Viktor Tikhonov—to let her sick husband travel abroad for a cure.

"Everybody knows Russian medicine is not so good as in the U.S.," Matveev said. "But Tikhonov didn't believe us. He wanted to see the papers from the clinic. Then he decided to put Vladdie in Burdenko, the best military hospital in the Soviet Union."

That required more bribes. Matveev estimated he spent around $30,000 at the initial clinic and another $30,000 at Burdenko.

"Everybody in Moscow wants some money," he said. "Everybody wants a nicer place to live, a better car. And working for a newspaper, as I did, gave me lots of connections to many different fields of life. I knew exactly with whom it would be possible to discuss this situation."

It was a clever plan: doctors couldn't figure out exactly what was wrong with Konstantinov, nor could they prove that there was nothing wrong with him. (Back in Detroit, the Wings kept up the ruse: when asked why Konstantinov wasn't with the Soviet Canada Cup team in early September, Murray replied that it was because of "a virus, a fatigue thing from what I'm told.")

The trip to the U.S. was approved with tickets for Konstantinov, Irina, and their daughter, Anastasia, to fly out of Moscow's Sheremetyevo Airport.

But Gushin remained suspicious, and Matveev learned he had put Konstantinov's name on a no-fly list, which would lead to him being detained if he showed up at the airport.

The plan changed from planes to trains.

But there was one development no amount of bribes could have eased. In August of 1991, a group of hardline Communist officials staged a coup in an attempt to overthrow Gorbachev and end his reforms. Tanks rolled through the streets of Moscow. Gorbachev was in Crimea while Boris Yeltsin, newly elected president, rallied the populace in Moscow, refusing to blink in the face of the agitators. He won, the hardliners lost, and by the end of the year, the Soviet Union had dissolved.

It was a fascinating time in world history, but for Konstantinov and the Wings, it created another hurdle. During the mayhem that enveloped Moscow, thieves broke into Matveev's car and stole his radio and his briefcase—which contained Konstantinov's forged medical reports and passport. It wasn't just the theft that bothered Konstantinov and Matveev—they were terrified the briefcase might end up with the KGB, the Soviet security agency that begat dread in Russians and foreigners alike.

"We were so upset," Matveev said. "We were in Vladdie's apartment trying to figure out what to do now when the phone rang. The guy said he was a big hockey fan, and he found Vladdie's documents. We knew it was the bandits who stole it. He said he would call back to arrange for us to meet him and pick it up."

Around midnight the bandit called back. By then, Matveev had tracked down a friend who owned a gun—he really did have wide-ranging connections—and together they went to the Kosmos Hotel to make the exchange. All the bandits wanted was some hockey gear and Konstantinov's autograph. It was the cheapest meeting Matveev had undertaken on the Wings' behalf.

Within a couple days, the two men were on a train to Budapest, Hungary, where Lites awaited with an immigration lawyer. Onward they went to Detroit. A few days later, Irina arrived with Anastasia.

It had been an incredible few weeks, from hatching the fake medical diagnosis, visiting multiple clinics, bribing dozens of people, riding out a coup, and recovering the briefcase.

Konstantinov debuted in a Wings uniform on October 3, 1991. A month later, "that nice Vladimir Konstantinov" was the subject of an NHL disciplinary investigation because of a melee that erupted in Boston after the final horn sounded. The Wings conceded video evidence showed Konstantinov punched and wrestled Bruins forward Jeff Lazaro to the ice in a headlock, but also noted the video countered accusations that Konstantinov gauged Lazaro in the face with his fingernails. (It was a wild night for the Wings: a Bruins fan punched Steve Yzerman, claiming it was in retaliation for Yzerman blackening his eye with the end of his hockey stick. After a night in jail, the fan admitted he lied and that Yzerman had not touched him.)

Konstantinov was 25 when he finished his rookie season with the Wings, posting eight goals, 26 assists, and 172 penalty minutes in 79 games. Lidström had more points (60), and both Bob Probert (276) and Gerard Gallant (187) had more penalty minutes, but for a Russian adjusting to his first year in North America, the Wings were very, very pleased with what Konstantinov gave them. Opponents had to pay attention when he was on the ice; he had a devilish way of pounding them into the boards and rubbing his elbows in their faces.

For all that the Wings did to open up the flow of Russians to Detroit, the Cold War at times raged within the team. At training camp in Konstantinov's second year, a career minor-league player by the name of Max Middendorf was tossed out of a scrimmage for hitting Konstantinov in the head with his stick and kicking him while he was underneath a scrum involving all 10 skaters on the ice. Skating up behind Konstantinov, Middendorf used the blade of his stick to scrape the back of the Russian's scalp and knock his helmet over his eyes. Konstantinov whirled and swung his stick, missing Middendorf. No one was injured seriously, but it was enough for Murray to eject Middendorf.

"Vladdie plays hard," Murray said. "He's a real competitor and he takes the game seriously when he's got a uniform on. He's got the stick up because people continually are running at him."

Konstantinov learned to lean into his reputation. "Vlad the Impaler" was one of his nicknames, but the better one was "The Vladinator." There was a video that played on the Jumbotron at Joe Louis Arena during games which inter-cut scenes from Arnold Schwarzenegger's The Terminator with shots of Konstantinov crashing into foes. A frightened man yelled, "He can't be stopped! He feels no pain! He feels no remorse!" At the end of the video, Konstantinov was shown wearing dark sunglasses, his arms folded as he said, "Hasta la vista, baby." George Thorogood's "Bad to the Bone" was used as his theme song.

It got lost because of the *other* game between the Wings and Avalanche in March 1997, but on the 16th of that month when the teams met in Denver, Konstantinov so infuriated Colorado's Claude Lemieux (whose dirty hit on Kris Draper in the 1996 playoffs ignited the Wings–Avalanche rivalry) that Lemieux botched a power play because he was so intent on getting even. As Lemieux skated to the penalty box, Konstantinov skated to his bench, laughing.

"I don't care if they hate me," he said afterward, a sentiment he repeated many times in his career. "I just play for my team and for Detroit."

In the mid-1990s, the Wings defense corps included Konstantinov, Lidström, Slava Fetisov, and Paul Coffey. Coffey (who was traded at the start of the 1996–97 season) was awarded the Norris Trophy given to the NHL's top defenseman in 1995, and Lidström was an NHL All-Star. Those two were gifted, skilled defensemen. Konstantinov (who would finish second in voting for the Norris in 1997) was skilled, but he also meted out punishment during every shift, making him the target of every opponent. The plus-minus rating is a rather nebulous statistic that shows a player was on the ice for more goals scored by his team than against it. It is not a particularly valuable statistic because a player can get a plus or a minus without being involved in a play, but it still said something that in 1995–96, Konstantinov topped the plus-minus category in the entire NHL with a plus-60. It was the highest rating a player had achieved since Wayne Gretzky's plus-69 in 1986–87.

"Vladdie plays with his heart," Larionov said in March 1997. "He's one of those few players who's got his own identity. Like Wayne Gretzky, you think of a guy with a sharp mind, a great playmaker. With Vladimir Konstantinov, you think of hardworking, tough. He's earned respect around the league with his toughness. And he will do anything to win. Anything."

Konstantinov was driven by nature. The son of a merchant marine sailor in the Barents seaport of Murmansk, Konstantinov stood out for how hard he worked at hockey practices.

"Vladimir, from a very, very early age, was very dedicated and very competitive," Petr Anikeev, who coached Konstantinov in a number of sports as a young boy, said during a visit to Detroit in 1996. "Some kids you have to push. Vladimir never needed that. I never had to push him. He always wanted to compete, to excel."

Konstantinov's instincts were bred into him, Anikeev said. "Vladimir was born where it is very cold climate, with severe winter conditions. Because of economic and social conditions, life is very tough. That's what builds character—the poverty, the hunger, the cold weather. In the winters we play hockey outside on the river and lake for six months."

When Konstantinov was 16, he was summoned to Moscow, where he played as a teenager among men for the Red Army in the Soviet Elite League. Tikhonov—the Soviet hockey legend who in 1991 tried to thwart Konstantinov's attempts to leave Russia—was so impressed with Konstantinov that he eventually pinned a "K" (for *kapitan*) on Konstantinov's sweater.

"One day, Tikhonov came to me and said, 'You will be captain,'" Konstantinov said. "That's all he said. He didn't talk much to the players. But if you made a bad pass, he'd get [mad] at you every time. If [your] man scored a goal, maybe you don't play the next game. As the coach, 'Why,' he said, 'don't [you] do your job. You watch the TV. You study now.' With Tikhonov there are no star players. If you don't do your job, you don't play."

Tikhonov respected how disciplined Konstantinov was—and how he withstood his coach's sometimes cruel treatment.

"Tikhonov pushed him and pushed him, and he was just a young person, a teenager," Igor Larionov recalled in 1994. "It was terrible sometimes."

Playing for the Red Army was demanding, but when he came to the NHL, Konstantinov had to deal with xenophobia— that incident with Middendorf at training camp wasn't an isolated event.

"He comes home more banged up now," Irina Konstantinov told the *Detroit Free Press* in January 1992. "Every other team hates him now. When he started to play in the NHL, everybody warned him to be careful, that other teams will pick on him because he's Russian. He decided the best way to defend himself is to attack."

It was all worth it, of course: soon after he signed a contract paying him $360,000 his first season, the Konstantinovs purchased a BMW for him, a Camaro for her, and got an apartment that overlooked the Detroit River. (They also called home a good deal: Irina Konstantinov said one month their bill was $1,700.)

Konstantinov had a way of leaving opponents raving. In January of 1994, Chicago Blackhawks All-Star center Jeremy Roenick seethed after one too many battles against Konstantinov. "He's going to get his one day," Roenick told the *Chicago Tribune*. "He better watch it. He's the dirtiest player in the league. Wicked stuff. I'm sure a lot of guys in this league owe him. We owe him more than he owes us." That was just what Konstantinov loved to hear. "Roenick, he [cries] like baby every time," Konstantinov countered. "I give him a little touch on the helmet. I'm not a dirty player."

Legions of opponents would dispute that, but no one could dispute what an effective defenseman Konstantinov was. He was more focused on preventing foes from scoring than producing points himself, but in June 1995, he scored in double overtime to give the Wings a 4–3 victory and a three-games-to-none lead in their conference Final against the Blackhawks. Konstantinov fired a 40-foot shot at the Chicago net, then turned and hurried to get back into position. When teammates informed him that he had scored, Konstantinov shouted, "Unbelievable, guys."

With about a month to go in the 1996–97 season, Konstantinov led the NHL with a plus-40 rating. "It's nice to lead," he said in March, a week before his 30th birthday, "but it's more important to win a championship."

On June 7, 1997, Konstantinov celebrated the championship he craved. Since embedding with the Wings at the start of the 1991–92 season, Konstantinov had experienced a second-round exit in 1992, a seven-game loss in the first round in 1993, the first-round upset of the 1994 playoffs when they were eliminated by the San Jose Sharks in Game 7 at home, the frustration of the 1995 playoffs when the advanced to the Stanley Cup Final only to be swept by the New Jersey Devils, and the emotions of the 1996 playoffs when the Avalanche sent them packing in the third round. At last, the season finished with pure joy, culminating in a 2–1 victory at Joe Louis Arena that completed the sweep of the Philadelphia Flyers. One of the photos of Konstantinov snapped as he took his turn with the Stanley Cup shows him smiling with an expression that says, "Unbelievable, guys."

He celebrated his next Stanley Cup in a wheelchair.

Konstantinov should have played a decade and beyond with the Wings. He was magnificent in his prime: the effectiveness with which he neutralized opponents, the impact with which he upended them—he was incredible to watch. Sometimes teams are fortunate enough to have one elite defenseman; in Konstantinov and Lidström, the Wings had two, plucked from the same draft. But a devastating turn of events robbed Konstantinov of his way of life six days after he had celebrated the Stanley Cup. The Wings did the right thing when they had a team celebration at a golf course, hiring chauffeured limousines to transport them after the event so that drinking champagne or beer from the Cup would not be an issue. But the limo occupied by Konstantinov, Fetisov, and team masseur Sergei Mnatsakanov was driven by a man who fell asleep and crashed the vehicle into a tree on Woodward Avenue in Birmingham, a suburb north of Detroit. The impact hurled Konstantinov into the mini bar, where his head crashed into the shattered glass. Konstantinov lay in a coma for two months. Doctors diagnosed him with that they called "scrambled brain," a condition that can shear neurons and cause swelling. He never recovered.

The tragedy of June 13, 1997, is part of Konstantinov's story, but it is not bigger than him. His attendance post-accident at games at Joe Louis Arena and Little Caesars Arena effected standing ovations from fans, including from those too young to have watched him play. He was a chance pick in 1989, he was worth all the subterfuge and bribery necessary to get him out of Russia in 1991, and for the six seasons he wore a Wings uniform, he was the fiercest of competitors and the funniest of teammates, a man who looked old and grizzled but who played with a light and exuberant heart.

14
Pavel Datsyuk

THE SUMMER OF 2001 WAS SUCH A HEADLINE OFFSEASON
for the Red Wings—Brett Hull, Luc Robitaille, Dominik
Hašek—that the mid-July signing of their sixth-round pick from
1998 was little more than an addendum. "We think he's a smart
player," it said in the news release announcing Pavel Datsyuk's
contract.

The Wings were coming off the disappointment of a first-
round loss in the 2001 playoffs, when the Los Angeles Kings
dispatched a roster that still featured many of the players who
had won the Stanley Cup in 1997 and 1998. Hull, Robitaille,
and Hašek joined the star-studded roster, fueling expectations
of another Cup.

Datsyuk was listed at 5'10" and 167 pounds when he came
to camp, not much heavier than when he had been drafted at
171st overall three years earlier. But it was never his physicality
that impressed, it was always the mental side of his game. And

that is how he earned a spot on the roster and made himself one of the headline stories of the fabled 2001–02 team.

"I remember the scrimmage on the first day of camp, he made an unbelievable backhand pass that not many guys can make," Nicklas Lidström said in 2023. "Put it across ice, saucer pass that landed on someone's stick who scored for a one-timer. That caught my eye. He didn't look strong, but he was good at protecting the puck and hard to knock off the puck. His skill set was one of the best in the league. So sneaky good, such a hardworking guy, back checking and stripping the puck off guys, not knowing who was behind him. He had so much skill, and he was such a hard worker."

Datsyuk's Wings story begins with Håkan Andersson, whose determination to scout players eclipsed all manner of threatening weather conditions. He first saw Datsyuk on a trip to Russia where the primary scouting target was Dmitri Kalinin, and one of the games Kalinin played in happened to be against Datsyuk, who was playing in the lower leagues for his hometown team in Yekaterinburg. As undersized as he was—the estimate was he weighed around 140 pounds at the time—Datsyuk bedeviled with the puck. He used his stealth to swipe it away from bigger opponents and then showed off his playmaking abilities by holding onto it when lesser players would have just gotten rid of the puck. Datsyuk made enough of an impression that not only did Andersson file his usual scouting report, he made a point to call Jim Nill, then the Wings' director of amateur scouting, to make sure the report was read. "This guy," Andersson told his cohorts in the organization, "is as smart of a player as Igor Larionov."

That comparison drew attention: Larionov was almost 35 by the time he joined the Wings in 1995, but he was as brilliant of a player late in his career as he had been in his prime, when he was a superstar center with the Soviet Red Army team. If there was another Larionov out there, the Wings wanted to know more.

Andersson's first attempt to get a second look at Datsyuk was waylaid by a monster snowstorm in Moscow. Passengers sat for hours on a plane tucked away on a runway, entertained—in a horror-movie kind of way—for a while when what looked like a giant flamethrower was used to de-ice the wings. It was late afternoon when the flight was cancelled. It was a long day going nowhere for Andersson, but there was a scout from another NHL team on the plane, and at least it meant he never got to see Datsyuk play before the 1998 draft.

Other NHL scouts may have heard of Datsyuk, but if they hadn't seen him, he certainly didn't do anything statistically in his draft year that would catch anyone's attention: playing in a second-level league for Dinamo-Energija Yekaterinburg, Datsyuk posted just three goals and four assists in 24 games.

For all of Andersson's glowing reviews, the Wings weren't quick to pick him. That they didn't use their first-round pick was understandable: even though it didn't come until 25th, third-from-last in the round, defenseman Jiří Fischer was a much more appealing choice. He made good on the selection, too, playing 305 games before a medical issue put an abrupt end to his career. But they also passed on Datsyuk twice in the second round (at 55th and 56th) and in the third, fourth, and fifth round, and even with their first pick in the sixth round, which was 20 spots ahead of their second sixth-round pick. Of those six draftees, the only player to appear in the NHL was the guy selected at 55th, Ryan Barnes, and he lasted two games.

Datsyuk lasted 953.

Born July 20, 1978, in what during the Soviet Union was known as Sverdlovsk, Datsyuk was nearly 20 years old when the Wings drafted him and 23 when he arrived in Detroit. He still looked so small, and it didn't help that he couldn't do a bench press during the physical at training camp, but the Wings brought him over from Russia because he had put up 28 points in 42 games in Russia's top league in 2000–01 and had looked at home playing on a line with Alexei Yashin during the World Championship. They were pleased enough with their draftee's development to want a look in person.

Once the exhibition games began, Datsyuk began to dazzle. He was tricky with the puck, stealing passes from men who were much bigger than him. Scotty Bowman praised him: "He was dangerous." So did Larionov: "He's a very gifted kid."

Datsyuk didn't say much because he knew very little English, but he had been savvy enough to insist that his contract demand that if he didn't make the Wings roster, he would be allowed to return to Russia to resume his career. No minor leagues in North America for him. To get a better look at Datsyuk, who played center, the Wings experimented with putting veteran Kris Draper on the right wing.

"Pavel has done his job," Nill said. "He has come in and caught everybody's eyes. He's played very well. The physical part of the game hasn't bothered him, and speed hasn't been a problem."

As the regular season got underway, Datsyuk gained a regular linemate in Boyd Devereaux, whose star had dimmed since he was the sixth overall pick in the 1996 draft. Bowman didn't give them much playing time—around 10 minutes per game—because the lineup was so loaded with stars, but they made the most of those minutes, and it didn't take long for Datsyuk to gain a fan base within the locker room.

"I didn't know anything about him before he came in, but right from the second day of camp, he's really stood out," Steve Yzerman said at Thanksgiving. "He's a tremendous talent—just a guy who is really, really good. He's been a real boost for the team."

For the first couple months of the season, Datsyuk and Devereaux played with a rotation of Robitaille, Hull, Tomas Holmström, and Mathieu Dandenault.

"At the beginning of the year, Pavel used to lose faceoffs," Robitaille said in late November. "Now, he's figured out ways to beat bigger guys. You see him in the third period—he won't take as many chances. It's funny because it doesn't seem like anyone is telling him this stuff. He just figures it out by watching the veterans. I think that shows a lot. This guy is going to be a superstar in this league."

It was a prolonged slump by Brett Hull that led to the assembly of one of the best lines of the 2001–02 season. Hull, one of the best goal scorers in the game, had gotten off to a rewarding start with seven goals and eight assists his first 15 games. But then he dried up, producing just two goals and three assists his next 15 games. "It's not really good when you're a goal scorer and you can't score," he said in early December.

Since he wasn't producing points, Bowman moved Hull onto the line formed by Datsyuk and Devereaux. In their first outing, Hull had six shots on goal. (The line was not an immediate hit: when Larionov was ready to return from an injury in mid-December, Datsyuk ended up being a healthy scratch for four games.)

By early January, though, the trio were a hit. "Pavel has done well since we put him with Devereaux and Hull," Bowman said. "He's improved all parts of his game and is a really good all-around player."

Hull, who at 37 was 14 years older than Datsyuk and Devereux, dubbed them "Two Kids and a Goat." The name was as big of a hit as the line was. "I'm having a gas playing with them," Hull said. In a 5–2 victory over the St. Louis Blues, the line provided every goal.

At the end of January, Datsyuk was selected to the NHL All-Star Game, recognition of his having produced seven goals and seven assists in a recent 15-game span. His every performance made a mockery of his having been bumped from the lineup to make room for others. There was the way he would throw a shoulder into an opponent and then skate away with the puck, the way he matched up against top players without any evidence of intimidation. Hull compared Datsyuk to "an orangutan—he goes this way and all of a sudden he's over there. He's very talented."

When Yzerman was sidelined by an injury, Bowman didn't resort to the easiest option—moving veteran Kris Draper from right wing back to center—but instead gave Datsyuk a bigger workload.

"I think he just continually has worked at his game and gotten better," Bowman said. "He's a dangerous, offensive threat. He's playing confidently."

In February, Datsyuk was one of 11 Wings (spread across five countries) who participated in the Olympics, playing for Russia alongside teammates Larionov and Sergei Fedorov. They took home the bronze medal.

Datsyuk returned from the Olympics recharged. In a game in late February against the Panthers in Florida, he raced by one opposing player and then drew two others to him before blindly threading the puck to Hull for the winning goal.

"Pavel was right in front of the goalie," Yzerman said. "There's maybe five guys in the league that aren't shooting that puck, and he fires a backhand pass 20 feet away from him. I wouldn't do that, and most players wouldn't do that in that position. Pavs just has that ability with the long reach and good hands that he can really hold guys off, delay, delay, and then he just draws them."

Datsyuk posted 11 goals and 24 assists in 70 games his rookie season in the NHL—not overwhelming statistics on their own, but he was adjusting to a far more rigorous schedule than he was used to in Russia, where he had only topped 40 games once in the five seasons before he arrived in Detroit. He was scratched as the playoffs approached in hopes it would reinvigorate him, but when he had one assist, a minus-3 rating and a 21 percent success rate on a faceoffs four games into the first-round series with the Vancouver Canucks, Datsyuk ended up being pulled from the lineup. When he returned in the second round, against the St. Louis Blues, Datsyuk delivered two goals his first three games. Larionov beamed: he knew that all his countryman needed to do was find a bit more confidence. Besides, the Wings had struggled as a whole in Round 1, dropping the first two games. "It's difficult for a kid like that to play at this level," Larionov said. "He had a great season, but the playoffs are different. He has to learn to play in these kind of situations, when the intensity is high and there is a lot of physical play."

It was mid-May when the Wings polished off the Blues in a five-game series. Around the same time, team management brought over one of the prospects from the 1999 draft: Swedish center Henrik Zetterberg. He had just won the Golden Puck as his country's top player in the Elite Series and international competition. Zetterberg wasn't eligible to play for the Wings that spring, but his arrival would go on to have a marvelous impact on their and Datsyuk's future.

The 2002 playoffs were a learning experience for young Datsyuk. After the Wings exorcised the Avalanche in Game 7 in the third round, he donned a Western Conference Champions commemorative cap as he walked into the locker room only to be pulled aside by Larionov and told that the Wings don't celebrate such accomplishments. Datsyuk removed the hat, wrapped it up in a championship T-shirt, and stuffed the items in his stall.

"I'm excited," he said. "That's all I understand. I don't understand much English. But all I can say is, I'm excited."

The "Two Kids and a Goat" line was together for all but four of the 23 games it took the Wings to capture the 2002 Stanley Cup championship. First formed in December after an injury to Yzerman left Hull without a center, the line worked because Datsyuk was such an incredible playmaker. Hull would not have tolerated playing with someone who couldn't get him the puck. "You have got to put that on his positive side," Bowman said. "It is not a powerhouse line." There were those on the team who believed one of the other reasons it worked was the language barrier between Datsyuk and Hull: "The good part is Pavel doesn't understand English, so that makes it easier for him," Yzerman said, meaning Datsyuk couldn't understand Hull's nearly non-stop talking.

Yzerman did not play in a Stanley Cup Final until his 12th year in the NHL. Datsyuk got there in his first year. He was a question mark when the season began, with team officials worried that he would hold up to the physical punishment that is an NHL season. But Andersson had it right the first time he saw Datsyuk: whatever he lacked in physique, his head impressed. That was on display in spades in Game 3 of the Finals, when, in the first of three overtimes, Datsyuk schooled Hurricanes Sami Kapanen and Marek Malik with moves that would have made Wayne Gretzky envious. Datsyuk finished fourth in voting for the 2002 Calder Trophy behind winner Dany Heatley and runners-up Ilya Kovalchuk and Kristian

Huselius, but to the Wings, Datsyuk was their rookie of the year. The night they won the Cup, Hull and Datsyuk found one another in the champagne-soaked locker room at Joe Louis Arena and embraced. "Friend," Datsyuk said. "Friend," Hull replied, his usual verbosity limited to one powerful word. In Russian, Datsyuk told teammate Maxim Kuznetsov to tell a reporter what it felt like to be in this situation: "Like seeing the sun coming up in the morning."

When camp began in September 2002, the buzz was that Zetterberg was that year's Datsyuk: a rookie crowd-pleaser. There was some experimentation with line combinations under new head coach Dave Lewis, but eventually the two ended up together. "We like to make plays," Zetterberg said. "Sometimes it's a little bit dangerous, but most of the time we try to not be so dangerous, to us." With Hull on the right wing, the trio was one of the Wings' best lines, until the playoffs began and Anaheim goaltender Jean-Sébastien Giguère spoiled the Wings' plans to repeat as champions. But better times were ahead, thanks to Datsyuk and Zetterberg, whose chemistry on the ice and friendship off the ice prompted teammates to call them the Euro-twins. "Those two kids can do a lot of magic together," Tomas Holmström said. Mike Babcock, who had been named coach in 2005, said, "The twins just seem to do it together."

By then, Datsyuk was a bona fide NHL star. His role expanded after Fedorov's departure in 2003, leading to an All-Star appearance in 2004, a two-year, $7.8 million contract in 2005, and the first of four straight Lady Byng Memorial Trophies starting in 2006. In 2007 he signed a seven-year, $46.9 million deal.

In 2007–08 Datsyuk paced the Wings with 97 points, joining Gordie Howe, Ted Lindsay, and Yzerman as the only players in history to lead the Wings in scoring in three straight seasons. That spring, he returned to the Finals for the first time since his rookie season, when he had posted six points in 21 playoff games. In his sixth season, he delivered 10 goals and 13 assists, averaging just north of a point over the 22-game 2008 playoffs. He and Zetterberg were a dream duo: "They're so good at finding each other," Lidström said. "They both have good speed when they're coming, too, so they're backing their [defenders] off, and even one-on-one, they're so good, too. The way they're able to find each other with passes—they're able to find each other all the time out there. They're really tough to defend when they play like that."

At the 2008 NHL Awards banquet, Datsyuk won the Frank J. Selke Trophy, given annually to the league's best defensive forward. He won it again in 2009 and 2010.

Datsyuk had the hands of an artist, but in a rare display, he showed he could use them as weapons, too. On the night they opened the 2010–11 season, the Wings downed the Ducks 4–0. The highlight of the game came when Datsyuk fought Corey Perry, who had four inches and 15 pounds on Datsyuk. It was a busy game for Datsyuk: he scored one goal and set up another in the second, and then fought in the third, earning a Gordie Howe hat trick—and admiration from the Wings' next opponent.

"I texted him, no fighting tonight," Marián Hossa said when the Wings were in Chicago to play the Blackhawks the next night. "When I saw it the first time, I was sort of frozen, like, watching the TV. That was something you don't see often, Pavel fighting." Patrick Kane was likewise delighted: "I thought it was pretty cool to see out of him. He didn't back down from Perry. Things got a little chippy, and it seems like he stood right up for himself. It's good to see a player like that do that."

It was the way Datsyuk used his hands to move the puck that enthralled the Wings most of all. In 2013 it was Datsyuk, Zetterberg, and Niklas Kronwall who were the headliners, and team management was eager to keep the talented trio around for many more seasons. Datsyuk was under contract through 2014 but agreed to a three-year, $22.5 million extension that would keep him in Detroit through 2016–17. It was a deal both sides came to rue. The glory and good times that marked the first half of Datsyuk's time in Detroit segued into challenging times and early playoff exits. The Wings returned to the Finals in 2009 only to lose and then came two straight second-round exits followed by a first-round exit in 2012. They made it to the second round in 2013 but lost in the first round in 2014, '15, and '16.

Datsyuk finished the 2015–16 season having become the sixth player in franchise history to reach 900 career points. He had played 953 games—and he wanted to go home. On June 18, 2016, Datsyuk announced that after 14 seasons in the NHL—never mind the one season left on his contract—he wanted to return to Russia. His daughter from his first marriage, who was born the summer Datsyuk celebrated his first Stanley Cup, was in Russia. His younger daughter, born during the 2014 playoffs, was two.

At his farewell news conference, Datsyuk revealed he had been thinking about going home since the labor dispute that wiped out the first half of the 2012–13 season. "When I come back, my mind is thinking that I want to go home. But I also want to keep playing here. I go with my mind and go with another three years. But it got harder and harder."

Datsyuk was 23 when he arrived in Detroit, and 38 when he left. He won a Stanley Cup and welcomed a child his first season in Detroit; his first season back in Russia, he helped SKA

St. Petersburg win the Gagarin Cup, and he and his second wife welcomed a son. When Datsyuk won gold at the 2018 Winter Olympics—in which NHL players did not participate—he joined the Triple Gold Club, having already won the Stanley Cup and World Championship.

Datsyuk was the self-proclaimed Magic Man during his time in Wings uniform, thrilling teammates and fans with the way he handled the puck. He was part of a grand stretch that saw the Wings thrive on Russian players, leading to a feast of Stanley Cups. As with Fedorov, Datsyuk left earlier than the Wings wanted him to—but for the time he was theirs, he was a marvel.

PART 5

TOUGH GUYS

15

Ted Lindsay

TO THE DELIGHT OF RED WINGS PLAYERS IN THE 1990S AND 2000s, Ted Lindsay was a regular in their locker room at Joe Louis Arena. His playing days had ended decades earlier, but after Mike and Marian Ilitch bought the team in 1982, there was a push to reestablish connections with the legends from the franchise's first dynasty. They were welcomed around the arena, and one of the fabled players who often took advantage of the invitation was Lindsay, whose physique in his 70s was marveled at by players in their prime.

"He's still in tremendous shape and he's got such an interesting image—a real tough guy from old-time hockey," Steve Yzerman said in 1997. "And he's a small man, a nice guy. It's kind of neat. The guys walk away saying, 'That was the killer of the '50s and '60s, and he's just like a really neat old man.'"

A neat old man who was fond of saying that "I hated everybody I played against, and they hated me. That's the way hockey should be played."

Robert Blake Theodore Lindsay, born July 29, 1925, was a young boy of about nine when hockey really took a hold of him. He lived in Kirkland Lake in northern Ontario, where the locals joked they had nine months of winter and three months of tough sledding. He played junior hockey for St. Michael's College in Toronto, and after putting up 29 points in 1943–44, Lindsay was invited to try out for the Wings. Jack Adams offered him a contract, but Lindsay hesitated because he thought he could have a bigger impact on his junior team. His junior coach, Paul McNamara, persuaded Lindsay to take the Wings' offer. Lindsay did—but not without showing signs of the labor activist he would become: Lindsay negotiated a $2,000 signing bonus (that was a staggering sum considering players made around $5,000 in annual salaries) and a clause that he could not be sent to the minors.

Lindsay debuted in a Wings uniform on October 29, 1944. He scored his first goal one game later, on November 2. He was a feisty, hard-nosed player, determined to not let anyone get the better of him. In his prime he was 5'8" and 163 pounds ("when I put my skates on, I'm 6-foot-5," he used to say) and augmented his small stature with a big heart. *Look* magazine described Lindsay, darting about the ice in his red uniform, as "a blood-red flash of cold fury" and "a picture of unmitigated villainy." Elbowing and kneeing were part of his routine, even after the NHL made them two-minute penalties. He used his stick as a cudgel, and one time in Toronto, an imitation rife. He received some 600 stitches during his career, most of them in his face.

When coach Tommy Ivan put Lindsay with Gordie Howe and Sid Abel in 1947, the three proved so effective they became known as the Production Line. When Lindsay was at his peak, in the early 1950s, the Wings were the best team in the NHL, winning the Stanley Cup four times in six years. It was Lindsay who began the tradition of parading the Cup around the ice, doing so for the first time at Olympia Stadium in 1950 after the Wings defeated the New York Rangers in seven games, including a double-overtime victory in the seventh game. Lindsay spontaneously hoisted the trophy and skated around so fans could get a close-up view of it. From his perspective, they were the ones who paid his salary, and they deserved to feel close to the ultimate reward.

Lindsay served as captain of the Wings from 1952–56, the embodiment of a leader who did whatever it took to help his team win. He taunted opponents, pushed referees, and stood up to Adams, the tyrannical coach and general manager who most players feared. Lindsay was known as "Terrible Ted" and "Scarface" because of the way he played and looked, but he was far from a goon. He was an excellent skater, shooter and passer.

Lindsay's prowess made him a favorite target for opposing fans. During the 1956 playoffs, he received death threats while the Wings were engaged in a series against the Maple Leafs. On March 24 Lindsay scored at 4:22 of overtime to secure the Wings a 5–4 victory and a 3–0 lead in the best-of-seven series. Lindsay decided to have some fun and turned his stick over, pointing it like a rifle at fans as they booed him. The gesture was captured by photographers, the black-and-white photo yet another story in Lindsay's colorful legacy.

(It wasn't just on the road that Lindsay engaged with fans; on November 11, 1954, minutes after the Wings had lost 1–0 to the Maple Leafs at Olympia Stadium, Lindsay went into the crowd to pursue a heckler, whose name was Bernard Czeponis. A photograph shows Lindsay, with Terry Sawchuk crawling over the wire fencing that was used on top of the boards before the days of Plexiglas, and Glen Skov ready to follow Sawchuk's example. Since the game had ended, the NHL essentially washed its hands of any disciplinary action.)

Lindsay was as intelligent as he was skilled, and through his years of playing, he came to realize that players were being short thrifted. In the late 1950s, Lindsay and Howe "went to see a fella named Jimmy Hoffa about starting a union," Howe recalled in a 1986 interview. "He told us there was no place for unions in sports."

Lindsay was undeterred by the advice from the Teamsters president. In 1957 Lindsay found out firsthand that league pension plans were kept secret from players. Around that same time, he found out how much better players in the National Football League and Major League Baseball were treated. What he learned convinced Lindsay that only through unity could NHL players hope to improve their standing. He and Doug Harvey of the Montreal Canadiens set out to organize their brethren.

"We wanted a situation where we could sit down with management and discuss things," Lindsay said in 1991. "It was difficult putting it together, but all of the players joined it and put $100 each into it, except for Toronto's Ted Kennedy, who just did not believe in it, which was fine. We did it because team management was dictatorial and there were abuses. They'd send kids down to the minors and the kids might have a lease on a house here and they'd have to pay that lease and for transportation to their new assignment."

When Adams discovered the efforts to organize, he went into the Wings locker room and moved from player to player as they were seated at their stalls, looking down at them as he asked if they were in favor of organizing. The only player who dared to look Adams in the eyes and say yes was Lindsay.

The first attempts at organizing fell apart after one season, but the groundwork had been laid, the seeds had been planted in players' heads to push back against the way things were. Back then, players were signed as teenagers and were bound to their club for life, unless traded, sold, or released. They had little in the way of bargaining leverage.

That all changed in June 1967 with the formation of the Players Association.

Lindsay's efforts immeasurably bettered players' lives, from their income to their medical benefits to pensions. His efforts were recognized in 2010 when the Lester B. Pearson Award, given annually to the most outstanding player of the regular season as voted on by fellow players, was renamed the Ted Lindsay Award.

The NHL was an autocratic league when Lindsay fought for players' rights, and Lindsay's organizing efforts infuriated Adams and Bruce Norris, who in 1955 had become sole owner of the Wings after ousting his sister, Marguerite. Adams traded Lindsay to the Chicago Black Hawks after the 1956–57 season, ending Lindsay's 13 years of stardom with the Wings. Lindsay played three seasons in Chicago. He retired after the 1959–60 season, and had his playing career ended then, it would have still been remarkable: Lindsay was the career leader with 1,635 penalty minutes and led all left wingers with 365 goals.

But Lindsay had more left in him. Fittingly, just as his career had taken off when he began playing with Abel on the Production Line, it was Abel who in 1964 persuaded Lindsay, then aged 39, to make a comeback. By then, Abel was the coach and general manager, and his faith in his old linemate was indefatigable. Lindsay happily accepted.

"It wasn't for the money because I was doing well, but the idea of retiring as a Red Wing was very attractive," Lindsay said in a 1995 interview in the *Detroit Free Press*.

On opening night of the 1964–65 season, a crowd of 14,233 fans gave Lindsay a standing ovation when he skated onto the ice.

"It sure made me feel that I must have done something right in my career that they still felt that way," Lindsay said. "Those were my fans, my people."

His fan club did not extend to NHL president Clarence Campbell, a former war-crimes prosecutor. When news broke that Lindsay was coming out of retirement, Campbell issued a statement: "It's the blackest day in hockey when a 39-year-old man thinks he can make a comeback in the world's fastest sport."

(Four months later, Campbell issued an apology: "This is one of the most amazing feats in professional sport. Lindsay has done what I thought was next to impossible. I, like many others, thought the game would suffer if a man of nearly 40 years of age could come back after being out so long. He has to be rated an amazing athlete.")

In January 1965 Lindsey was in trouble with the league for reportedly refusing to pay $75 in fines, which was grounds for a suspension. The fines stemmed from misconduct penalties Lindsay had been assessed in a game against the Toronto Maple Leafs on January 2, which carried fines of $25 and $50, respectively. Lindsay had been quoted in the press as saying he would tell Abel, the coach and general manager, not to pay the fines. (The procedure at the time was for the club to deduct the fines from a player's salary.) "If he doesn't pay, he doesn't play," Campbell said. There was more to it than the fines, though: Lindsay had also accused referee Vern Buffey of starting the trouble by swearing at a player and was quoted as saying, "I'm not going to sit for Campbell's Kangaroo Court. If they want to make something of it, they can do it in a regular court, and I'll have my own lawyer."

Lindsay ultimately apologized to Campbell and paid the fines.

Lindsay finished the season leading the Wings with 173 penalty minutes and was eighth in scoring with 28 points—not bad for the oldest player on the team. His efforts helped the Wings win their first league championship since Adams had jettisoned Lindsay.

"The comeback he did with the Wings in '64–65 after being out of the game was amazing," Scotty Bowman said in a 2019 *Detroit Free Press* interview. "He revived the team. It was quite a story at the time. He was only of the few who could do something like that because he was always a work-out guy."

It was a memorable season for Lindsay: on October 15, 1964, he played in his 1,000th career game. His return to the city he had called home for the first 13 seasons of his career enabled him to retire as a Red Wing, with 379 goals, 472 assists, and 1,808 penalty minutes in 1,068 games. A year after he retired, Lindsay was inducted into the Hockey Hall of Fame and in typical Lindsay fashion used the occasion to expose another of the league's inequalities: women were not allowed to attend the ceremony at that time. Lindsay didn't go to his induction because he wanted to bring his wife. The rule was changed the next year.

The time between Lindsay's retirement from playing and his emergence at Joe Louis Arena as a beloved alumnus with an enviable physique was more bluster than luster. He was named general manager in 1977 by Bruce Norris, 20 years after Norris had banished Lindsay for his efforts to organize players. The stint began well enough—Lindsay set off a buzz among fans with his initial marketing slogan, "Aggressive Hockey Is Back in Town," and he was named Executive of the Year after the Wings advanced to the playoffs in 1978, ending a seven-year absence. But by the next season the Wings were in disarray again. (They only made the playoffs once during the 1970s.)

In the spring of 1980, there was a crisis atmosphere around the Wings—they were losing again and, worse, they had a payroll that topped $5 million and had 82 players on it, double what was the norm. Half of those players weren't even deemed good enough to play in the NHL. Lindsay's mismanagement included giving what by the economics of the time were staggering contracts to Dennis Polonich and Greg Joly, who each got deals worth more than $100,000 a year.

Norris once again took aim at Lindsay. Norris met with Lindsay intending to fire him, but before that could happen, Lindsay suggested he should coach instead of manage. Norris agreed and installed Jimmy Skinner, Jack Adams' former acolyte, as general manager.

The crisis turned toxic, and when the Wings had won only three games by Thanksgiving of 1981, Lindsay was fired.

Lindsay's career as a hockey operations man was not successful, but in every other respect, he excelled. A fearsome and relentless competitor, Lindsay was also a thoughtful, intelligent man known for his humility, generosity, and kindness away from the ice. When a friend's son was diagnosed with autism, Lindsay established the Ted Lindsay foundation to raise money for autism research.

The Wings retired Lindsay's No. 7 jersey in 1991 and unveiled a statue in his honor in Joe Louis Arena in 2008. His picture hangs in multiple places at Little Caesars Arena, the Wings' home since 2017, including in the locker room. In the days after he died on March 4, 2019, only four months shy of what would have been his 94th birthday, the rink boards in all 31 NHL arenas featured a tribute to Lindsay in honor of his incredible career and trailblazing spirit.

16

Bob Probert

THE FIRST TIME BOB PROBERT REGISTERED A FIGHT WEARING a Red Wings uniform was three games into his rookie season. The Wings lost the match 5–0 to the Vancouver Canucks, but Probert was magnificent: he matched enforcer Craig Coxe punch for punch for a good minute, as officials hovered and fans hollered. The linesmen finally separated the two after Coxe landed on the ice, Probert on top of him.

Probert's toughness was an indelible part of his appeal. He was the heavyweight champion of the NHL for a good decade, before age and addiction wore him down. But Probert was much more than a hitter. In his third year, he came one goal shy of reaching 30 and was named to the NHL All-Star Game.

It was during the playoffs of that 1987–88 season that Probert was at his finest, that he was everything the Wings needed him to be—until he was at his worst, and they wondered yet again whether he was worth keeping.

On May 9, 1988, Probert recorded two goals in Game 4 of the Clarence Campbell Final against the Edmonton Oilers, giving him 21 playoff points. In front of an anxious crowd at Joe Louis Arena, Probert scored in the second and third periods to level a 3–1 deficit and force overtime. He had a chance to win the game in regulation but his backhander rang off the right goal post; in early overtime Oilers goaltender Grant Fuhr blocked Probert's point-blank shot. The Wings lost the game— but Probert came away having eclipsed franchise legend Gordie Howe's club single-season playoff record of 20 points in 1955.

Probert was the Wings' best player that spring. A knee injury suffered March 1 kept Steve Yzerman out of the lineup until the last three games of the playoffs, amplifying how much the Wings needed Probert—and he came through for them with the kind of performances they envisioned when they drafted him.

But one night after that phenomenal achievement— regardless of the score, Probert's name would be in the Wings' record books—Probert sullied all that he had accomplished by succumbing to the one fight he never would win: he went out to a bar and drank until a team official hauled him away, well past curfew.

Those 24 hours encapsulated everything that was great and everything that was destructive about Probert. When he made the team in the mid-1980s, a couple years after he was part of Yzerman's draft class, Probert's knack for scoring and fighting cast him as a rock star for fans starved for success. The team wasn't very good, and there wasn't much standing and cheering, but Probert and Joe Kocur, a duo that would be dubbed the "Bruise Brothers" for their pugilistic prowess, were beloved. They had a blue-collar vibe about them, an appearance of regular men who liked to work hard, play hard, and have fun.

But it was clear even before the Wings drafted him that there was nothing fun about Probert's relationship with alcohol. He got away with it for a long time because his scoring and his scuffles with enforcers outbalanced his entanglements with police, even when he did a stint as a federal prisoner. Probert would come back to the Wings, seemingly repentant; fans would greet him with a standing ovation, and hope sprang eternal that this time, the affable, entirely too pliable, and undeniably talented Probert would change.

Probert was part of the 1983 draft, a class that would bury the dead Wings reputation of the 1970s and rebuild the franchise. Jimmy Devellano, for whom it was his first draft as general manager of the team, saw Probert multiple times while traversing Ontario for potential draftees. Probert was easy on the eyes: at 17 he already stood 6'3" and weighed 206 pounds. He looked like a fabulous draw to sell tickets, too, being from Windsor, just across the river from Detroit. His statistics were mundane—28 points in 51 games for the Brantford Alexanders in the Ontario Hockey League—until the penalty minutes: 133 of them. That caught the attention of Devellano and his chief amateur scout, Neil Smith.

In Probert, Devellano and Smith saw the potential for a power forward, a guy who could score and keep opponents from taking liberties. He was an awkward skater in juniors, but the Wings liked much more about Probert than they faulted and grabbed him in the third round, at No. 46.

But skating was not Probert's only weakness. He started drinking when he was 14, and with that first can of beer, it was like popping the tab on an unquenchable thirst. In his book, *Tough Guy: My Life on the Edge*, Probert wrote of drinking between four and six cans on a regular basis while his father, Al, a former Windsor police officer, watched TV. Probert's father died of a heart attack at age 52 in 1982, a year before Probert was drafted. By 16, Probert wrote, he knew he had a problem with alcohol.

Probert stayed in Brantford for the 1983–84 season and made the Wings look like geniuses for drafting him when he more than doubled his production to 73 points in 65 games (the penalty minutes still impressed, too: 189 of them that year). Probert played so well he earned a spot in the 1984 OHL All-Star Game. The event was scheduled for February 7 in Guelph, and Devellano and Smith decided to make the three-and-a-half-hour drive from Detroit to see Probert play.

When they arrived, they found out he was scratched from the game. The night before the big game, ceremonial as it was, Probert had gone out drinking and broken curfew. That would be a pattern, too.

The Wings scolded Probert and told him he had to do better (the first of many times they had that conversation with him). As angry as they were, three months later, Probert was signed to a four-year contract. His appeal far outbalanced his peril.

After another year in junior hockey—interrupted when kicked off the Hamilton Steelhawks and, a month later, traded to the Sault Ste. Marie Greyhounds—Probert was ready for the professional leagues. He started with the Wings' American Hockey League affiliate in Glens Falls, New York, the Adirondack Red Wings, but was called up and made his debut November 6. The fight with Coxe—the first of several with him—was on November 11; five days later Probert fought Minnesota North Stars (and future Wing) defenseman Bob Rouse. Probert was demoted two weeks after he was promoted, criticized by coach Harry Neale for being "a little bit of a lazy player," and also "he'd probably be a little bit better if he was a little lighter."

Fat and lazy: not the terms a team wants to hear about a prospect at the start of his pro career. But the Wings had more pressing matters to deal with: they were terrible in 1985–86, winning just 17 games and finishing at the bottom of the NHL standings. Neale was fired midway through and replaced by Brad Park. In one of the first games Park coached, the Wings engaged in an all-out brawl with the Toronto Maple Leafs. Probert ended up serving a four-game suspension for a head butt that left Bob McGill briefly unconscious on the ice. (He eventually skated off on his own.) Probert had been recalled in mid-December, and in his second game back, which was against the Philadelphia Flyers, he fought Rick Tocchet and Dave Richter. In all, Probert fought 16 times in 44 games his rookie year.

That was the tough side of Probert. The troubled side erupted in April during his fourth stint being called up from the minors. He was arrested on drunken driving and speeding charges in Windsor when he was clocked going more than 100 kilometers per hour (roughly 60 miles per hour), double the posted speed limit. Once again, the Wings scolded Probert and said they were disappointed.

Three months later, in July, Probert was charged with assaulting a police officer in Windsor after getting into a scuffle while refusing to leave a bar at 1:25 AM. Probert was supposed to be at Hazelden Foundation, a treatment center in Minnesota, but his admission had been delayed when he came down with mononucleosis. It had been a busy first year of pro hockey for Probert: 21 points and 186 penalty minutes in 44 games with the Wings, and 152 penalty minutes with Adirondack—and two arrests.

Still trying to earn a regular role in Detroit, Probert dealt with a new coach, his third, when the 1986–87 season began. Jacques Demers joined the queue of Wings personnel who would plead with Probert to stop drinking, to no avail. Right before Christmas, Probert crashed his car into a utility pole in Windsor, picking up his third arrest of 1986. The Wings suspended him for five days without pay. He kicked off 1987 by losing his driver's license for a year and paying a $10,000 fine. He was admitted to a treatment facility in Windsor, though the fact he was able to continue to play in home and road games rendered the stay little more than a different place to sleep for a while. The Wings tried banning beer from the locker room as a gesture to help Probert, though when a season-high 19,140 fans watched them clinch a playoff berth on March 25, the talk afterward was that should the Norris Division title become theirs, there would be alcohol allowed.

"The yelling, the embracing, are just not the same without champagne," Demers said.

On May 1, 1987, Probert scored his first playoff goal; it even ended up being the decisive goal in a 4–2 victory that bought the Wings some breathing room after falling behind, three games to two, to the Toronto Maple Leafs.

"I couldn't have wanted anyone to score that final goal more than Probie," Demers said. "In the last two months he's turned his life around so much." Devellano, who had spent so much time scolding Probert, told reporters it was validation for the team's seemingly endless support for the 21-year-old. Yzerman, who had tried to navigate how teammates could best help Probert, was equally relieved.

"Probie's been on an emotional roller coaster all year," Yzerman said. "At first we pitied him. But that's not the way to do it. We're behind him all the way. We want him around for a long time.

"But he kept screwing up, getting in trouble. And our team got some criticism for the way it was handled. We've just accepted the guy's got a problem, and that he has to do it for himself. We keep a watchful eye out for him. We just let him know that he's not going to get away with anything. We're not going to allow him to hurt our team."

Yzerman spoke as a captain, a teammate, a friend—and as someone who benefitted directly from Probert's presence. Probert had been playing on the top line centered by Yzerman and with Gerard Gallant on the left wing. "Probie gets us room out there," Yzerman said.

Another goal followed May 7, and a third, May 9, as the Wings faced the Edmonton Oilers in the Clarence Campbell Conference Final. In fact, Probert was the only Wing to score in those back-to-back crucial games, which ended up being 2–1 and 4–1 losses, respectively.

"Bob Probert right now has been the most outstanding hockey player in this series," Demers said. "I am glad for Bobby. People are learning he is a lot more than what has been said and written about him."

Probert, who in his prime stood 6'3" and 215 pounds, had success crashing around the net. Rivals tended to give him space.

"My size might have a lot to do with that," Probert said. "They might think twice before they check me. I feel good, confident."

Yzerman gushed with praise. "Probie has been great all series, fantastic, working hard, good set of hands," he said. "He's got both his goals from around the net. He's playing with a lot of determination and working hard."

The Wings lost the series, but Probert's performance, after all the headaches and heartaches he had put the team through, was like a balm against the disappointment. "If we keep him in the right frame of mind," Demers said, "we've got ourselves a heck of a hockey player. I'm glad I stuck with Bobby."

Through it all, there was Probert, the bruiser. His fight card as a rookie read 16; the next year it was 17, plus two in the playoffs. In 1987–88 he fought 24 times, starting with Chris Kotsopoulos on October 16. (Probert also scored a goal that night.) There was another fight with Coxe in November, when the two traded punches for around 45 seconds before Probert KO'ed Coxe. That was five nights after Probert scored two goals and assisted on four others to lead the Wings past the New Jersey Devils 6–4. Linemates Yzerman and Gallant each had four points. "They belong to each other, that line," Demers said.

In October, Probert told reporters he wanted to "put all my problems in my past." In December he spent a night in jail for repeated violations of the probation stemming from a drunk driving arrest dating back two years. Probert had missed meetings with his probation officer and with Alcoholics Anonymous, and the judge wanted to send a message that that was not OK. At that time, Probert twice had been charged with drunken driving in Windsor and hospitalized three times for addiction treatment.

Probert was released on a Friday morning and that night returned to Joe Louis Arena and recorded a goal and an assist and a fight, earning a Gordie Howe hat trick, to help the Wings paste the Blackhawks 12–0. Demers brushed off the night in jail, saying that Probert wasn't "drinking or doing stupid things."

The night in jail seemed little more than a blemish on a beautiful season. In January, Probert was selected to play in the NHL All-Star Game. Probert had 23 goals and 45 points and a league-leading 273 penalty minutes in 45 games. Demers beamed: "From where he's come to the All-Star Game—wow!" At the time, Probert said he had been sober almost a year. The selection put him in a locker room next to the likes of Wayne Gretzky, Mark Messier, and Jari Kurri.

Everything was going so well. The Wings were winning, and Probert was having just the sort of impact the Wings envisioned when they drafted him: producing points and playing with physicality. When he was rewarded with a three-year contract in March 1988, Probert was enjoying the best season of his career with 28 goals, 59 points, and 360 penalty minutes in 66 games.

Probert's superb play was a key reason the Wings didn't falter without Yzerman, especially in the playoffs. They took out the Maple Leafs in six games in the first round; Probert had five straight two-point performances. It took five games to dispatch the St. Louis Blues; Probert had six points.

That set up a second straight conference Final against Gretzky and his Oilers. The Wings lost the first two games but gained Yzerman and a victory in Game 3. Probert's two-goal performance in Game 4 couldn't save the Wings from an overtime loss.

The 8–4 loss in Game 5 wasn't even the ugliest part of that event. The night before, Probert and Petr Klíma, along with Kocur, John Chabot, Darren Eliot, and Darren Veitch, went to an Edmonton nightclub named Goose Loonies. By the time assistant coach Colin Campbell and Smith, the chief amateur scout, found the players in a back room at 2 AM, three hours past curfew, Probert had been drinking heavily for most of the night. Klima had a broken thumb and wasn't playing anyway, but Demers dressed a listless Probert for Game 5 after calling the players "idiots" and "fools."

All the good will and good vibes Probert had engendered evaporated. It emerged that he had stopped taking Antabuse, a medication that makes people sick if they consume alcohol. Probert had kept up the mirage that he was taking it by substituting the pills with aspirin.

There was talk of admitting him to the Betty Ford Center in Rancho Mirage, Calfornia, and "not for two weeks but for three months," Demers said. "We are trying to get Probie in the best rehab center in North America."

Probert didn't seem to care about what happened in Edmonton or what the Wings wanted to happen next. He skipped the end-of-season gathering hosted by Mike Ilitch, ditching teammates and ownership, to vacation in Florida. He skipped the gym, bought a boat, spent the summer sailing, and showed up at training camp in the fall of 1988 out of shape and overweight.

Probert was spiraling. He missed a team flight home because he showed up at the wrong Chicago airport. The Wings demoted him to the minors; when they recalled him, he missed that flight, too.

After being suspended without pay—costing him around $1,300 per day—and hearing his name mentioned as a trade probability by team management, Probert finally entered the Betty Ford Center in October 1988. He lasted less than two weeks. His agent said he was in treatment on October 5; on October 13 Probert was back in Windsor and staying in a hotel under a false name. He couldn't go to the Joe because his suspension impacted his immigration visa status. When he finally did get there, he showed up 12 pounds overweight, ballooning to 227 pounds.

Just why the Wings found it so difficult to cut ties with Probert—Oilers general manager Glen Sather had offered "first-round draft choices" for him, according to Devellano—was on display when Probert finally made his first appearance of the 1988–89 season on November 27 at Joe Louis Arena. During pauses in the singing of the Star-Spangled Banner, several fans in a sellout crowd of 19,375 yelled, "Probie! Probie!" Many more stood and cheered when the 23-year-old lined up next to Yzerman and Klima just 16 seconds into the game against Washington. Probert's suspension had only lasted a month.

"They told us to bring him back, we brought him back, and I hope that's it," Demers said. "I hope the final chapter has been written about that. Maybe we can write more chapters about his goal scoring and his ability. There's not a meanness about him. You cannot dislike him. People who know him know what I'm saying. They want him to do well."

Probert was immensely popular with fans and he had just had a breakout performance in his third season in the NHL. But he didn't do much to generate cheers during the 1988–89 season, playing just 25 games and scoring four goals among six points.

Trade talks resurfaced, leading Probert to sulk. Before a game in early January, Probert was in the hallway when Devellano approached the locker room. Reporter Joe Lapointe described the scene in the next day's *Detroit Free Press*: "Probert looked one way. Devellano looked the other. Probert walked one way. Devellano walked the other. They didn't speak...Near the stick rack, Probert walked by a pair of sports writers. He carried a hockey stick. He grabbed the blade in one hand and the shaft in the other. He lifted the stick near the face of one reporter and twisted both pieces until they snapped in a spurt of splinters. 'Your head!' he said to a writer, with a mock-ferocious Friday-the-13th look on his face."

The Wings were running out of patience and suspended Probert again that January when he showed up late for a game for the second time in two weeks. He was also overweight again and wasn't reinstated until he had dropped 15 pounds, reappearing in the lineup on February 25.

One week later, he once again made headlines.

On March 2, 1988, Probert was charged with smuggling 14.3 grams of cocaine into the United States. He was arrested after a packet of cocaine fell out of his underpants during a strip search by U.S. Customs agents at the Detroit–Windsor Tunnel at 5:15 AM. At a 1 PM hearing in U.S. District Court before Magistrate Paul J. Komives, Probert stood mute to the charges which carried a potential prison term of up to 20 years and fines up to $1 million.

His attorney, Harold Fried, entered a plea of not guilty and kept his comments to reporters brief: "Hopefully, this will be a nightmare that will go away soon."

Probert was three months shy of his 24th birthday and already had been to five rehabilitation centers. The nightmare had, in fact, been ongoing for a decade.

In his memoir, *Tough Guy*, Probert stated he started drinking regularly when he was 14, knew he had a problem when he was 16, and started using cocaine when he was 21 after helping the Wings minor-league affiliate win the Calder Cup championship. By his own estimate, he spent $42,000 a year on cocaine. (At the time of his arrest, he was earning $200,000 a year.)

The Wings by then were used to Probert's scuffles with police and his arrests for driving while impaired, but the arrest at the border was a new nadir. It began when agents spotted beverage containers in the 1988 GMC Jimmy, which was driven by Probert. One of the passengers was Dani Wood, Probert's future wife. Agents ordered Probert, who appeared disoriented, to undergo a strip search, which revealed a mill used to grind cocaine and the cocaine itself. Describing his memory of the event in his memoir, Probert said he went into a restroom and snorted cocaine, emerging looking like someone who had inhaled a powdered donut.

The Internet has rendered information available to everyone everywhere more or less immediately, but in 1989 that was not the case. When players gathered at the Joe for practice later that day, they bombarded reporters with questions. "Did something happen to Probie?" Shawn Burr asked as soon as he saw a member of the media. The news left teammates sad and mad.

"It's tragic that it came to this," said defenseman Lee Norwood. "The team tried to help him with his drinking problem, and now this is just a new chapter in the book of Bob Probert. It's very unfortunate for the man and embarrassing for the team."

Klima, who team management concluded had encouraged Probert to go out drinking the night of the Goose Loonies incident, said he was "so surprised when I heard, I started shaking. I like that guy. I feel bad for him. And I feel bad for the guys in this room."

Gerard Gallant said that "you feel sorry for him, but he's had his chances, and he's got to realize that for himself...You hear things going around, but I never thought it was serious—like taking drugs across the border or something like that," he said.

Paul MacLean, who had been with the team less than a year, said that "it's been an ongoing situation since I've been here, and I'm not sure how much it really affects us. I mean, we're not the ones sitting in jail."

Probert was released from custody after posting 10 percent of his $50,000 bond; the terms of his bail included restriction of travel within the U.S., urinalysis, and counseling for addiction.

The NHL expelled him indefinitely. The Wings stopped paying him.

Two days after the arrest, Probert was spotted shooting pool in a downtown Detroit bar. Federal officials asked a judge to revoke Probert's bond because he had left a treatment facility and gone drinking.

Probert pleaded guilty to cocaine importation and remained in a treatment facility—where his visitor and phone privileges had been cut—while awaiting sentencing. He was sentenced to three months in prison in October, where those appearing on his behalf included Devellano, Demers, and Mike Ilitch. Probert told the judge that he was sorry for what happened. "I want a chance to prove...that I can be a positive role model for young kids and that I am committed to a life of sobriety."

(Probert being arrested for smuggling cocaine was a weird enough story on its own, but it got weirder in early November, when a 65-year-old self-employed financial broker named Dan DeFrancesco of Hamilton, Ontario, was charged with trying to pay the U.S. Customs commissioner $1 million to lose evidence in the criminal drug case against Probert. Probert had no knowledge of the man's attempt, and Probert's attorney dismissed the man as a "quack" after a brief encounter at a restaurant. DeFrancesco was eventually indicted by a grand jury in Buffalo, New York, where DeFrancesco had made his attempt at bribery.)

Probert began his sentence at the Federal Medical Center, a medium-security prison in Rochester, Minnesota, on November 7, 1989. (The prison has had illustrious inhabitants over the years, including televangelist Jim Bakker and three-time failed presidential candidate Lyndon LaRouche.) While Probert was incarcerated, an immigration judge ordered him to be deported upon finishing his sentence.

Probert was released on February 5, 1990. Eleven days later, he made a visit to Joe Louis Arena, stopping by the dressing room for the first time since his last game on March 1, 1988. "It was good to see the guys again," Probert said. The visit was short: he had a date in court to plead with Immigration officials for permission to rejoin the team while serving out the remainder of his sentence in a halfway house.

He was allowed to stay in the U.S. and work while his immigration appeal waited to be heard. On March 22 he played his first game in more than a year. He only played in four games in 1989–90 but managed to score three goals—and get into three fights. Once again, Probert was saying all the right things: that he realized he had a substance abuse problem; that every time he got into trouble, alcohol or cocaine was to blame; that he recognized he needed help.

In the fall the Wings welcomed Probert back to training camp. Probert fought twice in the season opener, first with Allan Stewart and then with Troy Crowder. Crowder threw a punch that caught Probert near his right eye, opening up a gash and sending Probert to the locker room for stitches. When he scored in the home opener, fans treated Probert to the loudest ovation of the night. For all that he had done and been through, he remained a fan favorite. He played so well, he was rewarded with being named an alternate captain.

While Probert was away, the Wings had endured their own turmoil, missing the playoffs in 1990, which cost Demers his job and led to Bryan Murray being named coach and general manager. Murray told Probert he didn't want him to fight, just to play.

Things really did seem like they were going in the right direction: in October a judge ruled Probert could play in the U.S. during his immigration appeal (his status was finally resolved in December 1992), which was a huge relief. Probert reestablished his reputation as the heavyweight of the NHL, highlighted by a New Year's Eve bout with Chicago's Stu Grimson, who Probert would fight a total of 13 times in his career. The season-opening bout that Probert lost to Crowder was avenged in January. By the end of the season, he had 16 goals and 39 points—and 315 penalty minutes—in 55 games, along with three points 50 penalty minutes in six playoff games. The Wings lost a seven-game series to the St. Louis Blues (in what marked the beginning of the historic 25-season playoff streak) but as disappointing as that was for the team, Probert had done what they had asked and he received a three-year contract extension. Murray was serious about wanting Probert to play, not fight, and signed Crowder in the offseason. (Back then, the New Jersey Devils had the right to ask for compensation because Crowder was a Group I free agent. They asked for Probert; an arbitrator awarded them forwards Randy McKay and Dave Barr.)

Probert still fought 19 times in 1991–92, but he also produced 20 goals and 44 points, both of which were second-best in his career only to his All-Star 1987–88 season. One of his best fights came February 9, 1992, when ebullient New York Rangers forward Tie Domi challenged Probert despite standing 5'8" to Probert's 6'3". The two slugged it out for 45 seconds with Domi opening up a four-stitch cut under Probert's right eye before officials separated them. Domi skated to center ice and mimicked buckling a belt, deriding Probert's heavyweight status and delighting fans at Madison Square Garden. It was, Domi said, a World Wrestling Federation move: "Macho Man Savage does that."

Their anticipated rematch in March fizzled when Domi sat out with a knee injury.

It wasn't just Probert who was doing well: the 1991–92 season saw the Wings welcome two rookie defensemen named Nicklas Lidström and Vladimir Konstantinov. The Wings won 43 games, the most since Ilitch bought the team in 1982 and cruised into the playoffs having finished atop the conference.

They beat the Minnesota North Stars in Round 1 but were swept by Chicago in Round 2. Probert had seven points in 11 games and a relatively tame, for him, 28 penalty minutes.

When the 1992–93 season began, early hype centered on the December 2 game between the Wings and Rangers. Domi talked and talked about the rematch, to the point then NHL president Gil Stein weighed in during a conference call in late November. "I'm considering what to do," Stein said in response to comments made by Domi in a *Toronto Sun* article. "He's quoted as saying, 'I'm going to get an instigator; I'm going to fight, and I'm going to dedicate it to people who cry when we fight on TV.'" Probert didn't want to engage in a verbal battle, saying, "That's just not my style."

The pugilists squared off less than a minute into the game. Probert egged him on with two shoves to the chest. The gloves came off, the punches flailed as much as they flew before Probert knocked down Domi, and then quickly threw another punch before officials intervened. Probert skated to the penalty box, Domi rose from the ice, smiled, and waved to the crowd. The best part of the fight was the scene on the Wings' bench, where Yzerman mocked Domi by mimicking his wrestling belt taunt.

(After considering what to do, Stein ultimately fined and suspended Domi, as well as then-Rangers coach Roger Neilson, for what was ruled a premeditated fight. The ruling was announced in January shortly after Domi had been traded to the Winnipeg Jets and the same day that Neilson was fired by the Rangers.)

Probert appeared in 80 games, scoring 14 goals and registering 292 penalty minutes. A first-round exit at the hands of the Toronto Maple Leafs led to another change in coaching and the hiring of Scotty Bowman.

Eight seasons into his NHL career, Probert had registered 122 fights. The toll started to catch up with him in 1993–94, when he missed eight games with a broken tailbone and then came back only to sprain his right knee. He played 66 games, but his offense was limited to seven goals and 17 points. He still racked up the penalty minutes—275 of them—and registered 20 fights, including fighting Kocur, his former Bruise Brother who had been traded to the Rangers in 1991. Probert's best fight of that season came on February 4, 1994, against Pittsburgh's Marty McSorley. The two heavyweights slugged it out before 19,875 fans at Joe Louis Arena, who stood and roared as the punches kept coming and coming. Clocked at around one minute, 40 seconds, Probert at one point knocked McSorley off his skates and pulled him back up to punch him some more. McSorley countered with heavy punches that knocked Probert back against the boards. One of the spectators on the Wings bench was Kris Draper, who had just been called up the month before.

"The first time I saw Probert fight in person, he fought Marty McSorley," Draper said in 2023. "And this fight had to have been two minutes long, over 100 punches thrown. Everybody was standing up on the bench watching. It was a complete slugfest. It was just like, *wow.* It was unreal."

The players looked exhausted when officials finally pulled them apart. Probert said it was the most tired he had ever been after a fight.

In April, Probert was spotted drinking in a Greektown gathering of friends that included his pregnant wife, Dani. The next day, Probert was called into Murray's office (he was still general manager), where Murray delivered the message: "Bob, you may or may not be playing with the Detroit Red Wings next year, but we're worried about you as a person. If you kill yourself, we're going to feel awfully bad."

That conversation happened April 3. Three months later, on July 15, Probert got drunk and crashed his Harley Davidson motorcycle into a car in the early afternoon in metro Detroit. Witnesses told police Probert had been speeding and driving erratically. He suffered cuts, bruises, and a separated shoulder, the damage limited because Probert had the incredibly good luck to land on the only sliver of grass in the intersection. A police investigation revealed Probert had a .31 blood alcohol level, well above the .10 limit for drunken driving; he also tested positive for cocaine. The report also detailed that Probert had threatened police and hospital emergency workers, telling them that "when I get out of here, I'm going to hunt you down and kill you." Around the same time, it became public knowledge that Probert was facing trial in Dallas on charges that he assaulted a woman in a bar the previous December. Once again, the NHL banned Probert.

The Wings had had enough. On July 19 they severed ties with the problematic pugilist, granting him his freedom to seek employment elsewhere in a terse, six-paragraph news release.

"Through both adversity and favorable times, we have done our utmost to help Bob and to do what we felt was in his and the team's best interests," senior vice president Jimmy Devellano said in the statement. "This is another of those times. We appreciate his contributions to the Detroit Red Wings. We wish him the best."

The NHL expelled Probert for a year, but he returned in 1995–96 with the Chicago Blackhawks, who initially looked like they had made a smart investment when they signed Probert to a four-year, $6.6 million deal three days after the Wings bid him the best. Probert scored 19 goals and had 237 penalty minutes his first year with the Blackhawks, but after that early success, his numbers plummeted. He took to using steroids to prolong his career, hanging on for another six seasons. The Blackhawks placed him on waivers after the 2001–02 season, and Probert retired on November 16, 2002, just 65 games shy of reaching 1,000. His final NHL regular-season statistics read 163 goals, 221 assists, 384 points, and 3,300 penalty minutes in 935 games. He played 474 games with the Wings, recording 114 goals, 145 assists, 259 points, and 2,090 penalty minutes.

Retirement did not mellow Probert, nor keep him from drinking. In 2004, he resisted arrest in Delray, Florida, writing his name as "The Bad One" on booking documents. The next summer, when he was 40 years old, Probert was charged with assaulting a police officer who responded to a call placed by Probert's wife from their lakefront house.

Probert's popularity with fans in Detroit never wavered; they greeted him with a standing ovation at Yzerman's retirement ceremony on January 2, 2007.

Probert died of a heart attack July 5, 2010, one month after his 45th birthday. At his funeral Yzerman delivered the eulogy.

Probert was posthumously diagnosed with an enlarged heart and with chronic traumatic encephalopathy (CTE), a degenerate disease caused by repeated blows to the head. Some of his ashes were scattered by Probert's family and Kocur, his old Bruise Brother, in the penalty box after the final game at Joe Louis Arena, which Probert had played such a key role in bringing to life starting in the mid-1980s and lasting a decade. He played with panache and punch, scoring and scuffling and besting a playoff record set by one of the greatest players in the game. Probert's reputation was entangled with his many off-ice problems, but his cherished place in franchise history is his legacy.

BROTHERS IN ARMS

After a much-needed victory in early November 1987, Red Wings coach Jacques Demers spoke effusively of his two toughest players, Bob Probert and Joe Kocur. "The Bruise Brothers did their job," Demers said. "When they do, people stand around and watch. They don't want to get involved."

Probert and Kocur were teammates for six seasons with the Wings, forming a punishing tandem. There were nights the sometime roommates would sit in the locker room before the game and study the opposing roster, deciding who would fight whom. Their fights were a hit with fans. On March 22, 1988, in a game against the defending Stanley Cup champion Edmonton Oilers, the Bruise Brothers ignited the crowd at Joe Louis Arena midway through the second period. Probert set a club record for penalties in a season when he exchanged punches with Marty McSorley; the 379 minutes in penalties surpassed Kocur's record of 377 set two seasons earlier. Before the game ended, Probert was at 381. A minute after Probert fought McSorley, Kocur scored to put the Wings up 2–1.

The two were teammates from 1985–86 until Kocur was sent to the New York Rangers on March 5, 1991. During that time together, Kocur registered 144 fights, and Probert, 82. (Off-ice problems limited him to 29 games combined in 1988–89 and 1989–90.) The trade—Kocur and defenseman Per Djoos were swapped for forward Kevin Miller, defenseman Dennis Vial and the rights to forward Jim Cummins—was unpopular with fans, and with Demers, who by then was a radio broadcaster with the Quebec Nordiques.

"So, they've traded my son, eh," Demers said. "Joey was one of my favorites...Joey was a real Red Wing at heart."

Kocur was 26 and in his seventh season with the Wings. He was part of the 1983 draft, selected at No. 88. (The Rangers' general manager at the time of the trade, Neil Smith, was an amateur scout with the Wings from 1982–89.) The trade wasn't popular in the locker room, either.

"Joey literally fought for guys like me and Shawn Burr, always there for this whole team," Steve Yzerman said. "I'll always be grateful for that part of it. I know Joey went through a lot of soreness and problems in his hands just to give us some room on the ice."

Burr broke into the NHL with Kocur in 1984–85: "You lose some toughness on the ice, but the important thing is you lose a friend."

Probert called Kocur "a good player, a tough player, a good guy to have in the dressing room. It's really hard to see a guy like Joey go."

The two were asked shortly after the trade about the possibility of fighting one another, and both downplayed it happening. But it did.

On December 17, 1993, the Bruise Brothers turned into the Bloodied Brothers. Their bout in the first period sent the 19,875 fans at Joe Louis Arena into a frenzy. Kocur bloodied Probert's nose, but Probert finished strong, slamming Kocur into the boards and pulling off his sweater and helmet. Linesmen broke it up when Probert finally got his own helmet off.

"He swung at someone on our team, and I went over to stop him," Kocur said afterward. "The next thing I know, he hit me a couple times in the chips. It was fun." Probert pleaded innocence: "I didn't know it was Joey until I was already in it. At that point, you can't stop."

In New York, Kocur celebrated a Stanley Cup championship in 1994. Two years later he was sent to the Vancouver Canucks, but they released him after seven games. By then, Kocur had endured multiple painful problems with his right hand, from a major infection early in his career to reconstructive surgery during his time with the Rangers, which he needed because a tendon had torn and split across his knuckles.

Unable to find work in the professional leagues, Kocur ended up playing in a beer league.

He was still friends with Probert, who was with the Chicago Blackhawks then. Kocur asked Probert to play extra tough against his former team to remind them they could use someone like Kocur. (It helped that in December 1996, the Wings were still eager to ensure that they wouldn't be bullied out of the playoffs again, like they had been in the 1996 Western Conference Finals by the Colorado Avalanche. Yzerman was among those pushing for Kocur to get another chance.)

Probert obliged, running Detroit goaltender Chris Osgood during a December 12, 1996, game, which led to Blackhawks enforcer Enrico Ciccone taking liberties with multiple Wings.

The Wings signed Kocur at the end of December. On January 5, 1997, the friends fought again, this time in Chicago, on Kocur's first shift. The bout ended in a draw. Kocur then pounded Cam Russell's face till it was bloody, just to emphasize the Wings had made a good hire.

"The last time, Brendan Shanahan and Darren McCarty had to fight," Wings coach Scotty Bowman said. "That's no good for us. I think Joe's going to be fine when we get him into NHL shape. He's actually going to be better than we expected."

Kocur would go on to be a part of the Grind Line with Kris Draper and Kirk Maltby, celebrating Stanley Cup championships in 1997 and 1998.

17
Darren McCarty

KRIS DRAPER DID NOT KNOW JUST HOW CLOSE HE WOULD become with the big winger he faced while playing in the Ontario Hockey League, but as soon as he first saw Darren McCarty, he left an indelible impression.

"I played against him in juniors, didn't really know him that well," Draper said in 2023. "You could tell he was going to do whatever it took to make the team; he had such a determination about him. Sure enough, he fought his way into the NHL and fought guys that were legit heavyweights. The thing about Darren was, the personality and the love that he had of being a Red Wing. The way he played the game, he was the ultimate blue-collar player. He worked for it. And he played it up perfectly. The fans loved him on the ice and off the ice. He was a man of the people. He loved entertaining and the role he had to play. That was Mac. He was always going to stick up for his teammates."

McCarty cemented his reputation in Wings lore on March 26, 1997, when he stuck up for Draper and struck down Claude Lemieux, whose gutless hit in the 1996 playoffs had bestowed him with No. 1 villain status in Detroit. It was McCarty's fourth season with the Wings, and he already had established his value to the franchise.

It was former general manager Ken Holland who brought McCarty into the organization, selecting him at No. 46 in the 1992 draft largely on the advice of a guy named Paul Crowley, who Holland had hired as a part-time scout. The overarching goal for the Wings in that draft was to get tougher and stronger, to find players who would make the team harder for opponents to bulldoze, as the Chicago Blackhawks had done to the Wings in the 1992 playoffs. Bob Probert was still on the team, but his fellow tough guy, Joe Kocur, had been traded to the New York Rangers in what was a deeply unpopular move with fans in March 1991. A year later, in the 1992 draft, the Wings wanted big, strong wingers, and McCarty fit that description.

He was 20 years old when they drafted him, passed over in the prior two drafts because his skating was poor and his statistics unimpressive. But as grew into his body—he was 6'1" and 214 pounds in his draft year—he also grew his game, posting 55 goals and 72 assists in 1991–92, his 127 points a 60-point increase over the previous season. McCarty also had 177 penalty minutes, the third straight season with his OHL Belleville Bulls that he had topped 100 minutes in the penalty box.

"Darren wasn't a great skater, but he had a lot of grit and inner drive," Holland said in 2023. "We thought he was a guy who could help us."

McCarty put up decent numbers his first year with the Wings' American Hockey League farm, the Adirondack Red Wings, producing 36 points and 278 penalty minutes in 1992–93. When he showed up for training camp with the Wings in the fall of 1993, the team had a new head coach in Scotty Bowman, who had been tasked with turning the Wings into a champion after another playoff disappointment that spring. McCarty's skating had improved enough that, given his willingness to be a combatant, he had moved up the depth chart on right wing and was considered a serious contender to make the big club. That he was a bit of a showman certainly didn't hurt. In an exhibition game in mid-September, he pummeled Chicago's Cam Russell, quickly taking down the Blackhawks forward and taking advantage of the linesmen being busy separating other players to skate from the corner out onto open ice, strip off his sweater and shoulder pads, and strike a pose as an old-time bare-knuckled boxer. The fight ended his night on his second shift, just 4:44 into the game, but his performance went over well with Wings management, and McCarty knew it.

"Just doing what I have to do," he said. "I don't go looking for it, but if it happens, I'll do it to help my teammates."

His willingness to fight earned McCarty a spot as Probert's new tag-team partner. When the season began, Bowman gave McCarty an early look on a line with Probert and either of Shawn Burr or Micah Aivazoff. McCarty recorded his first NHL goal on October 21, 1993, and also registered a fight. Bowman liked what he saw.

"McCarty has a lot of emotion and has shown the ability to score at every level," Bowman said. "He knows how to play the game, and that's a big factor."

McCarty's physical style left him on the sidelines at times—a bruised foot, a shoulder, what was termed a "moderate" concussion—but his rookie NHL season was a success: he appeared in 67 games, had 26 points and 181 penalty minutes, and even found time during the season to get married.

His role expanded in 1994–95, the year the Wings finally cut ties with Probert after yet another incident involving alcohol and the police. The two would eventually square off against one another, on December 12, 1996, in a short-lived fight that saw McCarty throw the majority of punches.

As much fun as he had had in his rookie season, the 1996–97 season was the highlight of McCarty's career. The Wings had such a plethora of stars—Steve Yzerman, Sergei Fedorov, and, as of the start of that season, Brendan Shanahan—that Bowman used McCarty on a line with Shanahan and Igor Larionov, mixing brawn and brains and bravado. It led to McCarty posting what would stand as career highs with 19 goals and 49 points.

No regular-season game better summed up why McCarty was such a favorite with teammates and fans than when the Avalanche made their second appearance at Joe Louis Arena with, at last, Lemieux in the lineup. Near the end of the first period officials distracted by collision between Larionov and Peter Forsberg—two of the most cerebral, fight-averse players in hockey—McCarty coldcocked Lemieux, setting off a chain reaction of battles that would be celebrated and relived for many years. Multiple players fought that evening, but it was McCarty's battering of Lemieux that satisfied the blood lust that had simmered since Lemieux's blindside hit the previous year that sent Draper to hospital with a disfigured face. That it took place right in front of the Wings' bench, giving Draper ringside seats, added to the justice of it all. At last, the hit was avenged.

Maybe because it was such a one-sided conflict, officials didn't even deem what happened between McCarty and Lemieux a fight when it came to doling out penalty minutes. All McCarty got for that transgression was a double minor for roughing. McCarty did get five for fighting in the second period, when he tussled with Adam Deadmarsh and also picked up another roughing penalty to get 11 minutes total for the evening. As if that wasn't enough, McCarty capped the evening by giving the hyped-up crowd at JLA something else to cheer, scoring in overtime to give the Wings a victory over their fiercest rival.

That was the second most memorable goal McCarty scored in 1997. On June 7, in Game 4 of the Stanley Cup Final against the Philadelphia Flyers, McCarty took a pass from Tomas Sandström and strode into the Flyers' zone. Philadelphia defenseman Janne Niinimaa shadowed McCarty and tried to force him to give up the puck, but McCarty moved the puck to his backhand, pulled it to the outside, through Niinimaa's legs, and kept striding. Niinimaa lost his balance and in desperation, swung his stick at McCarty. McCarty kept going, pumping his legs, eyeing Philadelphia's net, maneuvered the puck to his forehand, drew the goalie out, deked back to his backhand, and tucked the puck into the net. The goal would stand as the one that clinched the 2–1 victory, and with that, the Stanley Cup.

"Mac showed against the Flyers that he could make moves," Grind Line linemate Kirk Maltby said in 2023. "His skating wasn't great, but he always worked at it. He had a great shot and hockey sense. He had a little bit of everything. He was a very versatile player. He's one of those guys that whatever the coach asked of him, he would at least try to do it. He's such a big personality and he loved his teammates, the city of Detroit, the Red Wings. He would do anything for the team, for the city, to win."

McCarty was an on-again, off-again member of the Grind Line, the enormously successful line that featured Maltby on the left wing, Draper at center, and either of McCarty or Kocur on the right wing. They wore down opposing stars and scored timely goals. Off the ice, McCarty started a band called Grinder that, to the delight of Wings teammates, recorded a song called "Step Outside" that was played during warm-ups before a game in Dallas in October 1998. McCarty took some heat for it, but he loved it. The band raised money for the medical treatment of Vladimir Konstantinov and Sergei Mnatsakanov, who had suffered life-altering injuries in a limousine accident a week after the Wings won the Cup in 1997, and McCarty did everything he could to make that a success. A natural performer—remember his bareknuckle pose in Chicago—McCarty thrived in front of a microphone. He sang, he fought, he scored big goals, and generally thrived. McCarty had come clean during the 1996 offseason about his battle with alcohol, telling the *Detroit Free Press* that "if I didn't pass out, I wouldn't stop drinking." A stay at Maplegrove Center for Chemical Dependency in West Bloomfield, Michigan, helped him learn how to deal with that.

McCarty also started the McCarty Cancer Foundation in honor of his father, Craig, who passed away in 1999 from multiple myeloma.

As popular as McCarty was with teammates and fans, he was a hit with Bowman because "he had such good hockey sense," Bowman said in 2023. "He wasn't a great skater, but he understood what he had to do, how to play. He had a lot of perseverance."

McCarty helped the Wings win another Cup in 1998, recording 11 points in 22 playoff games. A third Cup followed in 2002, during which McCarty celebrated the only hat trick of his career, coming in the third period of Game 1 of the Western Conference Finals against Detroit's old rival, Colorado. McCarty scored all three on Patrick Roy, completing the natural hat trick on Maltby's rebound and sending a cavalcade of hats to the ice at the Joe.

McCarty's hard-nosed style wore on his body, and throughout his career with the Wings, he never did play a full season's worth of games. In 2003–04 he was limited to 43 games. The Wings were on a downswing; the core that had won the three Cups between 1997 and 2002 was aging, and a changing landscape led to the implementation of a salary cap when the NHL resumed play after losing the 2004–05 season to a labor dispute. Teams had to be compliant to a new accounting system, and McCarty's reduced effectiveness made him vulnerable. The Wings bought out his contract, severing ties and leaving McCarty an unrestricted free agent in search of a new employer.

He found one with the Calgary Flames, signing on August 2, 2005. McCarty spent two tumultuous seasons with his new team, struggling to score and dealing with off-ice issues including divorce and bankruptcy. When he failed to record a single point in 32 games with the Flames, it seemed McCarty's NHL career would end with a whimper.

McCarty, who had had four children with his first wife, moved back to Detroit. It was a tough time, but eventually, the friendship forged with Draper helped revive McCarty's career and brought him back to the Wings.

"It was kind of tough and kind of sad for me at that time," Draper said in 2023. "We were best friends and incredible teammates. I know that he was fighting some demons for a long time, and our friendship was basically non-existent. There was nothing going on between us. I'd reach out, I'd reach out, I'd get nothing. I'd see him, it was pretty uncomfortable. I knew he was in a tough place but to me, he was going to be a friend for life. I just kept telling him, no matter what you are going through, I'm here for you. He didn't take me up on that until the summer of 2007. He called, and I was excited to hear from him. He said he'd like to meet for coffee, and I asked when, thinking it was never going to happen. So, I said, 'Can we meet right now?' And then I said, 'You want to meet at a coffee shop or come over?' He came to my house and sat down and he's like, *I think I can play, I think I have some hockey in me.* He said, 'I need your help.' I'm like, *Mac, I'll set stuff up for you, 100 percent, but you have to do it.* And he did."

Draper offered McCarty a chance to reopen the door to playing hockey with a stint with the Flint Generals, then an International Hockey League team partially owned by Draper. McCarty played 11 games. He was 35 years old, but he still had an outsize personality, and for all the struggles he had endured—with alcohol, marijuana, bankruptcy, and gambling—McCarty remained a popular figure with Wings fans; as with Bob Probert, on-ice triumphs eclipsed off-ice battles. Ken Holland, the general manager who had drafted McCarty back in 1992, brought him back to the organization on a tryout with Detroit's AHL team, the Grand Rapids Griffins. Ten points in 13 games earned McCarty a contract with the Wings, and he was called up from the minors on March 7, 2008.

"All of a sudden Kenny told me we are going to call Mac up," Draper said. "I had tears in my eyes being a part of it, seeing how far he came, to get him back to the NHL and to the Detroit Red Wings. First game, it was Mac, Kirk Maltby, and me, and it was one of those nights all three of us will never forget. He was a great teammate."

McCarty played just three games in the regular season, but appeared in 17 playoff games, helping the Wings to win another Stanley Cup. He split the last season of his career between the Wings and the minor leagues, retiring in December 2009 having played 758 NHL games; 659 of them were with the Wings. The determination he had shown in juniors was there when he made the team, when he slew Lemieux, when he scored on the Flyers, and when he resuscitated his career to finish it where he belonged: with the Wings.

PART 6

HOW SWEDE IT WAS

18

Tomas Holmström

TOMAS HOLMSTRÖM WAS ON A PHONE CALL IN 2023 WHEN he described what it was like for him to fly back from Detroit to his house in Sweden. "It takes forever to get home, like 24 hours," he said. "Detroit to Amsterdam, then up to Stockholm, and then Stockholm up to the North Pole."

It was exactly that sense of humor that was such a big part of Holmström's immense appeal during his time with the Red Wings. If there was a joke involving Holmström, nobody laughed harder than he did.

Not that he wasn't concerned when he arrived for training camp in 1996, fresh off meeting future best friend Nicklas Lidström while playing for Sweden at the 1996 World Cup. Lidström was entering his sixth season with the Wings, but there was curiosity about the 6'0", 200-pound forward he had in tow.

"We were told this Swedish guy is coming over, this Tomas Holmström," Kirk Maltby said in 2023. "Back then before the

Internet, not a lot was known about overseas players. Someone said his nickname was the Demolition Man. We were all, *ooh, the Demolition Man*. We were joking about it."

It was the Wings' Swedish scout Håkan Andersson who brought Holmström into the fold, having first watched him at the Swedish national camp in 1991, where Holmström stood out even against such hockey luminaries as Peter Forsberg and Markus Näslund. Andersson noticed Holmström's ability around the net, noticed how feisty he was when battling defensemen trying to get the puck away from him, and how he overcame poor skating ability through sheer determination. The Wings drafted Holmström in the 10th round, at No. 257, in 1994. None of the other seven players they drafted after the second round made it to the NHL.

The nickname was bestowed on Holmström by the public-address announcer for his former club, Lulea, shortly after the Sylvester Stallone/Wesley Snipes *Demolition Man* movie came out in 1993.

While his future teammates wondered about Holmström, he wondered how he would become their teammate.

"I knew the team was pretty stacked," Holmström said in 2023. "In '95 they lost to New Jersey in the Finals and then the next season they won 62 games. So, it was like, *wow, here we go. Where am I going to play?* But then Dino Ciccarelli left, and I was like, *perfect.* That was an opening for me. That was my role, to be in front of the net."

(Scotty Bowman, who in addition to coaching also carried director of player personnel duties, had tried for more than a year to rid the team of Ciccarelli, disliking him for his penchant for taking dumb penalties, and finally traded him to the Tampa Bay Lightning in August 1996 for a conditional draft pick.)

Holmström played in 17 of the Wings' first 32 games in his rookie season. In one of his first appearances, he got into a scuffle with Los Angeles Kings defenseman Rob Blake—a hefty 6'4", 220 pounds in his prime—and landed on the ice after a punch in the face. As new as he was to the Wings, Holmström was all in during the famous March 26 game against the Colorado Avalanche, getting into a fight with Mike Keane.

Holmström played 47 games with the Wings in 1996–97, and only once in the playoffs. At one point he approached team owner Mike Ilitch to put in a word for him with Bowman. Recalling the conversation years later, Ilitch said he laughed and told Holmström, *no, that's not how things are done.*

Holmström chuckled when he thought back on it.

"I was probably just thinking that I know I can do it, that I can play in this league, just give me a chance," he said in 2023. "I was probably thinking, why not turn to the big boss? I knew I could play."

There's a story those who were around when Holmström first arrived still cherish decades later, how he wore No. 15 his first season, then relinquished it to veteran Dmitri Mironov. When Holmström cast about for a new number, Bowman suggested No. 98, joking that would be the year he would return to Sweden. Holmström chose No. 96 for the year he arrived.

Holmström may have been frustrated early on under Bowman, but if Bowman hadn't found Holmström useful, he wouldn't have lasted in Detroit. He played 57 games in 1997–98, recording 22 points, but when the playoffs began, Holmström was on a line with Sergei Fedorov and Vyacheslav Kozlov, two of the most talented forwards on the team.

Holmström used the '98 playoffs to prove what he had been saying since he came to Detroit: he could play in the NHL. When it was all over and he was celebrating his second

Stanley Cup championship—Holmström had 19 points, only one behind Fedorov, but Fedorov averaged 20 minutes per game to Holmström's 11.

At the rally before an estimated 1.2 million people in downtown Detroit on June 18, two days after they clinched the Cup, Holmström showed off that humor that was part of his charm. Grabbing the microphone, he asked the crowd, "You want me to speak?"

It was Steve Yzerman who replied: "No, no. You do your best when you just smile and shut up. The strength of our team isn't necessarily in the big names or the big-time players. It's in the foot soldiers, the guys who grind it out every day without attention, guys like Homer, that we're the Stanley Cup champions."

Holmström replied, "I love you fans. Let's party!" To which Yzerman followed up: "Now you know why I didn't want him to speak."

Holmström's command of English was debatable, but he understood how to communicate on the ice. He knew he had to be in front of the net in order to hold down a job. That takes willpower and discipline and a different sort of toughness than the kind displayed by, for example, Vladimir Konstantinov, who was a world-class clothes-liner with the way he could knock down opponents. Holmström's toughness was in his refusal to be bulldozed away from the crease.

"I had read he was a hard-nosed player, and he showed that right away in training camp," Lidström said in 2023. "He played a little bit like Vladdie in that he would hit anyone—he wasn't punishing like Vladdie, but he finished his checks against anybody. He was there to earn a spot and he didn't care who he was playing against."

Lidström and Holmström have a decades-long running joke about how many of Lidström's goals Holmström "stole" by getting his stick on the puck just before it went into the net (Holmström generally estimates it is in the tens; Lidström deems it to be around 30 to 40).

"Nick could put the puck pretty much anywhere he aimed," Holmström said. "So, I would tell him, you see my stick, shoot for my stick. And he didn't have to make it a big slap shot, just get the puck in there for me, and I will get it on my stick, and then it was battling for position."

Lidström would purposely shoot the puck wide to take advantage of Joe Louis Arena's famously bouncy end boards; all the time spent in practice enabled Lidström to know how to get just the right torque that would lead to a juicy rebound for Holmström, who he knew would be in position.

"You have to be brave to get in there in the first place and then you get slashed, and you get knocked down, and you get back up and back in there," Lidström said. "And he had someone taking slap shots at him, too. So, it takes a lot of courage to do what he did, and Homer had that courage. He had the willingness to take a beating because he knew eventually the puck would get there. He had great hand-eye coordination. When the puck was moving on the blue line, he was able to move with the puck, and still screen the goalie. Not many players have that skill. He was so good at moving to screen goalies all the time."

One of Holmström's biggest fans was the man who made the joke that 1998 would see him return to Sweden. "Homer was really, really effective," Bowman said in 2023. "He accepted his role and he never complained. If he missed a game, it was because he was really, truly injured. He was a big part of our success."

Holmström won a third Stanley Cup in 2002 and a fourth in 2008 and in 2023 he was still upset that in 2009 the Wings squandered two-games-to-none and three-games-to-two advantages and lost the Stanley Cup Finals to the Pittsburgh Penguins: "I'm still bitter about '09. I should have five Stanley Cups."

There was no bitterness, just pure joy two years later when, on February 10, 2011, Holmström played in his 1,000th NHL game. As of 2023, only two other players selected in the 10th round had accomplished that feat: Kimmo Timonen, who played 1,108 games, and Bret Hedican, who played 1,039. Holmström is the only one of three who logged all of his games—1,026— with the same team. That put him in the company of Lidström, Yzerman, Gordie Howe, and Alex Delvecchio, all of whom played at least 1,000 games with the Wings.

A couple of days after the milestone, after practice was done, Henrik Zetterberg burst out of the Zamboni gate riding a custom snowmobile, a gift to Holmström from his teammates. It was a nod to Holmström's hometown of Piteå, located in the northernmost county in Sweden. From the moment he arrived in Detroit, it had been a source of delight.

"Part of the fun of Homer was his accent," Maltby said. "Nick had none, but Homer, we always used to say he was from as far north as the North Pole. He would combine words or just use the wrong words. But he was good about it: he was always laughing along with everyone. We used to ask him to pass our Christmas wish lists to Santa Claus because we figured they were neighbors."

Holmström, of course, loved it. "It was such a special gift," he said. "I will never get rid of that. When Z came out, I couldn't believe it. I'm really proud of it. I was there in a good era, but if I didn't do my job, I would never have played 1,000 games."

It was that indefatigable work ethic that in the second half of his career led to Holmström playing on a line with Zetterberg and fellow young star Pavel Datsyuk.

"Those two, they didn't want me to leave the net," Holmström said. "Sometimes I would rush out to help Pavel because he had two guys on him, and he would tell me, 'No, don't come, it will be too crowded. You let me deal with the two guys and you stay by the net.' So, okay. That was how he wanted it. Usually, you want to help your teammates, but he didn't want that. But it was a good thing because if he had two guys on him, then Hank was open, and he could get the puck on net. That was a good mix."

Holmström announced his retirement in January 2013 after waiting through the labor dispute that nullified the first half of the 2012–13 season. He played his last regular-season game on April 7, 2012, and his last playoff game on April 20. He finished with 243 goals and 530 regular-season points and 97 points in 180 career playoff games. The Demolition Man had turned himself into a franchise man, with memorable performances that left a glowing legacy.

"With Tomas, what he did was pretty incredible," Maltby said. "To be in that net-front role, in that era, was incredible. I think Homer is one of the best net-front presences ever. He was always down there by the net, and it didn't matter that he was getting crosschecked by the Chris Prongers of the world and hacked and whacked by the Eddie Belfours of the world. Homer was one of those guys, you had to kill him to keep him down. The backs of his legs would be black and blue from all the bruising, from all the abuse he would take, but he was such a competitor. He put up with anything to win and he mostly did it with a smile on his face, every day."

19
Henrik Zetterberg

THE RED WINGS RECEIVED A NICE BIT OF NEWS DURING
THE Christmas break in 2001 when they found out Henrik
Zetterberg made Sweden's Olympic roster. They had chosen
him in the seventh round, 210th overall, in 1999—a draft they
were at almost reluctantly. But two years later, Zetterberg had
made the cut over several Swedish NHL forwards, and he was
only 21 years old.

Zetterberg's appeal in the '99 draft was based on his smarts.
He was only around 5'9", 155 pounds at the time, but he held his
own against bigger, faster players because he was always using
his head, always reading plays one step ahead, always making
smart plays with the puck. Not enough to warrant early-round
draft talk, but he left an impression on chief European scout
Håkan Andersson and chief amateur scout Jim Nill, and their
decision to draft him turned into the best decision the Wings
made that year. Attempts to chase another Stanley Cup in the
1999 playoffs had led then-general manager Ken Holland to

trade away the team's first-round pick and two second-round picks, and all the Wings got in return was two rounds of playoff hockey. Selecting Zetterberg would at least go on to push the team toward fresh playoff success.

By the time he joined the Wings for the start of the 2002–03 season, Zetterberg's game had grown to a point he was put on a line with Brendan Shanahan and Sergei Fedorov, two multi-Stanley Cup champions and NHL superstars. Zetterberg already knew several Wings, having been teammates with Nicklas Lidström, Tomas Holmström, and Fredrik Olausson at the Winter Olympics in Salt Lake City; other Wings, including Steve Yzerman, Chris Chelios, and Shanahan, were among Wings players representing other countries. Zetterberg further familiarized himself with his new team during the 2002 playoffs, which he and 2000 draftee Niklas Kronwall observed as spectators, all the way through to the 2002 Stanley Cup celebration.

The exceptionally smart playmaking ability that stood out when Zetterberg was a teenager flourished as his body matured. (He was 6'0", 180 pounds at his first camp, closer to 200 pounds in his prime.) He scored 22 goals as a rookie, producing 44 points in 79 games and finishing as runner-up for the Calder Trophy; it put him in the company of fellow rookie-of-the-year runner-ups Yzerman, Lidström, and Sergei Fedorov. It was in January 2003 that then head coach Dave Lewis decided to see how Zetterberg would look on a line with veteran winger Brett Hull and young center Pavel Datsyuk, a sixth-round pick from the 1998 draft. It turned out to be a brilliant move; Zetterberg and Datsyuk had such magic together that teammates took to referring to them as the Euro Twins.

"I was thinking of the Wonder Twins from the TV series," Kris Draper said in 2023. "They would say, 'Wonder Twins activate,' and they would have superpowers and go out and dominate. So, I kind of took it off that—'Euro Twins activate and go into superstar mode,' and go win us a game. I started kidding around with that and guys were laughing and saying, 'Oh my god, the Euro Twins. This is hilarious.' It caught on and next thing you knew, Pav and Z were known as the Euro Twins around Detroit and around the NHL."

It wasn't just on the ice the two jelled; close in age the two became close comrades.

"We have lots of fun, outside, inside," Datsyuk said in 2004. The two spent hours indulging in PlayStation's FIFA soccer and developed a pregame ritual of kicking around a soccer ball in the hallways outside locker rooms. They were roommates on the road and were each other's steady companions for dinners and movies. (Datsyuk had fun with this in the 2004 playoffs, when he told a reporter that "we like to watch romances and drama. After [the] movie we cry.")

They brought fresh star talent to the Wings at a time when they were dealing with Fedorov's departure after the 2002–03 season and Yzerman's retirement after the 2006 playoffs.

"They're pretty unique players," Yzerman said during the 2004 playoffs. "They've become, very quickly, top players in the league. They're tremendous offensive guys but play well in their own end as well. They're tough to match up against because they play hard and they're very smart and very strong. They work extremely well together."

Lidström, who only dealt with defending against them in practices, described what it was like: "You have to spend a lot of time in your own end chasing them. Pavel is a bit more tricky with the puck, but Hank gains a lot of ice just kind of holding you off on the side, whereas Pavel can stickhandle right through you, turn back, and go against the flow almost. They're both really tough to play against."

The 2005–06 season was a breakout one for Zetterberg, who scored 39 goals among 85 points in 77 games. He delivered consistent performances, a sound two-way game, and was so reliable that if a winger wasn't scoring, a few games on a line with Zetterberg generally got the points coming again. The playoffs ended with a six-game, first-round loss to the Edmonton Oilers, but not for lack of effort from Zetterberg: he had points in five straight games and six overall.

"Every time he had the puck, he did something good with it," Holmström recalled in a 2023 interview. "And you couldn't take the puck from him—he had that wide stance and good glide. He wasn't a big guy, but he used his speed and strength and made everyone around him better."

It was a stellar year all around for Zetterberg, who in 2006 won gold medals at the Olympics and World Championship. He eclipsed his NHL numbers in 2007–08, when he scored what would be a career high of 43 goals among 92 points. By then he was an alternate captain, recognized as one of the team's leaders with a letter on his sweater.

Zetterberg opened the 2008 playoffs with a two-goal performance, sliding across the ice to finish a perfect set-up by Datsyuk on the first goal. "We've seen that before, Pav gets Z the puck," Kronwall said after the 3–1 victory. "Hank's been playing great for us all year, and he finds a way to come up with these key goals."

Zetterberg scored five goals in the four games it took the Wings to dispatch the Avalanche. When the playoffs ended, he had 13 goals and 14 assists. His 27 points set a club record for points in one postseason and matched Pittsburgh Penguins superstar Sidney Crosby's playoff output, but Zetterberg's 1.35 points-per-game average edged Crosby's 1.23 average. The two were a sublime matchup to watch, and Zetterberg's impact for the Wings was as much from his offensive production as his immaculate penalty killing. In Game 4, he killed a five-on-three Pittsburgh power play almost by himself. In Game 5, he gave the Wings chance after chance to win, including diving to block a shot in the third overtime period.

In Game 6 Zetterberg scored what would stand as the Stanley Cup-winning goal; he assisted on the first goal of the 3–2 victory. He was recognized for his outstanding playoff performance by being awarded the Conn Smythe Trophy, the clearcut favorite as the most valuable player of the playoffs. It was further reinforcement of what a good decision the Wings made when they drafted him.

"We went to the tournament where he first caught our eye to scout Mattias Weinhandl," Jim Nill said. "We liked him, but Zetterberg kept doing things to be noticed. He was always working. He was really weak and really small, but we saw something in him and marked him down on our notes."

Ken Holland, the general manager, described Zetterberg after the 2008 playoffs, as "a special player. He brings it every shift, every day, every practice. Our team follows him."

As Lidström had been the natural successor to captain the Wings when Steve Yzerman retired in 2006, so was Zetterberg the natural next in line when Lidström retired in 2012. Holland told Zetterberg the news in mid-July after a round of golf at Meadowbrook Country Club, but the official announcement was delayed until January 15, 2013, because of a labor dispute. Zetterberg was handed a sweater with a "C" on it after a practice at what was then called Compuware Arena in Plymouth, Michigan.

"Henrik is a natural leader, intelligent and confident," Yzerman said. "He's a complete player who can also be counted on no matter the situation. He will be an outstanding leader for the Red Wings."

Zetterberg described himself as really proud.

"More than anything," he said, "this is a very big responsibility, to represent the Wings in everything. You look back at some of the former captains, it is very big shoes to fill. But I read a quote from Stevie Y, when he became captain in '86. He said it made it a lot easier by having a locker full of leaders. That's the same for me now."

Datsyuk, an alternate along with Kronwall, called it "exactly the right decision. He deserves it. He [is a] leader in locker room, out of locker room. It's hit to target."

Like Lidström and Yzerman, Zetterberg was a quiet leader; humble, demanding—most of all of himself—and vocal when needed. An intense competitor, he had come out of the seventh round of the 1999 draft and established himself as a key part of the reason the Wings stretched their success for a decade-plus beyond the retirement and departures of the older players that won Stanley Cups in 1997, 1998, and 2002.

Zetterberg's performance in the first round of the 2013 playoffs was masterful. The Wings were the lower seed, faced with starting on the road against the Anaheim Ducks. With the Wings facing elimination in Game 6, Zetterberg came through with a goal in the third period and another in overtime to force a Game 7. He scored again that night to complete the upset. Zetterberg had five points in the two games the Wings faced elimination.

The second-round series against the Chicago Blackhawks pitted Zetterberg against Jonathan Toews, a budding superstar with a game similar to Zetterberg's. It was reminiscent of Zetterberg's one-on-one battles with Sidney Crosby in the 2008 and 2009 Stanley Cup playoffs: two players, determined to lead their team to victory. The Blackhawks won the round, but Zetterberg was brilliant till the end, scoring a goal in the final game.

It was around this time that back pain that had bothered Zetterberg on and off through his career worsened. He was 33 and missed nearly a month in December 2013 because of a herniated disk. He returned in late December and was part of the festivities when the Wings hosted the 2014 Winter Classic, taking on the Toronto Maple Leafs at Michigan Stadium in Ann Arbor. (Zetterberg had an assist.) He missed some time again in late January but gutted through playing in early February and deemed himself in good enough condition to captain Team Sweden at the 2014 Winter Olympics in Sochi, Russia. That didn't last, however; Zetterberg had to withdraw after one appearance (during which he scored a goal). "I just can't play any more here," he said in mid-February 2014. "It's the same problems as before, only 20 times worse. It's impossible for me to play." Fellow Olympians were sympathetic: when Slovakia's Zdeno Chára eyed Zetterberg carrying a backpack and headed toward a bus, Chara grabbed the bag and carried it for Zetterberg.

A few days later, Zetterberg left for the United States, where he would see a medical specialist. He had surgery February 20th, when doctors found a floating piece of a disk dislodged in a nerve in Zetterberg's back. He pushed himself to return during the playoffs and made it into the last two games of what was a brief first-round series between the Wings and Boston Bruins; Zetterberg scored his lone playoff goal in the fifth and decisive game.

Zetterberg's inner drive pushed him to continue his career. He appeared in 77 games in 2014–15, recording 49 assists, and played 82 games in each of the following two season.

The milestones started to pile up: eighth player in franchise history to score 300 goals (November 6, 2015). Fifth player in Wings history to record 300 goals and 800 points, putting him in the company of Gordie Howe, Alex Delvecchio, Yzerman, and Fedorov. On April 9, 2017, he celebrated the final game at Joe Louis Arena in milestone fashion, as it coincided with Zetterberg's 1,000th game.

Zetterberg played one more season, posting 56 points in 2017–18, the franchise's first year at Little Caesars Arena. He showed up at training camp the following autumn, but it was only to make what had been a long-awaited announcement: his back, his body, could not take any more training. He played 1,082 regular-season games, recording 337 goals and 623 assists, along with a plus-160 rating, along with 120 points and a plus-41 rating in 137 playoff games. Only two players from his draft class eclipse those regular-season numbers: Henrik Sedin (1,070 points in 1,330 games) and brother Daniel Sedin (1,041 points, 1,306 games) but they were drafted third and second overall, respectively.

Zetterberg was a pro's pro, a consummate competitor. Scouts for the Wings first noticed him because of how smart a game he played, and that never faded. Together with Datsyuk, he carried the Wings franchise for a decade, demanding excellence while retaining a low-key, affable personality. Their lack of draft picks in 1999 prompted Wings brass to joke about just trading the few they had and going home; instead, in the seventh round, they found salvation.

20

Mining Sweden

When the Red Wings won the Stanley Cup in 2008, a third of the team had been mined from Sweden.

The Scandinavian superpower of hockey has a special place in franchise history. There hasn't been a single five-man unit like the Russian Five, but Sweden gave the Wings one of the best defensemen to ever play the game and several elite forwards.

Before teammates started calling Nicklas Lidström the "Perfect Human," they called him "Super Swede" in recognition of his superbness and his nationality. He was the first headline Swede but not the first Swede to play for the Wings. That recognition belongs to Thommie Bergman, whose performance at the 1972 Winter Olympics in Sapporo, Japan, drew the interest of multiple NHL teams. He was 6'3" and 200 pounds in his prime, with a mean streak not associated with Swedish players. He had an assist in his NHL debut, on October 7, 1972, and a fight in his third game on October 14 with Philadelphia

Flyers enforcer Dave Schultz, the guy who set the NHL record for most penalty minutes in a single season, at 472. Bergman didn't know who Schultz was, but the fight sent a message that Bergman wasn't going to be pushed around.

The 1970s, especially the first half, were a miserable time for the franchise, which fell into such disrepute fans took to calling them the Dead Wings. Bergman was a rare bright spot, especially that first season, when he posted 21 points to go along with 70 penalty minutes in 75 games. He left the franchise in the mid-1970s to play for the Winnipeg Jets in the World Hockey Association, returning to Detroit in 1978–79. Bergman returned to Sweden after the 1979–80 season having played 246 games for the Wings, posting 65 points and 243 penalty minutes.

Bergman was one of three Swedes to play for the Wings in the 1970s. The others were Dan Labraaten, a forward who scored 30 goals in 1979–80, and Tord Lundström, a forward who appeared in 11 games in 1973–74.

The Wings didn't have another Swede on their roster until Börje Salming finished his NHL career with them in 1989–90. By then Salming had gained fame in North America playing for the Toronto Maple Leafs and been named to six consecutive NHL All-Star teams.

At the conclusion of the 1988–89 season, Salming was the NHL's oldest player at 38 years. He was also a free agent, and Wings general manager Jimmy Devellano, whose astuteness extended to understanding the need to be a showman, decided to sign Salming. It was only for one year, and while Salming's best hockey clearly was in the past, the move generated attention in Detroit because of Salming's status and it was also a way to rankle the Leafs, who considered Salming theirs.

Devellano was delighted to talk about it.

"Borje has had a fabulous NHL career with the Toronto Maple Leafs and has been a tower of strength for them on defense," Devellano said at the time. "He will provide us with leadership and give us another solid defenseman."

Salming said it was tough to leave Toronto, but "Detroit is a great organization."

On the whole, given how much wear and tear he had been through, Salming gave the Wings above-average hockey, leading them with a plus-20 in 49 games at season's end. Still, there was no talk of a sequel; the Wings bid Salming farewell at season's end, and he returned to Sweden to continue his notable career. In 1996 he became the first European player inducted into the Hockey Hall of Fame.

What really put Sweden on the map for Wings fans was the 1989 draft. Neil Smith, the chief amateur scout, and Christer Rockström, the team's Swedish scout, had seen enough of Lidström to covet the young, physically unimposing defenseman. It was tricky: while Swedish forward Mats Sundin was the first overall pick in '89 (by the Quebec Nordiques), teams favored North American players under the perception they were tougher and cared more about the Stanley Cup. Smith was so eager to draft Lidström, though, that a week before the draft, Rockström called Lidström and told him not to come to the event.

"We were worried someone would see him and take him before we could get him," Smith said in 2021. "We didn't want anybody to think of him, to talk about him, to say anything at all."

Smith even convinced Lidström's agent, Donnie Meehan, to keep quiet.

The subterfuge worked: Lidström was available when the Wings' turn, at 53rd, came up in the third round, and a fervent sales pitch by Smith and Rockström led Devellano to draft Lidström.

It's almost indescribable the impact he had on the franchise. Lidström was a foundational piece for the second dynasty, an anchor on the defense for two decades. No player was more dependable, more superb, more perfect. In 20 seasons Lidström missed just 42 games, and a dozen of those were in his last year, 2011–12. The Wings never missed the playoffs while Lidström was on the team.

"From the minute he played his first NHL game, he looked totally comfortable," Steve Yzerman said on the occasion of Lidström's induction into the Hockey Hall of Fame in 2015. "I never saw him get rattled. He never had a bad day at the office, never reacted or acted inappropriately on or off the ice. He was the most low-maintenance player I have ever seen." As general manager, Yzerman would go on to hire Lidström, naming him vice president of hockey operations. Yzerman joked at the news conference announcing the hire that Lidström would "have to earn" being called the perfect vice president.

By 1993 the bias against non–North American players had abated enough that the Wings drafted a Swedish defenseman named Anders Eriksson with their first-round pick, at 22nd. His biggest contribution to the franchise was to be included in the package the Wings sent to the Chicago Blackhawks in 1999 in order to trade for defenseman Chris Chelios. In terms of massive return on minimal gamble, Tomas Holmström holds a special place in Wings history. Hailing from so far north in Sweden teammates would ask him to pass on their Christmas list to Santa Claus directly, Holmström turned being drafted in the 10th round, at 257th, into a career topping 1,000 NHL games and four Stanley Cups. He and Lidström became close friends, and their innate understanding of one another extended to the ice, where Lidström knew he could aim a shot at the net and Holmström would be there to tip the puck or get the rebound. Holmström wasn't a great skater—the joke was he was the only player to come out of Sweden who couldn't skate, but Holmström amended for that deficiency with willpower. Scotty Bowman made a joke early in Holmström's career, when he switched numbers from 15 to 96, that he should have picked 98 for the year he would be going back to Sweden, but there was no greater endorsement of Holmström's value than the fact once Bowman realized what Holmström could do, Bowman wanted him the lineup.

Five years after drafting Holmström in the 10th round, the Wings once again looked to Sweden when they made their pick in the seventh round in 1999. Like Holmström, Henrik Zetterberg emerged from the later rounds to reach 1,000 games. Zetterberg became such an integral part of the Wings that when Lidström retired in 2012, Zetterberg was the obvious choice to take over the captaincy.

It was a good couple of years for the Wings' mining of Sweden at that time, as the 2000 draft brought Niklas Kronwall into the fold. Even as an undersized teenager he displayed a knack for upending bigger opponents, sizing them up on open ice and delivering a blow that would send them crumbling. The hits even begat their own nickname: Kronwall-ed. Part of what made the phenomenon so popular was that in person, Kronwall was 6'0" and 190 pounds, hardly physically imposing—and personality-wise, he was as thoughtful and polite as they come.

Kronwall played a hard style of hockey, and he endured a slew of injuries as a result: a broken leg in 2004, a torn knee in 2005, a fractured sacrum that sidelined him the entire 2007 playoffs. By 2017 his left knee was in such pain he underwent stem cell therapy.

The 2002 draft yielded Jonathan Ericsson in the ninth round; at 291, he was the last player chosen. The Wings squeezed 680 games out of the 6'4" defenseman; he did not qualify under NHL rules to have his name engraved on the 2008 Cup, but the Wings awarded him a Stanley Cup ring for being a part of the team.

Two years later the Wings didn't make their first pick until the third round, but Johan Franzén was the only one of the eight players the Wings selected in the 2004 draft who made it to the NHL. A chance skate-by in a practice bestowed him with a nickname he begrudgingly came to like: Steve Yzerman skated next to the 6'3", 220-pound forward one day during a practice in Los Angeles and said he was like a mule; the moniker stuck. "The Mule" was a beast, a strong skater whose sheer size frustrated opponents trying to strip him of the puck. He had a stretch in the late aughts where he was one of the Wings' best players. On March 30, 2008, he scored his sixth game-winning goal of the month, eclipsing Gordie Howe's record of five. Howe was at the game against Nashville at Joe Louis Arena, on what was his 80th birthday. Less than a month later, on April 26, in Game 2 of the second-round series against the Colorado Avalanche, Franzén recorded his first hat trick. He came through with another in Game 4 to reach nine goals in the series eclipsing Howe's record of eight goals in one playoff series, set over seven games against Montreal in 1949.

Franzén also set a franchise record with 11 playoff goals in one year.

His time with the Wings has a sad coda. Repeated blows to his head cut short his career at 602 games and left him dealing with post-concussion syndrome. He was limited to 33 games in 2014–15 after a blindside hit in a January game against Edmonton, missing the rest of the season. Franzén valiantly attempted a comeback, but two games into 2015–16, he was placed on long-term injury reserve. When he was around the team in the playoffs, he spoke of the heartbreak he was dealing with off the ice, when persistent, overwhelming headaches prevented him from playing with his two young sons.

Gustav Nyquist was another superb pick out of Sweden, drafted in the fourth round, at 121st, in 2008. He played 481 games for them, but with the team in decline and in need of draft picks, he was traded for future assets at the 2019 deadline.

It was shortly after that trade that Yzerman was named general manager. He looked to Sweden in making his first pick in the 2020 draft, selecting forward Lucas Raymond at fourth overall. A year later, Yzerman chose another Swede in the first round, drafting defenseman Simon Edvinsson at sixth overall.

The Wings were seven Swedes strong when they won the Cup in 2008: Lidström, Kronwall, and Andreas Lilja on defense; Holmström, Franzén, Mikael Samuelsson, and Zetterberg among the forwards.

From the franchise's inception in Detroit in 1926 to 2023, 36 Swedes had skated in a Wings uniform, some for a handful of games, three for more than a thousand. In comparison, only 17 Russians had appeared wearing the winged wheel in that same time period. The Wings have had incredible success mining Sweden, finding players who helped turn the franchise into a Stanley Cup champion.

PART 7

THE BRAIN TRUST

21

Jack Adams

JACK ADAMS' LEGACY WITH THE RED WINGS IS THAT OF builder and destroyer, of supporter and underminer, of champion and chump. He worked for the franchise for 35 years, from its second year in Detroit when it was known as the Cougars though a reign of seven Stanley Cups. From 1927 to 1962, he served as coach and then general manager. It was NHL president Frank Calder who suggested Adams to the men in charge of the Cougars, who were looking for someone to come in and run their fledging hockey team. When James E. Norris bought the club in 1932, he kept Adams—but never on a contract; year by year, the two shook hands that Adams would remain.

Calder's recommendation was well warranted: John James Adams, born June 14, 1894, in Fort William, Ontario, turned his love of hockey into a successful career as player. In 1918 he won the Stanley Cup with the Toronto Arenas, although he did not play in the Final. He was drafted into the Canadian military but, with the war ending, was discharged the same year. In 1919, he joined the Vancouver Millionaires and played in the same league as the Victoria Cougars, who would become the foundation of the Red Wings after the dissolution in 1926 of what was then known as the Western Hockey League. Adams, a hard-nosed 5'9", 175 pounds in his prime, starred in the 1922 Stanley Cup Final, scoring a hat trick in the first game and finishing the series with six goals in five games, though the Millionaires lost to the Toronto St. Patricks. The following season Adams returned to Toronto and joined the St. Patricks team, playing on a line with Babe Dye, who had scored nine goals in the '22 Final. Adams had four good seasons with the St. Patricks, twice scoring 21 goals. He finished his playing career with the Ottawa Senators, where he won his second Stanley Cup as a player in 1927, a few months shy of his 33rd birthday.

In 1927 Art Duncan, who had been player, coach, and general manager of the Detroit franchise, was traded to Toronto and replaced by Adams. The team was germinated by players who had won the Stanley Cup in 1925, but the Cougars that were winners in Victoria, British Columbia, were losers in Detroit. They didn't qualify for the playoffs the first two years, lost in the quarterfinals in 1929, failed to qualify again in 1930 and '31, and lost in the quarterfinals in '32. When Norris took over, he used his wealth to improve the team, and the newly christened Wings won their first playoff series on March 28, 1933. Hooley Smith scored twice for the Montreal Maroons, but Herbie Lewis, Ebbie Goodfellow, and John Gallagher each scored their first playoff goals to give fans at Olympia Stadium a 3–2 victory to celebrate.

Adams, who had won the Stanley Cup as a player in 1918 and 1927, won his first as a coach in 1936. Detroit finished first in the American Division. That was the year the Wings set a record for longest overtime game in Stanley Cup playoff history at 176 minutes and 30 seconds. Mud Bruneteau scored at 16:30 in the sixth overtime period, giving the Red Wings a 1–0 win and a 1–0 series lead. (It was also the record for longest ice hockey game ever played, broken March 12, 2017, when Storhamar defeated Sparta Warriors 2–1 in an eight-overtime game in Norway. Joakim Jensen finally ended the marathon with a goal with 2:46 remaining in the 11th period. It featured 217 minutes and 14 seconds of play.)

The Wings would eventually sweep Montreal in three games en route to winning the Stanley Cup. Though the Great Depression's hold affected every avenue of life, the Wings provided a rare bright spot. With Vezina Trophy winner Normie Smith in goal in 1936–37, they again finished first in the American Division. They beat the Canadiens three games to two in the semifinals and finished the Stanley Cup Final against the New York Rangers with back-to-back shutouts to repeat as Stanley Cup champions.

The following season was a forgettable one, as an arm injury hampered Smith, and the Wings ended up finishing in last place in their division, missing the playoffs. They returned to the playoffs in 1939 and in 1941 began a stretch where they made the Stanley Cup Final three straight years.

The 1942 Final is infamous in NHL lore for two reasons. One, it is trotted out whenever a team loses the first three games of a playoff series and a historical perspective is provided on how rare it is to overcome such a deficit. The Wings had a three-games-to-none lead—but four games later, it was the Toronto Maple Leafs who claimed the Cup. As of 2023, the feat had never been duplicated in a Stanley Cup Final.

The second reason directly involved Adams. Bruneteau—the hero from the '36 overtime game—and Sid Abel scored by midway through the second period to give the Wings a lead, but the Leafs made it 2–2 going into the third period. Carl Liscombe scored early in the third, set up by Gordie Howe and Bruneteau, but Syl Apps replied for the Leafs two minutes later. Nick Metz scored with about seven minutes to play. The final minute was chaotic: Detroit's Eddie Wares was assessed a misconduct penalty and refused to leave the ice. Referee Mel Harwood signaled for a faceoff and dropped the puck while Wares was still on the ice, leading to a too-many-men call against the Wings. When the game ended, Adams berated Harwood and finished the tirade by punching the referee in the face. NHL President Frank Calder—the man who had recommended Adams for the Detroit job back in 1927—suspended Adams indefinitely. Goodfellow coached the next game, which the Leafs won 9–3. The Wings only scored one more goal for the rest of the series.

The 1942–43 season—the first of the "Original Six" era—saw the Wings finish first in the regular season and avenge the '42 Final by ousting the Leafs in the semifinals, which, with only four teams making the playoffs, was also the first round. The Wings swept the Boston Bruins in the Final, giving Adams his fifth Cup.

When he retired as coach in 1947, Adams had a record of 413 victories, 390 losses, and 161 ties, along with a 52–52–1 record in the playoffs. (The one playoff tie stemmed from 1932, when the Detroit Falcons—as the franchise was called from '30 to '32—played to a 1–1 final score with the Montreal Maroons in the first game of a quarterfinal series. Montreal won the round with a 2–0 shutout in the second game because the series was decided on total goals.)

Tommy Ivan succeeded Adams as coach, while Adams focused on maintaining an enviable farm team that would produce Gordie Howe, Ted Lindsay, Sid Abel, Terry Sawchuk, Red Kelly, and Alex Delvecchio. When the Wings won the Cup in 1950, Adams became the first person to win it as a player, coach, and general manager. During his time with the Wings, they won the Cup in 1936, '37, '43, '50, '53, '54, and '55.

As brilliant and demanding as he was, his dictatorial style tarnished what could have been a decade of Cup celebrations. It was Adams who announced to the Wings in December 1952 that their new president was Marguerite Norris, chosen by her father before his death to succeed him as president. Marguerite kept Adams on, but as had been the case under her father, held him accountable. But when Bruce Norris ousted his sister shortly after the 1955 championship, all restraint disappeared, and a dynasty was derailed.

Speaking decades later, Lindsay simultaneously complimented and criticized Adams.

"I owe a lot to Adams," Lindsay told the *Detroit Free Press'* George Puscas in 1994. "He was a great salesman for hockey. There wasn't a club breakfast or luncheon he'd skip if they'd allow him a chance to speak and sell the Wings. He was great at it. I owe my career to him; he gave me a chance. But the truth is, he wasn't much of a general manager. When we won the Stanley Cup in 1955, Jimmy Skinner was the coach, and Adams was the general manager. We needed only to boost up our defense to continue winning. Montreal wanted us to give up Terry Sawchuk. We had Glenn Hall as our reserve goalie. We could have gotten Doug Harvey from Montreal for our defense, and that would have kept us winning. But Adams didn't want to make Montreal stronger.

"If we had made that trade, I feel we would have won the Cup at least five more times. Instead, Montreal then won the Cup for the next five years."

Adams' reputation was tainted by the decisions he made in what would be his last decade with the franchise. He was known for his willingness to shake up team chemistry over the years, but what he did after the 1955 championship destroyed what could have been a dynasty for the decade. On April 14, the Wings won the Cup for the fourth time in six years. Gordie Howe, Red Kelly, Ted Lindsay, Marty Pavelich, Marcel Pronovost, and Johnny Wilson had been part of all four championships, and the overlap from '54 and '55 included Delvecchio, Glen Skov, Earl Reibel, Vic Stasiuk, Tony Leswick, Benny Woit, and Terry Sawchuk.

Six weeks later, Adams cleaved the roster. On May 27 he sent Leswick, Wilson, Skov, and Woit to Chicago. One week after that, on June 3, Adams sent Sawchuk, Stasiuk, Marcel Bonin, and Lorne Davis to Boston.

"We would have won at least three more Cups had those trades and others not been made," Lindsay told Bill Dow in 2005 for a story in the *Detroit Free Press*. "Our team had a winning personality and great chemistry. Not to knock the guys we got, but they didn't have Red Wings in their blood."

Of the nine players received in the transactions, only Warren Godfrey and Bucky Hollingworth were still around after the following season, and within three years, Sawchuk, Wilson, and Leswick were reacquired.

"When you send nine guys out of a hockey club, it doesn't matter who you get, the problem is you don't have the chemistry anymore," Wilson said. "Montreal and Toronto didn't destroy their teams. They were smart and maybe sent one or two guys out."

Pronovost, who appreciated how Adams treated him personally, also criticized the moves.

"It would have been different if the team was aging, but it wasn't," he said in 2005. "It seems Jack valued his hockey club on personalities rather than abilities, and he thought having won so often it was his influence that won the hockey games. But he wasn't the one putting on the skates."

Adams continued to treat what had been a championship roster like a chump. In 1957 he traded away Lindsay, in a petty move encouraged by owner Bruce Norris over Lindsay's attempts to organize a players' union.

In that same trade to the Black Hawks, Adams gave away Glenn Hall, who was the runner-up for the Vezina Trophy, which recognizes the league's best goaltender.

"It was pathetic how Adams destroyed that team," Lindsay said in 1994. "Of course there was an uproar about it. But Adams generally was respected for what he had done for the Wings in other years—and then, he thought he was God anyway and could do no wrong."

In April 1962 Adams was finally shown the door after nearly four decades with the franchise. In 1974—six years after Adams passed away at age 73—the NHL introduced the Jack Adams Award, given annually to the most outstanding coach in the league.

Adams could be a despot, and his wheeling and dealing of players earned him the sobriquet "Trader Jack." The greats of the organization—Howe, Lindsay, Kelly—excoriated Adams in later years for what he did to the roster following the '55 championship. But Adams had deep respect among his players, too—he knew what a special player he had in Howe and looked out for him, and before he turned on Lindsay for his union-organizing efforts, Adams played a key role in

Lindsay's development. That Adams cared about the Wings was undoubtable. They won seven Stanley Cups under his guidance and became ingrained in the fabric of Detroit.

"I will say this about Jack Adams," Pronovost said in 2005, "you have to give him credit as the person who promoted and established hockey in Detroit and Michigan."

22

Jimmy Devellano

THE BEST HIRE MIKE ILITCH EVER MADE WAS HIS SECOND choice to take charge of his beloved new hockey club. Jimmy Devellano drafted Steve Yzerman and Nicklas Lidström, drafted the Bruise Brothers, drafted the guy who was the catalyst for the Russian Five, and steered Ilitch to bring the best coach in hockey to Detroit.

Jack Adams set a golden standard for general managers in Detroit, running the Wings for 35 years and winning the Stanley Cup seven times. But he operated in the Original Six era, at a time before the draft, before the salary cap, before the National Hockey League doubled in franchises from six to 12 and onward past 20.

Devellano, known in hockey circles as Jimmy D, was named general manager in July 1982. He had impressed Mike and Marian Ilitch in interviews, speaking to them at length about the importance of drafting well. Devellano had an attractive résumé, having worked his way up from scouting to assistant general manager with the New York Islanders beginning in 1972. His appeal to a team in as bad a shape as the Wings were then was crystalline: the Islanders won 12 games in 1972–73 (their inaugural season) and two years later they won 33 and made the playoffs, going all the way to the semifinals. In 1980 they won the first of four straight Stanley Cups, and those Cups were won on the backs of the players Devellano had been key in drafting: Bryan Trottier, Mike Bossy, Denis Potvin, and Clark Gillies.

What Devellano had done with the Islanders was exactly what the Wings needed to reignite the team and its fan base. They didn't have the excuse of being a team that had just been founded—it was so much worse: they were an Original Six franchise that had missed the playoffs 14 of the last 16 years, and Devellano was their fourth general manager in 10 years.

"I'm going to surround myself with a lot of competent people," Ilitch said when he became owner. "I'm not going to interfere in the hockey area because I'm not qualified."

The list of managers between Adams, who was ousted in 1962, and Devellano's arrival 20 years later ran from Sid Abel to Ned Harkness to Alex Delvecchio, a second stint for Ted Lindsay, and Jimmy Skinner. Abel and Lindsay were Production Line legends, but their skills on the ice did not transfer to the front office.

Bruce Norris' parting gift to Ilitch, whose purchase of the team was finalized right around the time of the 1982 draft, was that the Wings didn't pick until 17th despite finishing 20th because of a trade made by Skinner. That came the year after the Wings didn't have a first-round pick at all in 1981.

Skinner was at the news conference when Ilitch introduced himself as the team's new owner on June 3, 1982. Skinner had worked for the Wings for 37 years, and while Ilitch okayed Skinner overseeing the selections at the draft, which was only a week away, it was going to be Skinner's last real duty with the team. He stuck around for a bit afterward in a self-described "consultant role" but knew his days shaping the roster were over. He told a reporter he didn't want to make any more deals because "it wouldn't have been fair to the new general manager."

Ilitch's first option to run his hockey team was Minnesota North Stars general manager Lou Nanne, but the team's owner, Gordon Gund, wouldn't give Ilitch permission to interview Nanne. Gund told Ilitch that the North Stars had Nanne "on a six-year deal," and that was that.

Had Ilitch brought in Nanne, the Wings' path would have been drastically, possibly devastatingly, different. Instead, Ilitch hired Devellano, then the 39-year-old assistant general manager of the Islanders. Devellano showed his savvy in his introductory news conference, when he distanced himself from how things had been running under Norris.

"They worked on a 'try to do it this year' basis," Devellano said. "Patch, patch, patch. We will build the Wings through the draft. I know of no other way. My hope is to build a winner. The challenge is very exciting. It's a chance to do something on my own and build a franchise. That's why I'm here."

Devellano's plan called for the Wings to make the playoffs his first season and becoming a bona fide Stanley Cup contender within four years.

That was a bold plan in July 1982. Devellano inherited a dismal, dejected squad devoid of the sort of star player who ignites a team and excites fans.

"I think what you have to tell the fans is you have a man who is committed to building this, not just into a good hockey club, but into a great hockey club," Devellano said. "I know they've suffered a long time, but I hate to say they may have to suffer some more. I'm sorry, but I think that's the best way to do it, to build a successful hockey club."

Devellano spent much of his first year scouting with multiple trips to the neighboring Canadian provinces Ottawa and Quebec. Devellano had a keen eye for Pat LaFontaine, a sublimely skilled teenager who hailed from Detroit's suburbs and was a superstar for the Verdun Juniors. A better pick could not have been scripted: he was a local, he was incredibly talented, and he was highly marketable.

LaFontaine was who Devellano saw as the guy who could come in and make the single biggest difference for the franchise.

The Wings were bad in 1982–83, but not so bad that they were headed for the worst record and with that, the first pick. Devellano had other prospects he really liked—Yzerman, Sylvain Turgeon—but neither of those guys were from the Detroit area.

Devellano would say years later that he felt a little guilty over how much he talked about LaFontaine in the lead-up to the 1983 draft because it gave the impression he was the only player that would revive the Wings. Devellano talked about LaFontaine to the media and to the Ilitches, and, sure enough, the day after the June 8 draft, the stories in the Detroit newspapers focused as much on how the Wings had just missed out on LaFontaine (who was selected at third overall by the New York Islanders) as the young player they had picked, the one whose last name briefly required a pronunciation guide.

It is funny how things turn out sometimes. Devellano hadn't been Ilitch's top choice, and Yzerman wasn't the Wings' top choice. Had Ilitch succeeded in hiring Nanne, the Wings might not have gotten Yzerman—Nanne, at least in his position of picking first for the North Stars at the '83 draft, selected forward Brian Lawton. (Nanne actually tried to make a deal with Devellano in the days before the draft, suggesting the two flip picks because Nanne wanted to draft goaltender Tom Barrasso. But back then teams didn't—and still rarely do—use the first overall pick on a goaltender. Michel Plasse was drafted first overall by the Montreal Canadiens in 1964, but in its early stages, the draft was little more than an afterthought. Devellano declined because he knew Nanne's reputation for getting the better out of a deal, and because Devellano had three players—LaFontaine, Yzerman, and Turgeon—rated equally skilled, if not equally marketable, and was confident one of them would be available at fourth overall.)

Yzerman was a transcendent selection, but the '83 draft class was rich in contribution. Devellano drafted Bob Probert in the third round, and Petr Klima and Joey Kocur in the fifth round. Stu Grimson played the majority of his NHL career with other teams, but it was the Wings who drafted him, in the 10th round. Probert and Kocur were fan favorites, so willing to fight they became known as the "Bruise Brothers." Klima's arrival in Detroit after defecting from communist Czechoslovakia drew international attention. He made magic with the puck—and with Probert, all sorts of problems off the ice—and helped bring fans to their feet. Devellano drafted Probert and Kocur for their size and toughness, so that the Wings wouldn't get pushed around anymore. Klima had been a standout at the World Junior Championship tournament, enough so to warrant chancing a pick on a player who was behind the Iron Curtain.

The 1983 class set the Wings up for a decade, bringing excitement back to the franchise and season tickets holders back to the box office. But it was the 1989 draft that elevated the Wings to champions. Devellano and his staff—chief amateur scout Neil Smith and Sweden-based scout Christer

Rockström, delivered the best draft class in the history of the NHL when they selected Nicklas Lidström in the third round, Sergei Fedorov in the fourth round, and Vladimir Konstantinov in the 11th round. Lidström would go on to be awarded the Norris Trophy as the NHL's best defenseman seven times. In 1994 Fedorov was awarded the Hart Trophy and Selke Trophy. Konstantinov was known as one of the toughest defensemen in the NHL before a limousine accident cut short his career in 1997. Fedorov was the catalyst for what became the Russian Five, with the drafting of Vyacheslav Kozlov in 1991, and later acquiring Igor Larionov and Slava Fetisov via trades. The quintet was crucial to the Wings' 1997 Stanley Cup championship.

That four-year plan was ambitious from the start, and the fourth year under Devellano, 1985–86, turned out to be a franchise low with the Wings finishing 17–57–6 in last place. Devellano was safe in his job because five of the first players he drafted—Yzerman, Lane Lambert, Probert, Kocur, and Klima—had fans believing that the franchise was on the right track. The Wings had 2,100 season ticket holders in 1982, and more than 10,000 four years later. That helped balance the sting of finishing last.

Devellano's plan was working, it just took longer than anyone in 1982 would have liked to predict. Devellano never wavered from the path he put the Wings on, having learned from a lifetime of hockey what led to success. He grew up in the Toronto area, coached a youth team when he was a teenager, and soon found scouting a source of immense satisfaction. Early in his career, he adopted signing his reports "Hockey Is Happiness."

The Wings were happier in the early 1990s than they had been in the early 1980s, but that Stanley Cup drought was dragging on for near four decades. When the 1992–93 season ended with a first-round loss to the Toronto Maple Leafs, the spotlight fell on coaching. The Wings had superstar forwards in Yzerman and Fedorov and a defense corps headlined by Lidström and Konstantinov. The one element missing was a star coach. Since buying the team and putting Devellano in charge, the Wings had generally had stability behind the bench other than that dreadful '85–86 season, when they cycled through Harry Neale and Brad Park. Polano, Jacques Demers, and Bryan Murray had served in the three-year range, but after the 1992–93 season ended with being eliminated in the first round by the Maple Leafs, the Wings sought to replace Murray.

Two of the biggest coaching names at the time were Scotty Bowman and Mike Keenan. Bowman had just won his sixth Stanley Cup with the Pittsburgh Penguins in 1992 after winning five with the Canadiens. Keenan's résumé didn't feature any Cups at that point, but he was 44 to Bowman's 60 and viewed as a fiery motivator.

Ilitch personally pursued Keenan, and during the 1993 Stanley Cup Final, Keenan dropped strong hints he could have had the job. But Devellano went to Ilitch and persuaded him instead to pursue either Bowman or Al Arbour, whose long tenure as coach of the Islanders included four Stanley Cups. (Arbour had also played for the Wings in the 1950s, appearing in 149 games between 1953–54 and 1957–58).

"There was talk that Mike Keenan was headed our way, and I went to Mr. I and really discouraged it," Devellano said in 2021. "I was asked, 'Well, what do you want me to do? I need a coach that can help us win in the playoffs.' My answer to Mike Ilitch was, 'Let's hire either Scotty Bowman or Al Arbour.'"

Ilitch told Devellano, "Go get one of them." Ilitch left it up to Devellano to decide which one it would be.

Bowman was known as a brilliant tactician, just the sort of man to appeal to a team that seemingly had all the star players needed to bring the Cup back to Detroit.

The Wings were upset in the first round by the upstart San Jose Sharks in 1994, but in 1995 they advanced to the Stanley Cup Final. What started out as a two-year contract for Bowman led to nine seasons behind the bench, and four championships.

Devellano remade the Wings through scouting, drafting, hiring—and trading. A July 1986 deal for Glen Hanlon was among his best ones. The crux of the exchange had the Wings sending Lane Lambert, the team's second-round pick from 1983, and Kelly Kisio to the New York Rangers for Hanlon, an experienced goaltender. Hanlon backstopped the Wings to the conference Finals in 1987 and 1988, stoking excitement that the team was closer to its goal of winning the Cup.

"That trade really worked out well for us," Devellano said in 2021. "Glen Hanlon was a solid goaltender for us, and with him in net, we went to the final four in back-to-back years."

Devellano had always loved scouting, but the stress of being expected "to win three games a week," as he put it in 1990, was affecting his health, and he was ready for someone else to serve as general manager. Devellano was named senior vice president on July 13, 1990, eight years after he was hired but returned to the general manager role from 1994 to 1997. In 1996 he and Bowman, who shared director of player personnel duties, engineered the trade that catapulted the Wings across the finish line. The Wings began the 1996–97 season still smarting from being pushed out of the playoffs the previous spring by the Colorado Avalanche, unable to withstand the eventual Cup champions toughness. When Brendan Shanahan—a 6'3", 220-pound power forward who could score and throw a punch—became available, the Wings did what was needed to bring him to Detroit.

"We were starting to look like a Stanley Cup team," Devellano said in 2010. "Keith Primeau wanted out of Detroit, so we traded him, Paul Coffey, and a first-round pick for Brendan Shanahan. And that was maybe as good a deal as we ever made."

Devellano has called a deal he made in March 1997 "the move of moves." The Wings, eyeing a Cup run, wanted to strengthen their defense corps. They took advantage of an untenable situation in Toronto, where Maple Leafs fans relentlessly booed veteran defenseman Larry Murphy. The Wings acquired Murphy for future considerations, which essentially ended up being nothing.

Devellano had designs on adding another veteran defenseman a few years later. Ray Bourque had spent his entire career with the Boston Bruins, but by the late 1990s, the team was struggling, and Bourque, nearing the end of his career, was ready to change uniforms to pursue a Stanley Cup, which had eluded him in Boston. But a feud between Ilitch and Bruins owner Jeremy Jacobs undermined Bourque ever putting on a Wings sweater. By then, Devellano's moves already had made the Wings Stanley Cup champions again.

Devellano was inducted into the Hockey Hall of Fame on November 8, 2010. The man who had never played pro hockey began his NHL career in 1967 with the St. Louis Blues, volunteering to scout for free from his hometown of Toronto. He was on their payroll within a year and hired by the New York Islanders four years later in 1972. Ten years later, Devellano was hired by Ilitch to take on what seemed a Herculean labor.

"I found that when I arrived in Detroit in '82, because the team was so poor the whole focus of the city was on me," Devellano said in 2010. "I was supposed to be savior. I said,

'There's something wrong with that. I don't play. I don't score goals.' But the focus was on me because we were so devoid of talent. Prior to Mike Ilitch buying the team, the franchise was in tough shape. They missed the playoffs 14 of 16 years. They had 2,100 season ticket holders. I really faced long odds."

Devellano told the Wings early on during his first season that they wouldn't see much of him around Joe Louis Arena because he needed to be out scouting. Devellano hired his young acolyte, Neil Smith, to help with the scouting and set up a scouting department overseas in Europe at a time European players were looked down upon for not being as tough as Canadians. His colleagues snickered in 1989 when Devellano drafted Fedorov in the fourth round, but Devellano knew his decision would mean the Wings would own the rights to one of the best young players in the world, even with the Iron Curtain in the way.

In July 2022 Devellano celebrated 40 years of working for the Wings under the Ilitches. When they hired him in 1982, he told them he would win them a championship in eight years. It took nearly double that, but it only took a year for Devellano to bring in the draft class that would bury the "Dead Wings" nickname bestowed during the horrendous 1970s. Devellano remade the Red Wings into champions on the strength of being able to find good players, through drafts and through trades. His parting thought at his Hall of Fame induction, at which point he had added four Cups with the Wings to the three Cups he had won with the Islanders, was this: "It's been a lot of fun."

23

Scotty Bowman

MIKE ILITCH INITIALLY WANTED SOMEBODY ELSE WHEN THE Red Wings needed a new coach in 1993, but once he fully realized Scotty Bowman's credentials, the pursuit was on.

After one meeting, Bowman was equally enamored and ready to move on from the Pittsburgh Penguins.

"I met Mike and Marian, and we just hit it off," Bowman said in a 2023 interview. "They were looking for an experienced coach and I had experience. They gave me a really good offer and I said, 'I may as well try it.' The core of the team was there—Nick Lidström was there, Sergei Fedorov was there, Vladimir Konstantinov was there, and Steve Yzerman was the captain. He had been there 10 years when I went there. It was a good challenge, but they had a lot of good players, too. Their team was very much in the mix, and I just felt a good vibe from the Ilitches."

When the Wings hired Bowman, he was chasing 1,000 victories as a head coach. He had made his name behind the bench, and that he said in 1993, "is where I feel most comfortable. I've had a lifetime of coaching."

Bowman came to coaching earlier than he had anticipated. Born September 18, 1933, in Verdun, near Montreal, he was a good player when a frightening incident altered his life. During a game on March 6, 1952, a player named Jean-Guy Talbot used his stick to club Bowman over the head, slicing open his scalp. (This was long before players wore helmets.)

"There were only 30 seconds left in the game," Bowman recalled in 1995. "I think about that sometimes. What if the game had been 30 seconds shorter?"

Bowman underwent surgery to repair a five-inch gash (contrary to popular lore, he did not have a metal plate inserted). He attempted a comeback, but headaches and blurry vision soon put an end to his playing career.

Bowman was training to be a paint salesman when his first coaching chance came along with the Junior Canadiens. Bowman got his first NHL head coaching job on November 22, 1967, with the St. Louis Blues. One of the players on the roster was Talbot, but Bowman bore no grudge against the man who ended his playing career. "He wrote me a long letter explaining it, pouring his heart out," Bowman said. "I figure he just started me on my career 15 years earlier than planned."

Bowman took over for Lynn Patrick, coaching the previously dismal Blues to the Stanley Cup Finals. He left St. Louis in 1971 and was hired to coach his hometown Canadiens. After a first-round exit in 1972, his first season, Bowman guided the Habs to the Stanley Cup in 1973—and again in '76, '77, '78, and '79. From there he moved on to spend seven seasons with the

Buffalo Sabres and two with the Pittsburgh Penguins, winning the Cup again in 1992.

By then, Bowman's antics as a coach were legendary: He would ask players for matches, even though he didn't smoke because then he could read the matchbook covers and see where they had been. He would give a stick to a fan waiting for autographs at team hotels and find out what time players were getting back to their rooms.

Bowman could frustrate players, he could infuriate them, but the ones he wanted on his teams were the ones he believed could win the Cup. Players understood that.

Bowman was a few months shy of 60 years old when the Wings hired him. The Ilitches had owned the team for a decade, during which Jimmy Devellano's drafting had resuscitated the franchise through shrewd drafting. A stellar roster was highlighted by Steve Yzerman and Sergei Fedorov up front and Nicklas Lidström and Vladimir Konstantinov on defense. But the Stanley Cup had proved elusive.

When the Wings followed up a second-round exit in 1992 with a first-round exit in 1993, Ilitch had had enough.

"I think it's time to win the Stanley Cup, and Scotty Bowman will give us our best opportunity," Ilitch said on June 15, 1993, the day Bowman was introduced as the team's new coach. "I thought it was time to go to somebody who [has the] know-how to win, who knows what it takes to win the Stanley Cup. Scotty Bowman knows how to win. It's as simple as that."

It ended up being as simple as that, ultimately. But Bowman initially wasn't Ilitch's top choice to replace Bryan Murray, who stepped down as coach and remained general manager soon after the seven-game loss to the Toronto Maple Leafs. Ilitch wanted Mike Keenan, who at 44 was considered the NHL's best young coach—but Bowman had six Stanley Cups and had been inducted into the Hockey Hall of Fame in 1991. Devellano persuaded Ilitch that either Bowman or Al Arbour—Devellano's former colleague with the New York Islanders—would be a better choice than Keenan, and Ilitch left it to Devellano to deliver one of them.

In Bowman, Devellano knew he was bringing in a coach with a reputation as a genius—a quirky genius, but a genius who won.

The Wings had cycled through five coaches during Ilitch's ownership: three years under Nick Polano, a season split between Harry Neale and Brad Park, four years with Jacques Demers, and three under Murray. In Bowman the Wings got a guy who they knew would not be intimidated by ownership, management, players, the media, or fans.

Ilitch was sold on Bowman after two lengthy, face-to-face meetings in which he came to know the man as well as the coach.

"Scotty Bowman has tremendous depth, not only in hockey but on a wide variety of topics," Ilitch said. "He can tell you stories and incidents…It's incredible how he can take you from one era to another. He could have been a good entrepreneur. He has a real broad vision on a number of subjects. He's got a lot of perception and range."

Bowman wasn't without a job when the Wings showed interest, but his tenure with the Pittsburgh Penguins—who he coached to the Cup in 1992—came to an end when the team's general manager, Craig Patrick, decided that Bowman could only stay on "as director of player development, but not as coach," Patrick said in May.

That decision worked out perfectly for the Wings, who craved Bowman's reputation for getting the most out of his players. He was demanding and indifferent to complaints. Ilitch admitted during the news conference introducing Bowman as coach that, "we've got to put more emphasis on winning. I've tiptoed a little bit. Maybe I should say what I've felt more often." Known for his generosity toward his players—in 1987 he doubled their $13,000 playoff shares—Ilitch signed Bowman to a two-year deal worth nearly $2 million that made Bowman the highest-paid coach in the NHL. Bowman welcomed the challenge that came with such a contract.

"I know what the parameters are of the job," he said. "The Red Wings are now right at the very top of the league. This team was very close, especially the last two seasons. The most important thing I can bring to a team is that I don't like to lose. I may be tolerable when I'm winning."

Bowman had won 834 regular-season games and another 137 in the playoffs when he arrived in Detroit.

Coaching in his native Montreal, he won his first Cup with the Canadiens in '73 and four straight times from '76 to '79. Ken Dryden, the goaltender on those teams, wrote a book called *The Game* in which he splendidly described Bowman's personality: "Scotty Bowman is not someone who is easy to like," Dryden wrote. "He has no coach's con about him. He does not slap backs, punch arms, or grab elbows. He doesn't search eyes, spew out ingratiating blarney, or disarm with faint, enervating praise. He is shy and not very friendly.

"Abrupt, straightforward, without flair or charm, he seems cold and abrasive, sometimes obnoxious, controversial, but never colorful. He is complex, confusing, misunderstood, unclear in every way but one: He is a brilliant coach, the best of his time. He starts each season with a goal—the Stanley Cup—and he has no other...A good season is the Stanley Cup; anything else is not."

Bowman's disregard for ruffling feathers was in evidence as soon as the season began. Bowman scratched Shawn Burr, a veteran of eight NHL seasons, from the lineup in favor of Russian rookie Vyacheslav Kozlov. Burr responded by requesting a trade. "I've heard he's a master of playing with players' minds," Burr said. "I just want to work hard and play. I don't need anybody to pull my strings. I'm not going to lose sleep every night wondering if I'm going to play. I'll do anything to help this team win, except sit and watch. That's where I draw the line. If he thinks that little of me that I shouldn't play, then maybe they should trade me."

(Players experienced the quirkiness, too. When Bowman wasn't satisfied with how quickly players came off the ice for line changes, he employed an old relic. "It's actually an old football horn but sounds like a duck call," Bowman said. "I played the bugle in the band and have some experience with this. My family is Scottish, and everyone plays the bagpipes. If this doesn't get their attention, my next move might be to get something that sounds like those pipes.")

The Wings lost seven of their first 10 games in Bowman's first season, but they righted themselves and surged all the way to the top of the Western Conference standings (clinched, no less, with a 9–0 victory over the Canadiens in the penultimate game of the season). That was nice, but bigger things were expected of the Wings as they took on the eighth-seeded San Jose Sharks. When the Wings lost Game 7 at home, Bowman was so upset, he left the bench as soon as the game ended.

It was Murray who paid the steepest price for the shocking upset: he was fired June 3 by Ilitch. Bowman—who carried an $850,000 salary—was given the general manager duties he craved without the title, promoted to director of player personnel three weeks after Murray was let go. "I have great confidence in Scotty that he will make the necessary personnel decisions and adjustments to help our team remain a Stanley Cup contender," Ilitch said.

Devellano—the man who engineered Bowman's hiring—would handle business operations, along with newly promoted assistant general manager Ken Holland.

"I'm going to spend 90 percent of my time coaching," Bowman said. "Things I will be doing as director of player personnel are things I would have been doing, anyway."

Bowman's coaching philosophy was simple: get the right players on the ice. Before he was fired, Murray said Bowman had presented a list of 11 players he wanted traded, released, or demoted. Their identities were not revealed, but one of the first changes Bowman made was to trade for goaltender Mike Vernon. It cost defenseman Steve Chiasson, who had been an All-Star in 1993. But as Bowman would prove, a seemingly high cost was no deterrent to get the right player.

A labor dispute delayed the start of Bowman's second season until January 1995, but when the Wings did get underway, they played so well they advanced to the Stanley Cup Final. In some ways, the outcome of the '95 playoffs was even tougher to process than the upset in '94. The New Jersey Devils swept the Final, leaving Bowman flummoxed.

"I was embarrassed, humiliated, really," he said. "I have coached a lot of teams in the Finals. I have lost and won games, even the first year I was in the league with the St. Louis Blues. This is a showcase series, the Finals...It's unacceptable. I've never been in this situation very much, fortunately."

Bowman had coached two seasons—the length of his original contract—and the sting of the Devils reverberated. Players like Burr and Ray Sheppard, who were scratched late in the series, publicly questioned Bowman's decisions.

The last time everyone was together as a team was to commemorate the season with a group picture and then dine at the home of Mike and Marian Ilitch. The owners were certain of one thing: they still had the right man behind the bench.

"We had a marvelous season," Mike Ilitch said June 27. "We won three rounds. There are 26 teams in the league. We beat out 24 other teams. We did a great job. I'd like to have Scotty back. He did a great job. He made some contributions to the organization up and above his coaching. He brought in some good players."

Bowman was a finalist for the Jack Adams Award (he lost to Marc Crawford but would win in 1996; he first won it in 1977).

In July, Bowman signed a three-year deal that offered him the flexibility, after the first year, to step back and serve only as director of player personnel.

Bowman had made a relatively low-key trade in April 1995 when he acquired veteran Russian defenseman Slava Fetisov from the Devils, just a few weeks before Fetisov's 37th birthday. That was billed as a depth move. The biggest move Bowman directed involving a Russian came in October 1995, when he acquired Igor Larionov for Sheppard. Bowman knew what he was doing: Larionov had played a key role in the Sharks' 1994 upset, was highly respected among his fellow Russian players, and added to the depth at another crucial position: center. That it cost a goal-scoring player in his prime was immaterial to Bowman.

"I'm only interested in the best players for the team," he said.

Three days after Larionov was acquired, Bowman and the Wings made history by fielding what would become known as the Russian Five, the first time in NHL history five Russians were on the ice at one time for one team. Bowman said that "it would be foolish not to try it."

The biggest deal Bowman was a part of during his time with the Wings came on the eve of the 1996–97 season. The Wings had a malcontent player in Keith Primeau, who didn't report to camp after requesting a trade. Conveniently for the Wings, at that same time Brendan Shanahan had asked the Hartford Whalers for a trade. A deal was struck on October 9, 1996, bringing Shanahan, an elite power forward, to Detroit.

The Wings hired Bowman for his coaching, but his role as director of player personnel enabled him to get the players he wanted to coach, like Shanahan, Larionov, Fetisov, Kirk Maltby, and Larry Murphy.

"We got a lot of good breaks on a lot of those deals," Bowman said in 2023. "The Leafs needed to cut salary and get rid of Larry Murphy. The Oilers didn't see Kirk Maltby staying in the organization. Slava, we got him for depth, and we didn't know what a difference he would make. Once we got going as a team, it just seemed we got some breaks on those moves."

Bowman coached his 1,000th regular-season career victory on February 8, 1997, almost exactly three years after coaching his 1,000th career overall victory on February 2, 1994. As was Bowman's habit, he kept a puck and a copy of the box score as a memento. "It's nice you don't have to think about it anymore," he said.

It took until Bowman's fourth season, but finally on June 7, 1997, the biggest reason the Wings hired him materialized: he coached the Wings to the Stanley Cup championship. His tenure had included a stunning first-round upset, two straight Presidents' trophies, a then-record 62-victory season, a 41–23 record in the playoffs while winning nine of 12 series, two trips to the Finals—and the franchise's first Stanley Cup since 1955.

"That was the year I skated with the Cup," Bowman said in 2023. "I had always wanted to do that, so I put on skates. That was something I really wanted to do."

He had been robbed of the chance to ever attempt to do so as a player by that blunt force trauma when he was a teenager, but there he was, nearly 64 years old, celebrating his seventh Stanley Cup championship.

Bowman was having too good of a time to stop coaching. Another Cup followed in 1998. That summer, he underwent angioplasty in July and a knee replacement in August, and still he wanted to keep coaching. He arrived in Detroit in the summer of 1993 and nine years and three Cups later, on the night the Wings won the 2002 Stanley Cup, Bowman finally let everyone know that "I'm done. That was my last game."

Fittingly for a champion, his last game was a celebration of hockey's ultimate prize.

Bowman stayed on in Detroit as a consultant until July 2008, adding what would be his 10th Stanley Cup championship that summer. (He had also won the Cup in a front-office role with the Penguins in 1991.) He left the Wings to join the Chicago Blackhawks, where Bowman's son, Stan Bowman, was general manager. Bowman was a member of their front office when the Blackhawks won the Cup in 2010, '13, and '15, bringing his total number of Stanley Cup rings to 14.

"Although I only went to Detroit for two years the first time, I ended up staying a long time," Bowman said in 2023. "I would never have left Detroit except my son got sick, and that's the only reason I went to Chicago. He was in a tough bind, so I decided to go and help him. But my time in Detroit was very special."

PART 8

RIVALRIES

24
Montreal Canadiens

IN THE 1980S IN DETROIT AND THE SURROUNDINGS SUBURBS, a wave of people took to gathering around their TV sets on Saturday evenings to watch hockey.

It was not the Red Wings they tuned in to see; it was the hockey of the legendary Canadiens. They were a byword for magic in the sport, the home of Maurice and Henri Richard, Jean Béliveau, "Boom Boom" Geoffrion, Gump Worsley, Ken Dryden, and Guy Lafleur.

Detroit's proximity to Windsor, Ontario, meant Montreal telecasts could be seen on local TV nearly every weekend. CBEFT-TV was founded to serve the French-speaking population in and around Windsor, and the fact that the telecasts were in French wasn't a drawback in Detroit. Fans appreciated seeing an Original Six team and one of the Wings' great rivals of yore. Hearing it in French just added to the Canadiens' mystique.

The 1985–86 season was a particularly miserable one for the Wings, who were so bad they set a franchise record with just 17 victories. But on February 8, a standing-room only crowd of 19,671 packed into Joe Louis Arena to watch a game between the Wings and the Habs. Mario Tremblay—who would go on to play a key role in a pivotal chapter in the Wings' rivalry with both Montreal and the Colorado Avalanche—fired a shot from the top of the right faceoff circle that hit the right post and bounced into the net; it was the winning goal in a 5–3 victory for the Habs.

The crowd was the largest to see a Wings-Canadiens game in their 60-year history. The capacity of the Joe at the time was 19,275.

The Wings finished at the bottom of the standings in 1985–86, while the Canadiens won the Stanley Cup for the 24th time in franchise history. But three decades earlier, it was the Wings who presented the biggest challenge to Les Glorieux, back when Gordie Howe, Ted Lindsay, Terry Sawchuk, Alex Delvecchio, Marcel Pronovost, Red Kelly, Marty Pavelich, Norm Ullman, Glen Skov, Bill Gadsby, and many more were the backbone of what was a wildly successful era in Wings history.

The franchises played one another for the first time on December 23, 1926. The Canadiens date their history to 1909, but Detroit's NHL franchise arrived in 1926, and was known as the Cougars until 1930, and the Falcons from 1930 to 1932, when the Red Wings sobriquet took hold. Their new arena wasn't finished when the club arrived, so for the first season, the Cougars played their "home" games at Border Cities Arena in Windsor. That December night, Howie Morenz scored the first goal in what was to become a long-running series, giving the Habs the lead. Johnny Sheppard tied the game in the second period. Russell Oatman's goal midway through the third period put the Cougars ahead, but Sylvio Mantha tied the game to force overtime. Aurèle Joliat scored at 12:50 of overtime, settling the game at 3–2 in Montreal's favor.

The Canadiens beat the Cougars again in January (5–3) and February (4–1) and March (3–0). It wasn't until the following season, on November 27, 1927, before a home crowd at the newly opened Olympia Stadium, that the Cougars prevailed over the Canadiens with Percy Traub and Carson Cooper providing the goals in a 2–0 victory.

The franchises did not meet in the playoffs until 1937. Now known as the Wings, and in their 10th season under head coach Jack Adams, the Wings finished first in the American Division with a 25–14–9 record. The Canadiens finished 24–18–6 and took first place in the Canadian Division, setting up a semifinal versus the Wings. The teams split the first four games, each winning at home. Game 5 was back at Olympia, where Hec Kilrea scored at 11:49 of triple overtime to give the Wings a 2–1 victory. Herbie Lewis captained the Wings to their second consecutive Stanley Cup in a five-game series against the New York Rangers.

The Wings ousted the Canadiens in the quarterfinals in 1939 and 1942 and in the semifinals in 1949, winning the first four series between the Original Six teams. The Habs got their vengeance in 1951, when they ousted the Wings in the semifinals and foiled their chances of repeating as Cup champions. That marked the first of 10 consecutive Finals for the Habs, the only team to boast such an accomplishment even when the NHL only had six teams.

The 1950s heralded the heyday of the Wings–Canadiens rivalry. The rosters were stacked, and there was no greater individual rivalry than that between Howe and Maurice "Rocket" Richard. Howe was seven years younger than Richard, but the two players, both famous for wearing No. 9, were fierce competitors and often held up against one another as measuring sticks. Richard entered the NHL in 1942 and retired in 1960 as the league's leader in goals scored with 544. (Howe broke the record on November 10, 1963, in a game against the Canadiens at Olympia Stadium, where the 15,027 fans responded with a 20-minute standing ovation.) Richard spent all 18 seasons with the Canadiens.

Where Howe was a physically imposing 6'0", 205 pounds in his prime, Richard was 5'10" and 180 pounds of hotheaded toughness—and his temper triggered an ugly event that factored into the rivalry between Richard and Howe.

The two dueled for the league scoring title season after season, beginning in 1950–51. Howe obliterated Richard that season, recording 86 points in 70 games to Richard's 66 points in 65 games.

Howe won the race again in 1951–52 with 86 points, but injuries limited Richard to 48 games (and 44 points). He was back for the playoffs, but endured a scare that by today's standards render it remarkable that Richard played in the Final against the Wings. In the seventh game of the Canadiens' semifinal against the Bruins, Richard suffered a concussion and brief unconsciousness after he fell and struck Bill Quackenbush's knee. Though he was obviously woozy, in those days, it was common practice for players to be put back into games. Richard did indeed return—and scored the winning goal. It was the last point Richard recorded in the playoffs that spring, as he went scoreless in the four games it took the Wings to win the Cup.

The 1952–53 season saw Howe secure the scoring title with 95 points, 34 ahead of Richard's 61 points. (Lindsay was second with 71 points.) The Wings won the regular season title with 90 points, 15 ahead of the Canadiens.

It was a very good season for a number of individual Wings: Alex Delvecchio, Metro Prystai, and Red Kelly all finished in the top 10 in points. But as poised as the Wings looked to defend their Cup, it wasn't to be: the Bruins eliminated the Wings in six games, and it was the Canadiens who claimed the Stanley Cup.

The 1953–54 season was a return to form: Howe, again, won the scoring race, with 81 points, and Richard came in second with 67 points. Lindsay (62), Canadiens Bernie Geoffrion (54) and Bert Olmstead (52), and Kelly (49) and Dutch Reibel (48) rounded out the top seven spots in scoring, showing the dominance of the Wings and Canadiens.

The Wings claimed the regular season title for a sixth straight year, topping Montreal by seven points. The rivals met in a Stanley Cup Final that went seven games and featured two overtimes, including in the decisive match. Tony Leswick scored at 4:29 of the extra period on April 16, 1954, to bring the Cup back to Detroit.

Howe missed three weeks of play in November 1954 and finished the '54–55 season with 62 points, his lowest output in six years. The opportunity was there for Richard to take the scoring title, but one of the ugliest events in NHL history prevented that from happening. On March 16 NHL president Clarence Campbell suspended Richard for the remainder of the regular season (three games) and the playoffs for attacking a game official during the Canadiens' game at Boston on March 13. What came to be known as the "Richard Riot" took place at Montreal's next home game, which happened to be against the Wings, on March 17. Fans at and around the Forum rioted to the point the game was forfeited after the first period with the Wings ahead 4–1.

Richard had 74 points when he was suspended. In the penultimate game of the Canadiens' season, Geoffrion recorded a goal and two assists to reach 75 points. Fans at the Forum booed him when he surpassed Richard.

Richard never won the points race, finishing in second place five times.

Even without him, the Canadiens marched back to the Final, where the Wings awaited after having swept the Leafs in the semifinals. Through six games, the teams each won at home, setting up another Game 7. Howe scored his playoff-leading ninth goal in the game at Olympia Stadium, and Delvecchio scored twice as the Wings successfully defended the Stanley Cup with a 3–1 victory. Howe led all playoff scorers with 20 points, Lindsay was next with 19, and Delvecchio third with 15 points.

After winning the Stanley Cup for the fourth time in six years, the *Hockey News* predicted that "Detroit was plotting to imprison the Cup for all time."

It wasn't to be. The rivalry with Montreal should have outlasted the decade, but it was derailed by deceit and conceit.

When James E. Norris died in December 1952, control of the team was given to his daughter, Marguerite, as the old patriarch had decreed. She thrived in her brief role as the first female executive in the NHL, managing Jack Adams with an alacrity that belied his being 33 years her senior—and she being a woman in what was entirely a man's world. But Bruce Norris, the youngest son in the Norris family, conspired to oust his sister in the summer of 1955, and that put the Wings on a path from which they did not recover under Norris' ownership. Bruce Norris let Adams make petty, unfavorable trades that destroyed the Wings' dynasty—among the worst: Sawchuk in 1955, Lindsay in 1957—and with that came the demise of one of the great rivalries in old-time hockey.

When the franchises met in the 1956 Stanley Cup Final, the Wings only won one game. A quarterfinal matchup in 1958 ended with the Wings being swept. Roger Crozier's arrival in 1964 gave the Wings a boost, and they advanced to the Stanley Cup Final in 1966. Crozier won the first two games, but the Canadiens took the next four. Richard's brother, Henri Richard, scored 2:20 into overtime in Game 6 at Olympia Stadium, foiling the Wings' hopes of rallying before their home fans.

"It seemed so easy," 11-time Cup winner Henri Richard said in a 1993 Associated Press story. "We all thought we'd win forever."

From 1967 to 1977, the Wings only made the playoffs once. In 1978, with Lindsay as coach, they made the playoffs but lost in the quarterfinals to Montreal in a five-game series. It was the 12th playoff series meeting between the franchises, and with the loss, the Wings were down to a 7–5 advantage. Game 4 was the final playoff game at Olympia Stadium.

As the league expanded, and realignment led to the Wings playing in the western conference from 1981–82 to 2012–13, the rivalry between the Original Six franchises became more historic than habitual. It was a source of fond memories, but not fresh ones.

On December 4, 2007, the Canadiens celebrated the rivalry in a pregame ceremony at Montreal Forum. Gordie Howe was accompanied by Ted Lindsay, Alex Delvecchio, Marcel Pronovost, and Marcel Dionne. Jean Béliveau, Dickie Moore, and Jean-Guy Talbot were among those representing the Habs, who were two years away from celebrating their centennial. Richard had passed away in 2000, and Geoffrion in 2006.

The evening was also an opportunity for Canadiens fans to say goodbye to Chris Chelios, who at 45 years old was making his last appearance in the city where he began his NHL career a quarter century earlier. Booed throughout Canada for his brashness and American-ness, it was, of course, different with the Canadiens: 21,273 fans gave Chelios a roaring ovation.

It was a regular-season game between the franchises in 1995 that helped stoke the rivalry that raged during the Wings' second dynasty. Mario Tremblay—the former Canadiens player—was coaching the Habs. Scotty Bowman was then two years into coaching the Wings; earlier in his storied career, he had coached Tremblay, who still resented Bowman for threatening to send him to the minors. (This was a stock trick Bowman used: he was known for pushing players' buttons in an effort to maximize their potential.) When the Wings beat the Canadiens on November 28, *Le Journal de Montreal* ran the following headline: "Bowman has the last word.")

If only that had been the last word. On December 2, the teams met in Montreal.

It was the final season before the Habs moved from the Forum to their new arena, the Bell Centre, as the Wings had done in 1979 when they moved from Olympia Stadium to Joe Louis Arena. The old rinks that had been home to the heyday of the rivalry were becoming a memory, too.

That night in 1995 was one that went down in history. The Wings had the kind of puck luck that sometimes strikes teams, when nearly every touch of the puck turns into a celebration of a goal. One by one Patrick Roy let them in—five goals in the first period, another four in the second period. His own team's fans jeered when he managed to make a save. It was the middle of the second period before Tremblay finally came to his senses and relented, signaling for a change in goaltenders. (The Wings scored two more on backup Pat Jablonski, winning 11–1.) Furious over the humiliation, Roy stormed past Tremblay to where Canadiens president Ronald Corey sat just behind the bench and told him, "It's my last game in Montreal."

Roy's furor was understandable. Even the best players have off nights, and he should have been pulled when that became obvious. Had Tremblay done that, it would have defused the situation. Instead, Roy forced the Canadiens to trade him, and his arrival in Colorado precipitated the best rivalry in post-expansion hockey: the Red Wings and Colorado Avalanche. It was a fitting epitaph for the rivalry that had defined the Wings during the Original Six era.

25

Colorado Avalanche

THE NIGHT PATRICK ROY STORMED HIS OWN BENCH AND told his boss he was done in Montreal precipitated the best and bloodiest rivalry in hockey in the late 1990s and early aughts, but the Wings came to rue their role in Roy's inclusion.

"I wish we'd never lit him up that night and that he'd remained in Montreal," longtime franchise executive Jimmy Devellano said years later. The Wings scored nine goals on Roy in an 11–1 victory on December 2, 1995, dealing the Canadiens their worst home loss in franchise history.

When it became clear that Roy, furious over not being pulled earlier than the middle of the second period, meant it when he raged to Canadiens president Ronald Corey that "this was my last game here," the Canadiens suspended Roy and set about trading him. "After what happened, for the credibility of our organization, we had to split between our organization and

Patrick," general manager Réjean Houle said. "It was a point of no return."

It was a hot time for rumors, one of which had the Wings sending Steve Yzerman and Mike Vernon to Montreal for Roy. That was outrageous speculation, but Houle did reach out the day after the incident to hear if there was interest.

"He called us, but we had just gotten Mike Vernon two years earlier," Scotty Bowman said years later. "I didn't think I could make a deal with them. We knew he would go somewhere, but we were hoping it wasn't Colorado."

The Avalanche—who began play in Colorado in 1995–96 after being relocated and rechristened from the Quebec Nordiques—already loomed as the Wings' main competition in the Western Conference.

The Nordiques had struggled financially but their roster was one to envy, boasting Joe Sakic, Peter Forsberg, Valeri Kamensky, Adam Deadmarsh, and Adam Foote. By the time the Avs began play the group also included Claude Lemieux, whose nefarious style sparked the rivalry.

As if that amount of star power wasn't enough to threaten teams dreaming of hoisting the Cup, the Avs were then able to add a two-time Stanley Cup champion and a three-time Vezina Trophy winner in Roy.

Devellano said later that had the Wings realized how quickly Roy would be dealt—the trade happened four days after the incident—they would have acted differently. "We would have started a bidding war if we realized that. We were really upset he ended up in Colorado. That was bad for us."

It's funny how things work out sometimes: the guy who lit the fuse on the rivalry with a reckless and irredeemable hit, Lemieux, likewise began his NHL career with the Canadiens—after the Wings passed on him in the 1983 draft, taking Lane

Lambert at No. 25 while Lemieux went at No. 26. Lemieux won the Cup with the Canadiens in 1986 and was such a central part of the 1995 New Jersey Devils team that swept the Wings in the Stanley Cup Final that he was awarded the Conn Smythe Trophy. Lemieux was infamous for his dirty play: in a game between his Devils and the New York Rangers on October 14, 1992, referee Kerry Fraser overheard Lemieux urge teammates to slash Rangers star Mark Messier's wrists hard enough to break them. Fraser gave Lemieux a 10-minute misconduct penalty.

That December game against the Canadiens was during the season the Wings set a record for victories. That they had shortcomings, still, would be exposed in the playoffs, but for 82 games the Wings shone like a supernova, consuming opponents and gobbling points at an unheard-of rate. They only lost one out of 13 games that entire December, and that was in overtime.

The Wings finished 1995–96 having won 62 games, setting an NHL record for most victories in the regular season, and finished with 131 points, at the time second only to the 1976–77 Canadiens. (The marks were eclipsed by the 2022–23 Boston Bruins, who finished with 65 victories and 135 points.) When the Wings were a minute away from winning their final regular-season home game, in a 5–3 victory over the Chicago Blackhawks, fans at Joe Louis Arena chanted, "Sixty-one! Sixty-one!" and when the buzzer sounded, players leapt over the boards and into a huddle, celebrating. "It was a great minute to be out there with everyone chanting," Darren McCarty said after the Wings broke the NHL's single-season record. "It's something we'll cherish for tonight and then forget about it until a few months from now, when maybe we'll have something else to cherish."

But there would be nothing else to cherish, just a crushing finish to the playoffs. Advancing to the Western Conference Final, the Wings faced off against the Avalanche and suddenly looked vulnerable. The first game was close, with Mike Keane scoring in the first overtime to settle it at 3–2 for Colorado. In the second game, Roy embodied why the Wings came to regret that night in December when they lit him up: he made 35 saves in a 3–0 victory. The Wings righted themselves with a 6–4 victory in Game 3 but lost Game 4. They staved off elimination at home with a 5–2 victory—along with the goals, the highlight was Vladimir Konstantinov's crushing check on Lemieux— sending the series back to Denver.

Their dream of winning the Cup died in the mountains, toppled by an avalanche of goals and a shove into an abyss of pain. Late in the first period, Draper was sliding backward along the half-wall by the benches, having just played the puck. Lemieux blindsided Draper, sending him face first into the dasher and crumbling to the ice. Avalanche captain Joe Sakic almost tumbled backward over him but was able to pull himself up in time. When Draper finally got up, his face was buried in a towel. The maintenance crew shoveled up the bloody ice and tossed it into a bucket. Draper had to go to hospital, where the damage included a broken jaw and shattered cheek and orbital bone.

Lemieux got a five-minute major and a game misconduct. The Wings got one goal during the power play and lost the game 4–1. McCarty, who had spoken of wanting "something else to cherish" when the regular season ended, described the elimination loss as "getting your heart torn out."

It wasn't just being eliminated that hurt, it was seeing a teammate injured and Lemieux act like he had done nothing wrong. "None of the players are going to forget it," Chris

Osgood said. "When he comes back to play the Red Wings next year, we'll be waiting for him. And he'd better be ready. He can say what he wants about going to the Finals. We know we're not going. We can deal with our situation. He'd better be ready to deal with what he's going to have to face next season. It's not a threat. It's just something that's going to happen."

The league levied Lemieux a $1,000 fine and a two-game suspension, and he spent the time whining and wailing that the NHL was influenced by the Wings. "If that same situation occurred with a club from a smaller market with half the press, the NHL wouldn't have had to deal with it," Lemieux said. "There was tons of pressure from the Detroit area." A week later, Lemieux celebrated as the Avalanche swept the Florida Panthers.

While Lemieux drank from the Stanley Cup, Draper drank from a sippy cup. He endured 16 days of milkshakes and codeine. He endured a fractured jaw and broken nose and spent his summer vacation at the doctor's office. Three months after the hit, he sported a ¾-inch star beneath his right eye and wore a retainer in the hopes of avoiding the loss of a tooth. He had no feeling in three teeth, so even when the wires came off his jaw and he could eat solid food, it hurt.

When the schedule for the 1996–97 season was released, the first thing Draper looked for was when the Avs would be at Joe Louis Arena. It was November 13. "I'm looking forward to it," Draper said in mid-August. "It will be interesting to see if he has anything to say when he comes to town. He felt no remorse for what he did to me, and I'm not going to forget that."

But Lemieux wasn't there for that game because he was recovering from abdominal surgery. Instead, the Wings focused on using the game as a gauge for whether they were better than six months earlier, whether the addition of Brendan Shanahan made them tougher. (The quick answer that night: no. The Wings lost 4–1.)

All the better to delay gratification. When the Avs were back at the Joe on March 26, Lemieux couldn't hide behind a doctor's note. Deafening boos greeted him when he stepped onto the ice. Soon, the jeers turned to cheers.

It was a night that became a legend, a game that became lore. There were as many fights as there were goals, and there were 11 of the latter. The first happened just short of five minutes in, when Jamie Pushor and Colorado's Brent Severyn were each given five for fighting, despite not throwing any punches. Five minutes later Kirk Maltby and Colorado's René Corbet jostled, though their scuffle was ended by officials before anything really began.

Part of what made the melee that erupted late in the first period so special was the two instigators: Igor Larionov—at the time 36 years old and known as "The Professor" for his cerebral, thoughtful approach to hockey and life—and Peter Forsberg—a soft-spoken Swede who used his hands to score, not scuffle. The two collided, and as Larionov fell backward, Forsberg swatted at Larionov's head, prompting Larionov to throw his arm around Forsberg and put him in a headlock as they fell to the ice. It wasn't planned, but it was the perfect foil: while officials dealt with that (back then, there was one referee and two linesmen), McCarty took advantage and coldcocked Lemieux. Lemieux surrendered without a fight, folding to the ice like a turtle protecting its soft self. McCarty pounded, fans roared, and soon the ice was awash in tossed sticks and gloves. Roy left his crease, gathering in speed as he sought to defend his teammate. He was intercepted by Shanahan, who used a leaping bear hug to bring Roy to a halt. In turn, Foote intervened with Shanahan. Vernon, who had left his crease when he saw Roy leave his, grabbed Foote. It was a chain reaction of grab-and-engage, and while the rest of the players on the ice partnered off, McCarty was still going. He dragged Lemieux across the ice like a sack of potatoes, depositing the non-combatant villain in front of the Wings' bench, within feet of Draper. When officials finally were able to separate the two, it was Lemieux's turn to have blood pouring from his face, to need a towel to stop the gushing.

Officials didn't even deem it a fight when it came time to dole out penalties. It was so one-sided, it was more like a thrashing. The best give-and-go fight of the night took place between the two most disparately sized players: Vernon, 5'9" and 170 pounds and Roy, 6'2" and 192. They traded punches, four apiece, and each delivered one big blow. Vernon won the balance battle, winding up on top as the two tumbled to the ice with two officials on top of them. Fans loved it—and so did teammates. "I had a big smile on my face watching the goalies fighting," Maltby said afterward.

Vladimir Konstantinov and Deadmarsh fought 15 seconds after the officials had finished doling out penalties for all the infractions that took place at 18:22. (McCarty got away with just two roughing calls.) The list of undercards in the second period included Shanahan, Foote, Aaron Ward, Keane, Tomas Holmström, Severyn, Deadmarsh, Pushor, Uwe Krupp, and McCarty, again. It was like the joke about going to a fight and a hockey game breaks out: in between all the bouts, the teams managed to play enough to make it 4–3 in favor of the Avs.

"For the first two periods, the issue of winning the game seemed to be completely irrelevant," Yzerman said.

But to the Wings, it certainly wasn't. They didn't just want to punch their biggest rival, they wanted to show they could beat them. And they did both. In the third period, when the punches stopped and blood dried and two supremely talented teams focused on hockey, the Wings overcame what had grown to a 5–3 deficit and tied the game, and 39 seconds into overtime, won it. McCarty streaked down the left side, and Shanahan fed him a perfectly timed pass that McCarty whacked past Roy. This time, it was immensely gratifying to light him up.

"It's a great rivalry, isn't it," McCarty gushed afterward. "Everybody's involved now. Man, that was fun hockey."

Draper, his face still bearing faint scars from the hit 10 months earlier, beamed.

"Mac is such a team guy and he wanted to stick up for me," Draper said. "I consider us best friends and I was happy he did what he did for me. If that's closure, that's perfect."

McCarty had left Lemieux's face bloodied, just like Draper's had been 10 months earlier, but there was still the matter of avenging the playoff elimination. Like the year before, the Wings found something to cherish during the regular season— but they wanted so much more.

The Wings defeated the Blues and Anaheim Ducks to once again advance to the Western Conference Final; three days later, the Avalanche advanced to set up a rematch. (Marc Crawford, the Avalanche coach, had wished for it after the March 26 game: "That team has no heart," he said. "Everyone is gutless on that team. I'd love to see them in the playoffs.")

The Avs won the first game, but in the second game, the Wings rallied from a two-goal deficit to win 4–2, leaving Lemieux so frustrated he broke his stick on his own net. Two games later, the Wings led the series, three games to one. Game 4 was another highlight in the rivalry. The Wings had a 5–0 lead (they would win 6–0) in the third period when Crawford went berserk, climbing the glass partition to get to the well between the benches so that he could better scream at Bowman. Bowman—nearly three decades Crawford's senior—

put his young colleague in place with just a few words. "I knew your father before you did and I don't think he'd be too proud of what you're doing right now."

Bowman, ever the gamesman, told reporters afterward that "his eyes were coming out of his head. So, he was pretty excited." Poorer, too: the NHL fined Crawford $10,000 for his behavior.

There were eight fighting majors, 10 misconducts, three game misconducts, two instigating penalties, and one goalie interference among more than 200 penalty minutes—and that was just in the third period.

The Wings were on the short end of a 6–0 decision the next game, blowing their first chance to clinch but delivered the knockout blow in Game 6, winning 3–1. During the postgame handshake line, Draper refused to shake hands with Lemieux, who refused to shake hands with McCarty.

"Obviously there's a lot of bad blood between these two hockey clubs," Draper said afterward. "But you look the players in the eye, and they shake your hands and you shake their hands. Some guys that don't like you a lot wish you good luck. I was just going through the line, and I looked at him, and as soon as he saw me, he just kind of turned away and threw his hand out. So that's an indication for me just to skate by, and that's why I did it. It would have been nice if he had something to say. But obviously he didn't. He feels he doesn't have to do that. That's fine. I looked at him, he looked away and stuck his hand out. That's not sportsmanship. That's not up to me to go grab his hand. I didn't do anything wrong."

Lemieux chirped back: "That says it all, that says it all."

McCarty offered his hand to Lemieux in the spirit of sportsmanship only to see his efforts rejected.

"He didn't want to shake my hand," McCarty said. "I'm not going to worry about it. He's not real high on my priority list."

Players would talk later of how the March 26 game unified them, how it brought them together as a team. When Lemieux hurt one of them, he hurt all of them, and the fight night coupled with eliminating the Avs from the playoffs was immensely cathartic. It carried the Wings to the Final and carried them all the way to celebrating with the Cup.

Seeing Lemieux turtle, the Avalanche eliminated, and the Cup back in Detroit was like a three-month euphoria binge. Had that been it for the rivalry, it would have been talked about for years. But there were so many satisfying chapters to follow.

When the Avalanche played at the Joe on November 11, 1997, Lemieux lined up against McCarty on the opening faceoff. Lemieux threw a punch that landed on McCarty's chest, but it was such an uneven bout it fizzled before there was any real fight. Lemieux should have known better: brawls are for spring.

When the teams met at the Joe on April 1, 1998, Draper predicted it wouldn't rival the March 26 game, but then again, "on April Fool's Day, you never know what's going to happen."

As much as the rivalry centered on Draper and Lemieux and McCarty, it was the sheer talent of both squads that made the meetings so special.

"Anytime you play Colorado, you expect them to be at their best," Shanahan said the day before the match. "You can never underestimate that team. We never will. We were underestimated last year, and it worked out for our benefit in the playoffs. We kind of snuck up on them. So, from our experience of being in that position, we're not going to take anything for granted.

"It's the kind of game that helps both teams. Usually, the style in which both teams play is a preview to the playoff style.

It's a chance for an intense style of hockey that sometimes in the course of a long season you get away from. No matter when it is during the year, we always seem to play each other intensely. Especially a couple of weeks before the playoffs, I think it's a pretty good preview."

Martin Lapointe was succinct: "If a crazy game goes on, that's just the way it goes. You never know what can happen out there."

It wasn't as crazy as March 26, but it was close: a six-on-six brawl broke out, each team went over 100 penalty minutes, and most importantly, the Wings won, again. It was Sergei Fedorov's handiwork with the puck that led to both goals in a 2–0 victory, but it was the fisticuffs of Osgood and Roy that kept fans on their feet. Near the midpoint of the third period, Roy dropped his gloves and challenged Osgood to a fight at center ice.

"I don't think Ozzy wanted to do it," McCarty said, "but he saw there was no other choice."

When the skirmish concluded, Roy again found himself on the bottom of the pile.

"I think he underestimated Ozzy," Draper said. "He didn't think Ozzy was going to come out, but he wasn't running away. It was good to see."

Gleeful chants greeted Osgood when he rose from the pileup, descending from the stands as teammates cheered from the bench.

"Not too bad for somebody who's never fought before," McCarty said. He had a ringside seat for this melee, stuck on the bench as chaos descended.

Fans loved it, and players loved the two points.

"I don't think there was anything premeditated about what happened," Yzerman said. "That's just what's going to happen when you've got two teams that always play hard against each other. But I certainly don't think what happened was a big shock."

The Avalanche were eliminated in the first round, robbing fans of a rematch. The Wings cruised all the way to a second Stanley Cup without having to face their toughest rival.

The Avalanche gained the upper hand in 1999 and 2000, eliminating the Wings both years in second-round series. In November of 1999, Lemieux was traded to the Devils, removing the central villain from the rivalry.

Dominik Hašek attempted to follow the tradition started by Vernon and continued by Osgood by fighting Roy when the Avs were at the Joe on March 23, 2002, but he never even got started. Hašek left his crease and skated up ice only to trip over Roy's discarded stick. Both goaltenders were in their mid-30s by then, and it was probably for the best they didn't tangle. Hašek won the duel when the two met in the playoffs that spring, especially late in the Western Conference Final when the Avalanche had taken a three-games-to-two lead. Hašek delivered a 24-save shutout, eight of his stops coming during Colorado power plays, as the Wings staved off elimination with a 2–0 victory and forced a Game 7 back on home ice.

"We have no doubts about our goaltender," Yzerman said after the game. "None."

It was Roy who looked doubtable. In the first period, Yzerman fired a close-range shot that Roy appeared to stop. He rose up and opened his glove only to find it empty; beneath him the puck was sliding toward the goal line. Before Roy could get to it, Shanahan poked it into the net, and the Wings, for the first time in the series, had the first goal. "I'd have to hang up my skates if I missed that one," Shanahan quipped afterward.

On May 31, 2002, the Wings once again lit up Roy. Detroit's first shot was a goal. So was the second. And the fifth. That was just halfway through the first period. This night Roy ended up playing 26 minutes and 28 seconds before being pulled; it was 6–0 when he shuffled to the bench.

In 2008 the Wings swept the Avalanche in Round 2 en route to another Stanley Cup championship. The rivalry had died down by then—most of the principal participants had been traded or had retired—but in their heyday, the Wings and Avalanche enraptured the hockey world. Lemieux was the linchpin who lit the fuse, but it was Roy who stoked the flames as two highly talented squads feuded and fought and found fame.

26

Toronto Maple Leafs

DETROIT'S AND TORONTO'S NHL FRANCHISES HAVE A RIVALRY that dates back to 1927, when the teams known as the Detroit Cougars and Toronto St. Patricks played one another at the Border Cities arena in Windsor, Ontario, which was Detroit's home before Olympia Stadium was finished. Johnny Sheppard scored in the first period, but Hap Day scored twice in the second period to give Toronto a 2–1 lead that would hold up as the final score. The teams met for the first time in the playoffs in 1929, which Toronto, by then renamed the Maple Leafs, won in two games by outscoring the Cougars by a combined seven to two.

Detroit's fortunes changed when the franchise was bought in 1932 by grain merchant James E. Norris, who renamed the team the Red Wings. The rivalry with the Maple Leafs grew stronger, and in 1936, the Wings won their first Stanley Cup by besting the Maple Leafs three games to one.

One of the most spirited playoff games in the history of the rivalry happened March 28, 1940, when the teams met in the Stanley Cup semifinals. The Leafs had won the first game 2–1 at Maple Leaf Gardens. The second game was at Olympia Stadium—but it was more of a bout than a game. The next day the *Detroit Free Press* ran a grainy picture of one of the brawls that erupted, captioning it, "Picture of a Hockey Team Going Down Fighting." The description explained what had happened: "There was some hockey for the capacity crowd to watch— enough to eliminate the Red Wings from further Stanley Cup competition for the season—but it was just sandwiched between fights and more fights. Counts of the number of separate brawls was lost but none among the members of the Wings and Maple Leafs was without his own individual little difficulty before the evening had drawn to a glorious finish."

The trouble began when Maple Leafs defenseman Rudolph Kampman injured Wings forward Cecil Dillon, leaving him unable to finish the game. That was in the first period. In the second period, Toronto defenseman Red Horner and Detroit defenseman Alex Motter fought one another so bitterly their brawl segued from the ice to the penalty box and into the arms of the police, who were called in when the players ignored game officials. Later in the period, Wings forward Don Grosso picked up Leafs forward Hank Goldup and tossed him over the boards, onto the cement floor. Goldup had to be helped off. In the third period, left wing Syd Howe had just scored to cut Toronto's lead to 3–1 when he and Gus Marker began a fight that ignited the all-out brawl captured in the photograph. The brawl lasted for around 10 minutes. The Wings lost the game, and as a fitting coda, Wings coach Jack Adams threw the last punch of the night to ward off a fan attempting to accost him.

The 1940 series marked the first of seven times the franchises met in the playoffs in the 1940s. Unfortunately for the Wings, they were generally on the losing end: in 1942 in the Stanley Cup Finals, again in 1945 in the Finals, in the semis in 1947, the Finals in 1948 and 1949. The one series the Wings won was in 1943, when they took a six-game series in the semifinals over the Leafs (en route to beating the Bruins to win the Stanley Cup). The '42 Finals is brought to light whenever a team loses the first three games of the Stanley Cup Finals because the Leafs escaped from that seeming chokehold to win the series four games to three. It was also the first Cup Final in history that went to seven games.

The fourth game was at Olympia Stadium, giving the Wings a chance to celebrate on home ice. Instead, the game ended in a riot, when Wings forward Eddie Wares argued so vociferously against a penalty call that he was fined $50 by referee Mel Harwood. Harwood then signaled for a faceoff and dropped the puck with Wares still on the ice, resulting in a too-many-men call on the Wings. After the game was over, with Toronto winning 4–3, Adams punched Harwood in the face. NHL president Frank Calder suspended Adams indefinitely. Ebbie Goodfellow, a future Hall of Famer who played center and defense in his 14-season NHL career, took over coaching duties.

Two years later, it was the Wings who lost the first three games of the Stanley Cup Finals. They staved off elimination with a 5–3 victory at Maple Leaf Gardens and built momentum with a 2–0 victory in Game 5 back at Olympia. Mud Bruneteau, who wrote his name into NHL history books in 1936 when he ended the longest game in NHL playoff history, scoring at 16:30 of the sixth overtime of the first game of the series between Detroit and Montreal, added to his playoff overtime heroics on April 21, 1945, when he scored in overtime to give the Wings a 1–0 win and push the series against the Leafs to a seventh game.

The rivalry moved into the 1950s with a headline incident. Gordie Howe, the Wings' young star, mistimed a check on Toronto's Ted Kennedy and instead crashed head-first into the boards, causing an injury so severe Howe had to undergo emergency surgery to relieve pressure on his brain. The Wings won the series four games to three but had to deal with Toronto fans in the Finals because the Ringling Bros. and Barnum and Bailey Circus were using Madison Square Garden during the two dates that were scheduled for games two and three. The Rangers opted to instead use Maple Leafs Gardens, knowing Leafs fans would jeer the Wings.

The semfinals in 1956 between the Wings and Leafs prompted one of the more famous hockey photos of the decade. An anonymous caller to a Toronto newspaper threatened to shoot Howe and Ted Lindsay during Game 3 at the Gardens. After Howe and Lindsay combined for three goals to shoot down the Leafs 5–4, Lindsay flipped his stick to mimic a rifle as he pointed it the crowd, skating a lap while making machine gun noises.

The 1950s were an era of great success for the Wings, sweetened by taking out the rival Leafs on multiple occasions. The Wings swept Toronto in the 1952 and '55 semifinals, and they beat them in five games in the 1954 and '56 semifinals.

The rivalry cooled as the Wings went into decline following Bruce Norris becoming sole owner in 1955.

It was five years after Mike Ilitch had bought the team that the rivalry took on renewed meaning. Ilitch stoked excitement with his own fervor, and fans responded to seeing the time and money he invested in turning around the franchise. Still, the 1985–86 season was miserable with the team winning just 17 games. One of the nadirs was a game against the Toronto Maple Leafs on January 13, 1986, when a brawl erupted in the third period that lasted nearly 20 minutes and resulted in 171 penalty minutes. The Leafs won the game 7–4.

A year later, in 1987, under new head coach Jacques Demers, the Wings and Leafs met for the first time in the playoffs since 1964. The Leafs won the first two games of the second-round series by a combined score of 11–4 at Joe Louis Arena. The Wings won Game 3 but were pushed to the brink of elimination when Toronto's Mike Allison scored midway through the first overtime in Game 4. The Wings rallied to win Game 5 at home and pulled off a victory again the next game at the Gardens. On May 3 Steve Yzerman, who had been named captain at the start of the season, was among the scorers as the Wings capped the comeback with a 3–0 victory in Game 7, sending them on to the conference Finals. Afterward, a reporter asked Yzerman how far the Wings were from their lowest point the previous season.

"Last year seems like centuries ago," Yzerman said. "It feels good to be a Detroit Red Wing right now."

Centuries apart from the previous season, a millennium from the previous ownership. Seeing the Wings come back and beat the Leafs against seemingly insurmountable odds strengthened belief among fans that what Ilitch and general manager Jimmy Devellano were doing the right things to restore the Wings to championship glory.

Six years later, the teams met in the playoffs for the 23rd time in the history of the rivalry. The outcome would have a transformative effect on the Wings.

The 1992–93 regular season was a successful one for the Wings, who finished first in the league in goals scored (369) and had five players who reached the 30-goal plateau. They finished second in the Norris Division, setting up a first-round series with the Leafs. It was 2–2 after four games, with each side holding down home ice. The Leafs won in overtime in Game 5, but the Wings went into Toronto for Game 6 and emerged with a 7–3 victory. Game 7 was back at Joe Louis Arena. It was 3–3 at the end of regulation.

Just two minutes and 35 seconds into overtime, Nikolai Borschevsky fired the puck past Wings goaltender Tim Cheveldae, giving the underdog Leafs the victory.

"I don't know what to say," Yzerman said afterward. "We had a lot higher expectations than to be out in the first round."

The defeat cost Bryan Murray the coaching half of his job and begat the process that would end with the hiring of Scotty Bowman. The consensus within the organization was that the Wings needed a demanding coach who could get the most out of players, and no coach fit that description better than Bowman. (Well, maybe one other coach—Yzerman lightheartedly nominated Dick Cordick, who coached Yzerman as a nine-year-old: "Our coach had to leave for about two months, and Jeff Cordick's dad came in," Yzerman said. "He was the scariest guy on the face of the Earth. He'd yell at us and he'd give us that look with his eyes. And I don't know if we lost a game the rest of the year. We won everything. He was something. I think it's good to be pushed, to be kicked in the rear and tested a little bit.")

The Wings suffered an even bigger upset in the first year under Bowman, winning the Western Conference with 100 points only to lose in the first round to the upstart San Jose Sharks in seven games. The organization wasn't about to jettison Bowman—who came to Detroit already having won six Stanley Cups as a coach—after one year; instead, it cost Murray the other half of his job, ending his run as general manager of the Wings. Technically, Devellano and Bowman shared management duties for the next three years, but Bowman's reach was on the player personnel side. Within a short amount of time, he used that power to trade a 50-goal scorer (Ray Sheppard) for 35-year-old center named Igor Larionov. In 1996 Bowman went back and forth with the Hartford Whalers in the talks that would lead to the acquisition of Brendan Shanahan. Shanahan was the power forward the Wings needed to stand up to the likes of the Colorado Avalanche in the playoffs, Larionov, the centerpiece of the Russian Five.

Bowman ultimately coached the Wings to three Stanley Cups—and that might never have happened had the Leafs not beaten the Wings in 1993 and forced them to make a change that would alter the franchise.

PART 9

GREAT LINES

27

The Production Line

JUST BEFORE CHRISTMAS IN 1986, THE RED WINGS GIFTED
fans a reunion that harkened back to the franchise's best days.

The event on December 23 at Joe Louis Arena was to honor
Sid Abel, who had retired the previous spring after representing
the Wings for 32 seasons as a player, coach, general manager,
and broadcaster. Guests included Gordie Howe and Ted
Lindsay, with whom Abel formed the famed Production Line
starting in 1947.

"I taught Gordie and Ted everything they know about
hockey," Abel joked. "And they did a pretty good job."

Among the gifts Abel received that night was a miniature
Stanley Cup with his name engraved on it, a pair of round-trip
tickets from Florida (where Abel moved upon retirement) to
Detroit, and a white Chevrolet Euro Sport driven onto the ice
by Tommy Ivan, who handed Abel the keys.

It was to Ivan who Jack Adams handed the keys to the Wings in 1947, when Adams stepped back as coach and named Ivan his successor. Howe was 19 and Lindsay was 22, and Ivan thought the two youngsters would be well served to play with Abel, who was 29. Abel turned out to be a perfect fit between the two dynamos—Howe was 6'0" and 200-odd pounds of pure strength, and Lindsay was 5'8" and 160-odd pounds of pure brawn.

"He molded a bunch of men together into a very good machine," Lindsay said of Ivan in 1999. "He understood men, understood that everyone had a different personality and different strengths."

The trio was nicknamed the "Production Line" in homage to Detroit's car industry. Their effectiveness lay in their skill sets—Howe and Lindsay were physical forces who powered their way into corners to emerge with the puck, and Abel would be near the net, ready for a pass.

"Sid would just turn those young guys loose in the corners, where they'd mix it up with the other team's tough guys," Budd Lynch, then the Wings' broadcaster, said in a 1991 interview. "Then Sid would go to the front of the net and, bingo, score a goal. Sid had been around long enough to know not to go into the corners."

The Production Line gained fame on home ice for originating the intentional angled shoot-in, where the puck would bounce off the notoriously tricky boards at Olympia Stadium and slide into the slot for a one-timer.

In 1947–48, their first season together, Lindsay led the Wings with 52 points in 60 games, and Howe and Abel each had 44 points.

"We were two seconds ahead of everyone else," Lindsay said years later. "We knew what was going to happen. The average guy waits to see what happens, and often it's too late."

The three grew accustomed to coming to camp, playing on different lines as Ivan experimented with line combinations— and inevitably ending up being reunited. "At times it upset me, but I figured if they could find somebody who could do a better job, they ought to give him a whack at it," Abel said. "But invariably they came back to me."

The Production Line reigned from November 1947 through 1951–52. Starting in 1948–49, the Wings won the regular-season title seven consecutive times. The first year of that winning streak, Abel and Lindsay each recorded 54 points, tied for third in the league. The following season, in 1949–50, Lindsay topped the NHL scoring race with 78 points, Abel was second with 69, and Howe in third place with 68.

By 1950–51 Howe was on his way to establishing his reputation as one of the game's stars. It was his fourth season in the league, and he dominated with 86 points, 20 more than Montreal's Maurice Richard, who finished second in points.

The 1951–52 season would be the last for the fabled line, with Abel traded to the Black Hawks for cash in 1952. They finished that season with Howe again leading the NHL in points with 86, Lindsay in second place with 69, and Abel in eighth place with 53 points, and with the Wings winning the Stanley Cup for the second time in three years.

In four of their seasons together, Lindsay was a first-team All-Star; he was second-team the other. Howe was twice named to the first team, twice to the second team, and Abel made the first team twice, and the second team once. They were so effective that Ivan, who generally was a stickler for positional play, let the three of them have free reign.

"They are both unorthodox, crisscrossing on the ice so that no one really is a right wing, a center, or left wing," Abel said of his line mates.

There was scant chance that opponents would be able to take advantage of them. "The only way to stop [Howe] is to crowd him, throw him off stride," Toronto Maple Leafs defenseman Kent Douglas once said. "But nobody even wants to get near Gordie Howe."

The Production Line skated around and through opponents for five seasons, the fluid patterns of Howe, Abel, and Lindsay forming a venerable and victorious weapon for the Wings during their first dynasty.

28

The Russian Five

IT SPEAKS TO HOW INTRICATE THEIR STYLE WAS THAT EVEN Scotty Bowman, a man who won nine Stanley Cups as head coach, could not distill their genius.

For an all too short time in the mid-1990s, the hockey world was gifted the wonder that was the Russian Five: Sergei Fedorov, Slava Fetisov, Vladimir Konstantinov, Igor Larionov, Vyacheslav Kozlov, and Igor Larinov. They colored the Red Wings with hues from their Red Army days, controlling the puck with a degree that resembled magic.

Three of the comrades—Fedorov, Konstantinov, and Kozlov—were already in Detroit when Bowman arrived in 1993; he engineered the trades that brought in Fetisov and Larionov, two players with such experience they had the respect of elder statesmen. Fetisov and Konstantinov paired on defense, and Larionov played center between Fedorov and Kozlov. Gifted individually, together they were glorious.

"I still wouldn't be able to tell you what strategy they were using," Bowman said in a 2023 interview. "It was just amazing what they were doing. The guy [who] seemed to be getting the breakaways was Vladimir, and he was the right-side defenseman. In the neutral zone, they circled the puck around, and next thing you know, this guy comes up the middle and he's got a breakaway. It was amazing. Slava was always talking on behalf of them. He would come to me and say, 'if there's something that really concerns you, let me know.' And that's what I said, 'Slava, I can't figure out how you're playing, but whatever you're doing, keep doing it.'"

Their control of the puck was the essence of their success, the Zen of why they were such a marvel to watch.

In April 1996 the Wings' contingent of comrades drew so much interest in their native country that *Sport Express*, a Russian daily newspaper that at the time had 800,000 readers, sent a reporter, Alex Gounk, on a 10-day journey to North America follow their exploits. "There is lots of interest in the Red Wings," Gounk told the *Detroit Free Press*. "It started after Sergei Fedorov came here. They feel that Russian Five play the best hockey in the world today."

Canada lays claim to the origins of hockey, but a continent away, little Russian children grew up playing bandy, a game of 11 skaters a side playing on a frozen soccer field. To understand why the Russian Five were so dynamic, it helped to understand bandy. Playing bandy on a 330-foot-long surface instead of the 200-foot NHL ice sheet, players had to learn how to move the ball using teamwork. Larionov explained why: "It's impossible to go coast to coast, so you advance the ball down the field by passing it to the guy beside you, like a rugby team moving down the field. It's a team game. You have to use your teammates. This is the root of our style. First you must move the puck. It should be moving all the time because when the puck is moving you can see the holes on the ice open up, you see the gaps between the defense."

There was tremendous pride involved, especially for Larionov and Fetisov, who already were legends in Soviet hockey by the time they rebooted their careers in North America. "We played against the best professional teams and we beat them," Fetisov said. "We won the international tournaments we played in, and always it was a road game for us. And people hated us because we were the Soviets. Not just the players, but the referees tried to beat us. We played against pro players here and we never got beat up. We proved we were the best in the world.

"In Russia, the players are selected by skill. Size doesn't matter. You have to skate very well, shoot the puck, pass, forecheck, and back-check."

Russians did not compete internationally in hockey until the late 1940s, and Soviet hockey entered its first Winter Olympics in 1956. The rivalry between Canada and Russia changed forever in 1972, when the Soviets played Canadian NHL stars in an eight-game showdown billed as the Super Series.

"We had been the best. We had always been the best," Ken Dryden, Team Canada's goaltender, wrote in his book *The Game*. "So, however we played it was the best way. And there could be no other way to play."

After the Soviets stunned Canada with a 7–3 victory in the opening game, Canada rebounded to win the series—barely. Its margin of victory: 34 seconds, the time left when Paul Henderson scored the winning goal in the final game.

"Our birthright was suddenly at risk," Dryden wrote. "A game that is in our blood was finally put on the couch and examined...In the 1972 series, we dominated those parts of the game to which our style had moved...In the end, it was enough, but disturbingly, the Soviets had been better in the traditional skills—passing, open ice play, team play, quickness, finishing around the net—skills we had developed that seemed to us the essence of play, but that we had abandoned as incompatible with the modern game. The Soviets showed us otherwise."

It was a style that, a quarter of a century later, Bowman deeply admired. He had been brought in by the Wings in 1993 because he was viewed as a hockey genius. His principal role was to coach, but he was also, after his first season, involved in player personnel moves.

When Bowman arrived, the Wings already had Fedorov, Konstantinov, and Kozlov on the roster thanks to shrewd drafting decisions. That left two legends to add: Fetisov, the former Red Army captain, and Larionov, both members of the Green Line, the best five-man unit in the history of Soviet hockey. They had won just about everything, from Olympic gold medals to World Championships to European championships to MVP awards in the Soviet Elite League.

Fetisov joined the Wings in April 1995 from the New Jersey Devils, who were happy to jettison a nearly 37-year-old defenseman who no longer fit into their plans for a third-round pick. To Bowman, Fetisov was the epitome of a winning pedigree: "He was a great player in his prime," Bowman told reporters at the time. Fetisov had joined the NHL in 1989, but after five seasons the Devils no longer found him useful. Bowman thought otherwise.

Giving up a relatively high draft pick for an aged defenseman was viewed with a degree of skepticism within the organization, but it paled compared to what Bowman gave up to get the missing Russian. Larionov was part of the San Jose Sharks team that in 1994 upset the Wings in the first round of the playoffs, and, as he stood behind the losing-team's bench, Bowman had a first-hand view of the difference that Larionov made. "If he wasn't around San Jose at that time, we would not have had any trouble beating them," Bowman would say years later.

Bowman wanted Larionov enough to trade Ray Sheppard, a 50-goal scorer who was six years younger than Larionov. It looked like a lopsided trade except to those who, like Bowman, appreciated what a cerebral player Larionov was. He and Fetisov had stood up to the mighty Red Army and all the red tape of bureaucracy to forge a path for Russian players to join the NHL freely, and now they were united in North America.

The five comrades played their first shift as a unit on October 27, 1995, in a game at Calgary. Kozlov scored in the first period, set up by Fedorov and Konstantinov; Larionov in the third period, set up by Fedorov. The Wings won 3–0.

It was the first time in the NHL that five Russians on the same team shared the ice. Wayne Gretzky, one of hockey's all-time greatest, was a fan: "They're better than any five-man unit I've ever seen in the NHL. Those guys are so creative. They know where the next guy is all the time without even looking. That's because of the system they came from. They play hard and they really throw the puck around."

Not so much throw as weave: it was their ability to control the puck, to be willing to retreat into their own zone rather than give away the puck, that made them almost indefensible. "They're so unpredictable," Chicago Blackhawks coach Craig Hartsburg said in 1997. "They have five guys on the attack. You don't know where they're coming from because there's really no set system. They play off instinct and skill. That's tough to defend."

At least one of them always was open for a scoring opportunity. They made it all look so effortless, transitioning the puck among them, gliding across the ice with a fluid ease. In an instant, they could transition from defense to offense, setting up while opponents were still figuring out where to position themselves.

"You have to think like a chess player—two or three moves ahead all the time," Larionov explained in 1996. "It looks easy from the stands, but it's not so easy. There has to be a mutual understanding. Sometimes Vladdie or Slava jumps up into the offense. You have to watch out and be aware. Otherwise, it will be anarchy out there."

Fetisov elaborated: "Immediately, you read the first move. When the puck turns over, everybody regroups. It's instinctive. We've been taught in tactical situations. It's structured, but we have lots of room for creativity. It doesn't matter—if the defenseman is in a good position to jump in the play, he can jump. Your teammates back you up."

That was in games. In practices, their teammates came to dread having to go against the Russians during drills, because, as Steve Yzerman explained, "You end up chasing the puck around for 45 seconds."

The concept of holding onto the puck rather than giving it away seems so simple and straightforward, but like Larionov said, it took being able to think like a chess player, and, as Bowman understood, it took having four likeminded players on the ice at the same time. Bowman's blockbuster trade with the Wings was acquiring Brendan Shanahan at the start of the 1996–97 season but acquiring Fetisov and Larionov showed an unmatched shrewdness.

When the 1995–96 season ended with the Wings having won a record-setting 62 games, the three Russian forwards ranked in the top five in points on the team: Fedorov was first with 107, Kozlov fourth with 73, and Larionov fifth with 71. All but Fetisov ranked in the top seven in scoring when the playoffs ended, but Bowman wasn't able to field the five as a unit as much in the playoffs because of the increased clutching and grabbing.

The concern within the organization over trading for two players in their mid-30s with as much mileage on them as Fetisov and Larionov came to the forefront early in the 1996–97 season, when injuries prevented Bowman from using the unit as much as he would have liked. It took their reunion at the end of October to break Fedorov out of the worst goal-scoring slump of his career when he ended a 10-game drought and had a goal and an assist in a 5–3 victory over the Montreal Canadiens.

"It was nice to be back together with the Russian unit," Fedorov said after scoring his first goal since the season opener. "We controlled the puck very well. It felt like I was back home at my fireplace."

On December 26, 1996, Fedorov amended for his October slump with a masterful performance, scoring every goal the Wings needed to top the Washington Capitals 5–4, in overtime. Konstantinov had four assists, Larionov had three, and Fetisov, one.

"Tonight was like a dream game, you score them all, and get the game-winner in overtime," Bowman said of Fedorov's performance.

The unit had been a regular feature at that time for about a month. "After we started playing together, he had a lot of quality chances, but he didn't score," Konstantinov said. "He didn't believe in himself, maybe that's why he wasn't scoring goals. I told him, if he can believe in himself, he can score the goals."

Cautious after the unit struggled with the increased clutching in the 1996 playoffs, Bowman didn't use the five as a group until the fifth game of the first-round series against the St. Louis Blues in 1997. Their cycling of the puck helped the Wings pocket a 5–2 victory and a three-games-to-two lead in the series.

"They really carried the load for them," Blues defenseman Marc Bergevin said.

In the third game of the second-round series against the Mighty Ducks of Anaheim, the Russian Five contributed four goals in a 5–3 victory. Among those watching were Jimmy Devellano, who had drafted Fedorov, Konstantinov, and Kozlov. "I'm so sick and tired of people saying the Russians don't get up for the playoffs, that they don't know the meaning of the Stanley Cup," Devellano said. "They've been through the wars, these guys. They know how to win and they're here to win the Cup."

Fetisov had turned 39 on April 20.

"Look at me," he said during the Ducks series. "It's probably much better for me to get season over as soon as possible to get rest. But we're playing for championship. We're winners. We all grew up with our national team when anything but first place was a tragedy. The NHL is the same situation. Everybody wants to win this Cup and put their names on this trophy, also. Russians are no exceptions."

They were an easy target for opposing fans, though: In NHL stops across the country, fans broke into chants of "U-S-A! U-S-A!" when the Russian Five were weaving their magic on the ice.

"We hear it," Konstantinov said. "What are they cheering that for? We just try to score a goal right away and get more attention from the stands."

Bowman used the Russians as a unit, but he also brilliantly parlayed their skills onto other lines—and used Fedorov as a defenseman at times. In the third-round series, when the Wings faced their nemesis, the Colorado Avalanche, Bowman used Konstantinov with Nicklas Lidström, uniting a pair that could handle 30 minutes a game.

One thing that didn't change, as May turned to June and the Wings entered the Stanley Cup Final against the Philadelphia Flyers, was the xenophobic jeers from opposing fans.

"I don't know why people hate us," Larionov said. "When we go on the road people hate us, maybe because they don't want to see some Russians kick some butt of the Americans. But what can we do? We can't really change that. It's a lack of intelligence, that's all."

Just how much they were valued by the Wings was laid bare by Yzerman, who as captain was the player to whom the Cup was presented on June 7, 1997. It was his choice who would carry it for a lap next. He handed it to Fetisov and Larionov, who each held up an end as they lapped the ice.

"Stevie gives it to us, and we appreciate it very much," Fetisov said. "I have been through so many situations, winning so many gold medals, but it was unforgettable moment to carry the Stanley Cup around and have so many fans cheering. It was an unforgettable moment."

Larionov described it as "a great feeling. It is a great honor for us, a great honor for Slava and me to take the Cup around the rink and have 20,000 fans cheer for us."

Larionov and Fetisov won the Cup again in 1998 and Larionov won a third one in 2002. Fetisov was elected to the Hockey Hall of Fame in 2001, followed by Larionov in 2008. A third member of the Russian Five, Fedorov, was elected in 2015.

The 1997 playoffs were, tragically, the last time the Russian Five played together. Six days after they won the Cup, Konstantinov suffered career-ending injuries in a limousine accident.

The Russian Five were beloved by Wings fans—and, naturally, fans in their homeland. In the days before the Internet enabled everyone to keep track of everything, hockey fans relied on newspaper reports about their favorite expatriates. David McHugh, a special writer for the *Detroit Free Press* in the 1990s, filed a report from Moscow in early June 1997 that shed light on how much interest there was in Detroit's Russians.

"The sympathy of Russian fans, undoubtedly, is on the side of Detroit," said the Moscow daily *Komsomolskaya Pravda* in its preview of the finals, adding, "On Canadian and American ice, it's as if the best times of Soviet hockey had returned."

The Wings victory in Game 2 of the Final topped the sports news on the evening newscast on NTV, one of the most popular stations, and every newspaper article on the Finals mentions the Russian Five prominently.

"Kozlov Could Be Mayor of Detroit," read one headline in *Sport Express*, the main sports daily, after Kozlov had a big goal in a semifinal victory against Colorado. "Fedorov's Goal Puts Wings in Final," read another. Each box score concludes with a separate section titled "Nashy," or "Ours"—the stats of all the Russian players.

It helped that "Red Wings" translates gracefully into Russian as "Krasnye Krylya"—and of course, in the land of Lenin, red had long been a familiar color.

The Wings won the Cup on a Saturday night. The following Monday edition of the Russian newspaper *Izvestia* topped its sports page with news of the Red Wings victory.

"Triumph: Five More Russian Names on the Stanley Cup" was the headline. Wings Vyacheslav Kozlov and Sergei Fedorov were pictured. Part of the report read: "On Tuesday, there will be a parade. The mayor of Detroit has named the Cup championship as a holiday for the whole city. Special honors await the magnificent Russian five."

29

The Grind Line

"Probably in the final run, the Draper-Maltby-Kocur line gave us the final ingredient. They let the star players know they could count on anybody." —Scotty Bowman, June 7, 1997

"How do you think I feel? I've got my left wing on the cover of SI, *and my right wing goes backhand, top shelf."* —Kris Draper, June 2, 1997

TWO YEARS AFTER THE NEW JERSEY DEVILS' "CRASH LINE" frustrated the Wings for four miserable games in the 1995 Stanley Cup Finals, the Wings had their own star killers.

The Grind Line had Kirk Maltby on the left wing, Kris Draper at center, and either Joey Kocur or Darren McCarty on the right wing. Kocur was on the first version of the line, but McCarty replaced him during the first round of the 1997 playoffs, when the Wings were battling the St. Louis Blues. In either iteration the group aggravated and annoyed the Blues, goading them into taking retaliatory penalties.

"We have a blast," McCarty said. "Drapes is the talker out there, I just laugh. Malts will say stuff, too, but Drapes is the one who talks. We all yell at each other and yell at the other guys. I just watch and laugh. I played with Drapes for a long time, and we always played well together, and Malts plays the same way. The first two guys forecheck, and then the third guy picks up. It's basic hockey. No special plays, just bump and grind."

The line was named during one of the times the Wings were in St. Louis for the six-game series. Draper mentioned how Kocur and Bob Probert used to be known as the Bruise Brothers, and how cool that was. Whenever the Maltby-Draper-McCarty/Kocur line was talked about, it was always about how good they were at grinding. The Grind Line—it sounded as good as they were.

"They can play a good role," Bowman said in May 1997. "It always gives a team a lot of confidence when they score goals. That's the big part, they feel pretty good about themselves. They've been rewarded because they've been playing well."

The franchise hadn't had a named line with traction since the Production Line of the 1950s. The Russian Five rolled off the tongue, but that was a unit, a five-man integration of icy precision.

The Grind Line was a hit, spawning T-shirts and bobbleheads and a *Sports Illustrated* cover. They were a master class in the art of how to frustrate stars from Brett Hull to Teemu Selänne to Joe Sakic to Eric Lindros. Draper was the speedy one, and the others, the physical ones.

"It's fun that we were able to complement each other and read each other," Maltby said. "With our style you get under teams' skins. It's good anytime you can get a guy to retaliate and take a penalty. We're a line that the other team is going to have to worry about getting crashed and banged on."

At its core, the Grind Line's effectiveness came from the style that gave it its name: they kept grinding down opponents, shift after shift. But the totality of the Grind Line's success came from how effective they were at both ends of the ice. When the playoffs were over, when the 20 games it took the Wings to bring the Stanley Cup back to Detroit were done, Maltby had five goals, and he and McCarty each had seven points. Draper had six points, and Kocur four. For a group that was primarily tasked with playing a defensive role, those were excellent numbers.

"We all knew our roles," Maltby said in 2023. "We were the Grind Line, not the Production Line, but we scored a few goals here and there. We could produce and helped out that way, but our primary function was to grind. Our friendship off the ice carried on to the ice. As much of a pain Drapes and I were and started scuffles, Mac would come in and finish it. I remember some player said to him, 'Those two guys are a-holes,' and Mac said, 'Yeah, but they're my a-holes.' He understood what his role was with us, we all did."

In Game 1 of the Stanley Cup Finals, it was Maltby who scored the first goal, breaking in on a two-on-nobody with Draper and giving the Wings a lead just 6:38 into the opening period. It was Kocur who made it 2–1, picking off a pass in the Philadelphia Flyers zone and beating goaltender Ron Hextall with a backhander that roofed into the net.

That was on May 31. On June 2 the latest issue of *Sports Illustrated* came out. The cover story was a feature titled "Hot Wings," and the cover image showed Maltby playing the puck while battling Sakic, the superstar captain of the Colorado Avalanche. The issue was a huge hit with the Wings, who throughout the playoffs had emphasized the need for contributions from everybody. Now here they were, nearing the end of a grueling but joyful challenge, and the cover boy for their efforts was not one of their North American stars, like Yzerman or Shanahan, nor the Russian Five, but a guy whose playoff performance embodied the whole team.

Maltby came to the Wings in a trade on March 20, 1996, wondering why a team that was on a record-setting pace with 53 victories wanted him. He was dealing with a scary eye injury that had happened about a month before, when he was clipped by Edmonton Oilers teammate Louie DeBrusk's stick during a practice. He was 23 years old and had appeared in 164 NHL games.

"We knew Maltby had a bad eye injury, but Glen Sather called me, and he said the Oilers wanted a defenseman for their farm team," Scotty Bowman said in 2023. "We had a guy, Dan McGillis, who we weren't going to sign. So, it made sense for us. We'll take a forward for a defenseman we weren't going to keep. Kirk was a really good acquisition for us."

McGillis went on to play 634 NHL games, though he only lasted two seasons with Edmonton. The Oilers had been disappointed in Maltby since drafting him at 65th in 1992 and didn't see him as part of their future. But Bowman saw potential in Maltby.

"He's a good, solid up-and-down winger," Bowman said. "He's more defensive than offensive. He plays a solid game."

What Maltby didn't know was that the Wings knew they needed to be tougher when it mattered—in the playoffs—and they saw the possibility of that in Maltby. He had made a big impression on higher-ups in the organization the previous season with a crushing hit on Paul Coffey that left the veteran defenseman with a sore back and unable to play for several games. It was exactly the sort of physicality the Wings craved.

There was some concern regarding the eye injury—"If I get a blow to it anytime soon, it could definitely damage the eye," Maltby said shortly after the trade—but wearing a visor ensured he would not need to change the way he played.

"I bump and grind," he said. "I like the hitting part of the game, getting into the corner and being physical."

Maltby scored his first goal in a Wings uniform on April 10, in the 5–2 victory over the Winnipeg Jets that tied the then-record 60 victories in one season.

"It was nice to help contribute to that record," Maltby said afterward. "It felt sort of like my first goal all over again."

The Wings won 62 games that season, but when the playoffs ended with bitter defeat at the hands of the Colorado Avalanche in the Western Conference Finals, Maltby again wondered if he had a future with the team. His name occasionally popped up in potential trade scenarios. When the 1996–97 season began, Maltby still wasn't sure where he really fit. Finally in early December, Bowman started using Maltby with Draper on the first penalty killing unit. It was a move designed to alleviate the wear and tear on Yzerman and Brendan Shanahan, who had been killing penalties.

It worked brilliantly. A few weeks later, Bowman followed through on Yzerman's suggestion to reach out and see if Kocur would want to come out of retirement and re-join the Wings. Kocur's arrival gave Bowman the flexibility to put together Maltby, Draper, and Kocur as a line. Gone were the days Maltby worried how he would fit in Detroit.

Kocur had been drafted by the Wings at 88th in 1983, the same year as Yzerman, and within a few seasons emerged as a fan favorite. Together with Probert, Kocur put on knock-out performances, bringing Joe Louis Arena crowds to their feet with his fisticuffs. In 1991 the Wings traded him to the New York Rangers. The move wasn't popular with fans, but it turned out to be beneficial during his comeback with the team.

By the mid-1990s, Kocur had washed out of the NHL and, after a five-game stint in the International Hockey League with the San Antonio Dragons, out of pro hockey altogether. He returned to metro Detroit, and settled for playing hockey in midnight adult leagues, popularly known as the beer league.

A Christmastime phone call in 1996 from Bowman changed all that. On December 28, Kocur signed a deal to return to the Wings. Yzerman and Sergei Fedorov were the only players left from Kocur's early days with the team. His pugilistic prowess in those days often left the knuckles on his right hand raw.

Kocur was able to convince the Wings' brain trust that he could still fight if needed, and that was key to his being offered a contract. McCarty and Shanahan could box with the best of them, but it did not benefit the Wings to have either serving a penalty for fighting.

Kocur came in at a fit 220 pounds—and with 2,270 penalty minutes in 685 games.

"My role hasn't changed in the 12 years I've played in this league," Kocur said at the time. "It's to be a physical player and do what I do."

Yzerman wanted Kocur because he was another guy who would toughen up the Wings, but Kocur also brought with him the experience of knowing what it takes to win the Stanley Cup, having done so in 1994 with the Rangers. He turned the 1996 Christmas call from Bowman into a nearly three-year stay.

The story of how Draper came to join the franchise is part of Wings lore. Where Maltby and Kocur appealed because of their physicality, the Wings sought out Draper because of his faceoffs.

Bowman scouted Draper when he played for the Adirondack Red Wings, then the club's American Hockey League affiliate. It was Adirondack general manager Doug MacLean who brought Draper into the organization, acquiring him for $1 from the Winnipeg Jets. The Jets had given up on Draper after just 20 games after drafting him at 62nd overall in 1989. Like Maltby, Draper wondered if he would end up fitting in with the Wings, wondered where he would play on such a skilled team.

Draper was called up on January 24, 1994, on what initially was projected to be a short-term situation. The Wings needed somebody to fill in for a bit. But Draper kept giving the Wings reasons to keep him. He played sound defense. He contributed a bit of scoring here and there, like goals in three straight games in early March. By mid-March, general manager Bryan Murray deemed Draper bumped Dallas Drake on the depth chart. "As much as I liked Dallas, Kris came in and beat him out," Murray said.

Bowman said that Draper "surprised our people in Adirondack with a pretty good scoring touch. We were looking for a faceoff man and a penalty killer. That's how he got the chance to play. He's given us timely goals. He also adds to our team speed. He's a hungry player." Draper's emergence enabled the Wings to add Drake to the package deal that brought goaltender Bob Essensa to Detroit from the Winnipeg Jets.

Later in the season, Bowman called Draper "a revelation."

"What I like in a role player are two things. They have to know their role and they have to accept it. I think he realizes when we're behind a goal, he may not play as much."

Early in his career, teammates called Draper "B.A." for breakaway, for his ability to use his legs to generate enviable speed. That facet of his game also earned Draper occasional looks on scoring lines, where his task was to hang back a bit in the offensive zone and be ready if needed to protect the defensive zone.

As returns on investments go—and nobody is even sure if that buck ever was paid—few can match what the Wings got in Draper. He ended up filling in for 1,137 games.

McCarty, who the Wings had drafted at No. 46 in 1992, was on and off the Grind Line as decided by Bowman. It was such an ace of a line for the Wings to have because when Bowman thought it prudent, he could move McCarty up to play with Shanahan, adding more muscle to a top line, while sacrificing nothing from the Grind Line because of Kocur.

It was Kocur who was on the T-shirts marketed in the spring of 1997, which featured the Grind Line members depicted in the caricature style where heads are much bigger than bodies. Those shirts were as big of a hit as the line.

The Grind Line played a key role in the Wings winning the 1997 Stanley Cup and in repeating as champions in 1998. Kocur retired in 2000, but the Maltby-Draper-McCarty edition was on the job when the Wings won again in 2002. When it was McCarty's return to re-join the Wings, a la Kocur style, in 2008, there was a brief moment in McCarty's first game back on March 28 when the Grind Line was reunited. Fans responded with a standing ovation. Three months later, the Grind Line helped the Wings win a fourth Stanley Cup.

PART 10

THREE OF A KIND

30

Sid Abel, Alex Delvecchio, Red Kelly

SID ABEL WAS THE SAVVY VETERAN WHOSE ROLE AS PIVOT man was integral to the success of one of the greatest lines in hockey. Tucked between the giant of a man that was Gordie Howe on the right wing and the undersized pest that was Ted Lindsay on the left wing, Abel was 10 years older than Howe and seven years older than Lindsay. Abel was part center, part mentor; he often had his younger teammates over for dinner, and while his wife, Gloria, who was Jack Adams' secretary, cooked dinner, Abel would go over the previous night's game. Long before there was video and instant replay, there was Abel: he used words and wisdom as teaching tools.

Born February 22, 1918, in Melville, a small city in Saskatchewan, Abel joined the Wings in 1938, becoming a full-time player in 1940. He recorded 18 goals and topped 40 points in both 1941–42 and 1942–43 and won his first Stanley Cup in 1943. Abel left the team to serve in the Royal Canadian Air Force during World War II. He returned late in the 1945–46 season, regaining his captaincy and after a brief interlude wearing No. 9, his No. 12.

Abel, Howe, and Lindsay started playing together in November of 1947 and finished that season among the team's top four scorers. In 1949–50 they were the top three scorers in the six-team NHL: Lindsay with 78 points, Abel with 69, and Howe with 68. Their prowess earned them the nickname, "the Production Line" in a nod to the city's automotive industry.

Abel had his own nickname, too: "Old Boot Nose," or simply, "Boot Nose." That came about after a game between the Wings and the Montreal Canadiens. Maurice Richard shoved Howe, who retaliated by pushing Richard to the ice. When Richard saw Abel laughing at him, Richard punched Abel so hard that it broke Abel's nose.

Abel won the Stanley Cup again in 1950. The Production Line was back in form in 1950–51, combining for 206 points. The line contributed 208 points in 1951–52, which culminated with Abel winning a third Stanley Cup.

Abel played 612 games in the NHL, all with the Wings save the last 42, which he spent with the Chicago Black Hawks. Jack Adams, the general manager of the Wings, traded Abel to Chicago for cash. Abel was a player/coach with the Black Hawks and in his last season, 1953–54, played just three games.

Abel dabbled in being a television broadcaster, and he was also a coach and general manager. He coached the franchise to the Stanley Cup Finals in 1961, 1963, 1964, and 1966. When he was named general manager in 1963, he talked Lindsay out of retirement.

Other than serving in World War II and a five-year stretch in the 1950s, Abel had a tenure with the Wings that spanned from 1938 to 1986. He was elected to the Hockey Hall of Fame in 1969. The Wings retired his No. 12 in 1995.

Before Nicklas Lidström, the Wings had understated perfection in Alex Delvecchio, the center who served as Abel's replacement on the second iteration of the Production Line.

Born December 4, 1931, in Fort William, Ontario, Delvecchio debuted with the Wings on March 25, 1951. When he stopped playing in November 1973, Delvecchio had logged 1,550 games; only Howe (1,687) and Lidström (1,564) played more games with one franchise. At the time of retirement, Delvecchio ranked second in the NHL with 1,281 points, trailing only Howe's 1,809 points.

Steve Yzerman was a youngster when Delvecchio was near the end of his career.

"I remember he was a centerman and I would ask my dad about him, watching him play," Yzerman said in 1998 after he passed Delvecchio to move into second place on the Wings' all-time assists list. "He's a guy that showed a lot of class, was a great player, always played in Detroit. I just thought it was kind of interesting and kind of unique what he did."

Delvecchio, who also played left wing at times, was known for his soft hands and sportsmanlike conduct. (His nickname, "Fats," was an affectionate one, given to him because of his round face.) He didn't deliver big hits, and he didn't bloody up the ice with his fists, but he would go into corners and dance out with the puck dangling on the end of his stick. In a career that lasted 22 full seasons and parts of two more, Delvecchio accumulated only 383 penalty minutes. He won the Stanley Cup in 1952, '54, and '55 and the Lady Byng Memorial Trophy in 1959, '66, and '69. Delvecchio's stardom led to appearances in 13 NHL All-Star Games.

Delvecchio was known for his durability, too: he missed only 42 games in his entire career, and 22 of those stemmed from a broken ankle suffered during the 1956–57 season.

Delvecchio served as captain from 1962 until his retirement in 1973, the longest tenure in franchise history until Yzerman. Delvecchio's 456 goals rank third in franchise history behind Howe (786) and Yzerman (692). Delvecchio's 825 assists rank fourth behind Yzerman (1,063), Howe (1,023), and Lidström (878).

Delvecchio was less than a month from his 42nd birthday when, on November 7, 1973, he was suddenly and dramatically named the new coach of the Wings. The announcement was made shortly after the team lost its ninth game of the season.

Delvecchio became the Wings' seventh coach in five years, succeeding Ted Garvin.

"I made the decision to change coaches this morning," general manager Ned Harkness told reporters at a news conference that included the presence of owner Bruce Norris. "I thought I had to make the switch under the present circumstances. When Mr. Norris asked me who I would recommend, I told him I wanted Alex Delvecchio. He has the leadership and the knowledge of hockey to make this team into a winner. And he has charisma."

Delvecchio described the move from sitting on the bench to being behind it as "the greatest thing that has happened to me. I think I can turn this club around. I just want to get with the players now and develop a good mood among them."

Seeing one of the franchise's most legendary players take on the coaching duties briefly stirred hope the Wings would revitalize. George Puscas, writing in the *Detroit Free Press* at the time of the 1973 oil crisis, commented that "if gas rationing comes, would you waste precious fuel driving to Olympia to see the Red Wings play? Two weeks ago, before Alex Delvecchio, surely you would not. But now, now you must think about it."

Delvecchio, who eventually would also serve as general manager, was not able to turn around the club. The Wings went 82–131–32 under his guidance, which ended in February 1977. There were reports he resigned, but in an interview in April, Delvecchio said he had been dismissed.

"I was ticked off," he said. "I was just 16 when I first signed with the organization. And I was 45 when I left. That's 29 years. That's a long time. And then just to be told that you're relieved, that they don't need you anymore."

That memory gave way to a much better one when Delvecchio was inducted into the Hockey Hall of Fame later that year.

On November 10, 1991, the Wings held a dual ceremony to retire Delvecchio's No. 10 and Lindsay's No. 7.

Leonard "Red" Kelly was an offensive defenseman for the Red Wings before the term was a regular part of hockey vernacular. Then he joined another team and starred as a center.

Kelly's remarkable NHL career began with the Wings in 1947. He stood out from the start, lauded for the way he could dash up ice with the puck, for the way he could thread passes to teammates. In 1949–50, the year Lindsay, Abel, and Howe finished, respectively, first, second, and third overall in NHL scoring, Kelly was the league's leading scorer among defensemen, recording 40 points in 70 games. He led league defensemen again the next season with 54 points and continued to do so every season until 1954–55, when he finished second, trailing Doug Harvey by four points.

In 1954 Kelly won the inaugural James Norris Memorial Trophy, instituted to recognize the NHL's top defenseman. That same year he won his third Lady Byng Trophy, recognizing gentlemanly and sportsmanlike play. During Kelly's 12½ seasons with the Wings, the franchise won eight regular-season championships and four Stanley Cups.

A broken ankle led to his departure. Kelly remembered the story in an interview nearly six decades later. "In practice, one of the players shot the puck along the boards and it broke my ankle," Kelly said. "They put it in a cast for three days. The team went on the road and lost three games. They asked me if I thought I could take the cast off and tape it up and play, because we were desperate. I said, 'Sure, I'll give it a try.' They taped it up to my knee, and I played for the rest of the year. The ankle was stiff. Wouldn't bend." (A story from the *Detroit Free Press* in February 1959 detailed a scene from the dressing room that day: "Defenseman Red Kelly was seated under a lamp, undergoing heat lamp treatment, which his injured foot has required for the last month.")

When a reporter asked Kelly—who could turn heads with his skating—why his performances seemed off, he mentioned the ankle. That lead to a story questioning whether Kelly was forced to play on a broken ankle. General manager Jack Adams was furious and punished Kelly (and the Wings) by trading him. The trade, in early February 1960, made headline news, blaring "Wings Trade Red Kelly to N.Y."

Adams tried, anyway, to trade Kelly, along with young forward Billy McNeill, to the Rangers for star defenseman Bill Gadsby and young forward Eddie Shack. Kelly loved Detroit, loved playing for the Wings, and opted to announce he was retiring rather than submit to the trade. That forced Adams to rescind his promise never to take Kelly back again because

PART 10: THREE OF A KIND

otherwise the Wings would have had to follow through with their request to put him on waivers with the intent that he retire. On waivers any club could have claimed Kelly for $20,000. The Wings got around it when Adams telephoned Kelly and asked if he would come back to the Wings. "We took him off the waiver list, and then we made the trade with the Toronto Maple Leafs. As far as we are concerned, Kelly is a Maple Leaf, and he will play for the Leafs."

Kelly, who had taken in the past couple games in the Olympia press box, had already talked with Toronto assistant general manager King Clancy by then: "Clancy wanted me to go with the Leafs and said it would be a good move for me since I went to school at St. Michael's in Toronto and had my farm and bowling alley at Simcoe."

Instead of Gadsby and Shack, Adams' insistence on jettisoning Kelly only landed defenseman Marc Reaume, who had points in 47 games over parts of two seasons with the Wings.

Kelly went on to win another four Stanley Cups with the Leafs. He retired after they won the Cup in 1967, finishing with 823 points in 1,316 games. He was inducted into the Hockey Hall of Fame in 1969.

The Leafs retired Kelly's No. 4 in October 2016. In 2019— six decades after Adams exiled Kelly from Detroit for the mere mention of his ankle—the Wings followed suit, recognizing Kelly's immense impact on the franchise.

31

Marguerite Norris, Colleen Howe, Marian Ilitch

On December 5, 1952, a headline ran across one of the pages of the *Detroit Free Press*: "Wings Lose Owner and 'No. 1 Fan' as Norris Dies." James E. Norris, the man who in 1932 bought a fledgling hockey franchise in Detroit and used his money and power to make the re-named Red Wings successful, died at age 73 from a heart attack.

The immediate presumption was that James D. Norris—who went by Young Jim—would become the next head of the Detroit hockey club. Ten days after James E. Norris' death, the contents of his will revealed his choice: his youngest child, Marguerite Ann Norris, would become the first woman ever to head a professional hockey team.

She was named president of both the Red Wings and Olympia Stadium. The announcement was made by general manager Jack Adams on behalf of the Norris heirs.

"Marguerite Ann was selected to follow the prescribed wishes of her father," Adams said in a brief statement that he telephoned to Detroit hockey writers.

A graduate of Smith College, Marguerite later had business training with Dun & Bradstreet in New York and West Farm Management in Chicago.

When coach Tommy Ivan was introduced to Marguerite a few days later, he inquired how to address her. "What should I call you when we talk hockey," he said. "Miss Norris? Miss Boss? Miss President? Miss Owner?"

She replied, "Margo will do." (Margo was "my father's choice," Marguerite explained, while "Marge is what my brothers and sister call me.")

Marguerite Norris accepted her new role with aplomb. "One minute I'm thrilled and the next I feel rather humble," the 25-year-old said a week into the job. "This is all so new and exciting, and I really can't say a thing yet about team operations."

Unlike her father, Marguerite planned to live in Detroit, in a mid-town apartment hotel. An avid sailor, there was talk she would bring her Star class boat, the Half Shell, to join the Detroit River fleet. "I sailed a great deal around Long Island and once, about 1948, went to the Atlantic Coast championships," she revealed in a newspaper interview. "I also played competitive tennis and I enjoy golf. And everyone in our family is interested in baseball, football, and boxing."

Marguerite arrived at Willow Run airport on December 15, 1952, accompanied by her brother Bruce and his wife. Clad in a grey wool suit and mink jacket—as noted in newspaper reports at the time—she stepped from the portable stair into a car to be driven to the Sheraton-Cadillac hotel for an introductory news conference.

She returned to Chicago to spend the holidays with her mother but was back in Detroit in the new year. On January 15, she took in a game at Olympia Stadium, watching Gordie Howe score twice and Sawchuk deliver a shutout in a 4–0 victory over the Boston Bruins.

Three months later, the Bruins delivered a stunning upset over the Wings, eliminating the defending Stanley Cup champions in a six-game semifinal. There was speculation afterward that the Wings might be sold, or that Olympia Stadium would be sold, but Adams soon laid that to rest. "Marge talks like she's planning to stick here," he said in mid-April. "Sure, we'll probably make some trades or sales. We do that every year, win or lose, to make room for our good young prospects. But we'll still have the same nucleus we've had for five straight NHL titles. Marge has been wonderful to work for. But I wouldn't be shackled."

Decades later, Howe revealed in his 2014 book, *Mr. Hockey: My Story*, that Marguerite had reined in Adams' penchant for wheeling and dealing.

"I don't know how Mr. Adams felt about his new team president, but I'm sure he wasn't thrilled about a woman in her twenties handing down his marching orders," Howe wrote. "I found her to be both smart and capable. Others I talked to felt the same way. She was good for the club, but unfortunately, she didn't stick around for as long as anyone would have liked. A few years into the job, she was ousted by her older brother, Bruce.

"In retrospect, it's easy to see how bad the family infighting was for the team. Marguerite was a much more thoughtful owner than her brother, who could be something of a bully. I don't think it's a coincidence that Marguerite's time in charge coincided with some of the greatest years in franchise history. As president she had enough juice to check Trader Jack's instincts to upset the apple cart."

Unfortunately for Marguerite and the Wings, her tenure came to an end in October 1955. Bruce Norris, the brother who had accompanied her upon her arrival in Detroit three years earlier, rose from vice president to president. The official reason given for Marguerite's departure was growing demands on her time from other business affairs, but Howe had it right: it was an ouster.

Bruce Norris' takeover led to the darkest days in the franchise's history. He had no backbone to stand up to Adams, whose changes marred what had been a championship roster. The Wings finished first in all three seasons under Marguerite's leadership and won the Cup in 1954 and 1955. Under Bruce's leadership they never won a Cup and eventually were derided as the "Dead Wings."

The Norris family occupy a special place in hockey history. James E. Norris was inducted into the Hockey Hall of Fame in 1958, three years after his death. Bruce Norris was inducted in 1969 (his brother, James D., was inducted in 1962). Marguerite Norris, the first woman president of an NHL team and the first woman to have her name engraved on the Stanley Cup, passed away in 1994. Thirty years after her death, she had yet to join her family in the Hockey Hall of Fame.

* * *

Where Marguerite Norris' tenure with the Wings was brief, Colleen Howe's impact lasted the length of her husband's career—and then some. She met Gordie in April 1951 at the Lucky Strike Lanes, near Olympia Stadium, and married him in 1953. Together they had four children: Marty, Mark (who would go on to play for the Wings, too, and serve as a scout in the organization), Murray, and Cathy. Colleen Howe set out to foster what she had lacked growing up in limited circumstances and raised by her great-aunt: a strong and secure family nucleus that would never lack for financial security.

Colleen Howe understood Gordie's marketing value long before that was common parlance in the sports world. She trademarked his nickname, "Mr. Hockey," and then for good measure trademarked herself as "Mrs. Hockey."

She understood the role that the wives of the players played—Adams, in contrast, preferred players to focus less on their brides and more on their games—and fought to have their value recognized, setting in motion what would, decades later, result in arenas creating luxurious spaces for the families of players.

In the early years, Colleen Howe was mostly in the news as Gordie's wife: in 1958 she was pictured in the *Detroit Free Press* taking part in a bowling tournament; in 1969 she was interviewed about his eating habits. "Gord has a wonderful appetite and is easy to cook for. However, his eating habits have changed somewhat since we were married. He used to be an oatmeal, meat, and potato man. But now he likes all kinds of salads, casseroles, and vegetables—except squash. He eats a good meal about five hours before a game and always has hot tea sweetened with honey just before the game. He picked up that idea from Ted Lindsay, and I guess it gives him a lift. Favorite food? Could be cottage cheese—he can eat it about three times a day."

A year later, she was featured in the *Detroit Free Press* in her capacity as one of the founders of the first Junior A team in the United States, the Detroit Junior Wings, lamenting the team's need for a general manager. "If I had the qualifications, I wouldn't hesitate to do it," she said. "This team means so much to Gordie and me and our family. We feel American boys should have the same opportunity to play hockey at this level, and we're the only area in the United States that has so many things going for it—the cooperation of Olympia and getting the building for our games."

Colleen also developed the first private indoor rink in Michigan, Gordie Howe Hockeyland in St. Clair Shores; she created the Howe Foundation, a charity to bring hockey to the less fortunate; and she became the first woman inducted into the U.S. Hockey Hall of Fame.

* * *

Like Colleen Howe, Marian Ilitch worked behind the scenes to make her name in hockey. She and Mike bought the Wings in June 1982; soon after, she set about working the phones to increase season ticket sales in her role as secretary-treasurer. She brought along several of the couple's seven children.

"We wanted to emphasize to the kids that it is a business and that the bottom line is that you must get customers in the door," she told the *Detroit Free Press* in an interview in June 1988.

Marian Ilitch generally operated as the silent, unseen partner to her husband, but those who worked for the team knew just how big of a role she really played. It was Marian Ilitch who talked down her husband when he wanted to offer the New York Islanders $1 million to relinquish Steve Yzerman as a draft pick in 1983, convincing Mike to put his trust in Jimmy Devellano. "She was a great sounding board for Mike," Devellano said in 2021. "She understood the importance of stability. She helped us make a lot of good decisions."

It was with good reason she had been named the treasurer at the start.

Mike Ilitch was the public face of the Red Wings from the time he rescued the organization from the miserable state it had deteriorated into under Bruce Norris' ownership. It was Mike who did everything he could to regenerate interest, pouring his time and money into renovating the Joe, experimenting briefly with a mascot (the Red Winger, a red and white bird that resembled a chicken), and in general talking up his prized new team.

As Scotty Bowman came to learn, Marian's input was quieter, but invaluable.

"They were a good tandem because she was a really astute business lady, and Mike was a big entrepreneur," Bowman said in 2023.

It had been three decades since an exchange in the hallway of the Joe, but Bowman remembered the details: it was 1994, and he had agreed to add director of player personnel to his head coaching duties. He didn't want to deal with contracts, except the one he already was negotiating involving Bob Rouse.

"It was interesting because Mike and Marian Ilitch had a meeting with [me] and Jimmy Devellano and Kenny Holland in the middle of the summer, in July of that year, 1994," Bowman said. "They set it up where Jimmy was going to do the contracts, and I could do the acquisition of players. The way they set it up, Marian would be the one that I would deal with.

"That '94–95 season, they had a budget, even though there was no cap, and it was $19 million. I'm pretty sure we were at $18.5 million, and Bob Rouse's agent wanted a contract for $1 million. We only had $500,000 had left, and the way Mike Ilitch had set it up, he said if you are going to sign any players, free agents, contact Marian. And make sure I'm clued in on it. So, he wanted a million and we only had half a million. I did phone Marian. I told her, 'We have to go over budget.' She said, 'I don't think that's a good idea right now.'

"So, I had to call Mike Ilitch and tell him that we have this player. I said, I understand that I have to run it through Marian and I did. But I told Mike, 'I just want you to know, we have to go over budget.' He said, 'Well, how good is he?' I said, 'Well, he's a pretty aggressive guy and a stay-at-home defenseman.'

"I said, 'he's rugged.' And that was Mike's favorite thing. He said, 'Can he help us win?' I said, 'Well yes, I would say he can help us win in the playoffs, because playoffs are a little different.' So, Mike said, 'Okay.'

"I said, 'Should I call Marian back and say I talked with you?' He said, 'No. I'll get slammed, but I'll handle everything.' So, that's the way he was. She was pretty funny about it the next time I ran into her. She and Mike worked really well together. They really understood how to make the team work."

32

Howe's 545ᵗʰ Goal, Bruneteau's OT Goal, Yzerman's Double-OT Goal

GORDIE HOWE'S RIGHT FOOT MADE THE PAGES OF THE *Detroit Free Press* in October 1963, with an accompanying photo.

The article that accompanied the grainy black and white photo referred to the "unkindest cut in hockey" belonging to Howe, whose right ankle showed the aftereffects of a collision with goaltender Terry Sawchuk the previous week. The cut required four stitches to close. Another picture showed Howe's right skate, where a small incision had been made in an effort to relieve the pressure on his ankle. It hurt, but Howe, being Howe, played.

There was a sense of urgency at the time because Howe was chasing his 544th and 545th goals, leading teammates to play, as Jack Berry wrote in the *Detroit Free Press*, a "look for Gordie" style. Howe had six shots on net in an October 24th game against the Chicago Black Hawks but failed to score.

It was just as well. Howe had entered the season with 540 goals, four short of Maurice "Rocket" Richard's NHL-best 544 goals. Fittingly, Howe tied the record against the Montreal Canadiens, on October 27. "Howe Ties Rocket—Bags Goal 544!" ran the headline in the *Detroit Free Press* the next day, along with an evocative description of the evening's main event. "A thundering, deafening, rolling, five-minute standing ovation followed Gordie Howe's 544th regular-season goal, the one that ties him with retired Maurice Richard for the National Hockey League record." Howe explained the play, at 11:04 of the third period and with the Wings on a power play, that brought an eruption from the 14,749 fans that had packed into Olympia to watch him celebrate. "Bill Gadsby threw it to Bruce [MacGregor] and Bruce threw it to me and I threw it in. Then five guys hit me."

MacGregor was at the left boards and fired the puck over to the goal mouth. Howe banged it past goalie Gump Worsley, but the celebration was marred by the final score favoring the Canadiens 6–4. "It takes some of the joy away when you lose the game," Howe said.

After the game Montreal coach Toe Blake approached Howe to congratulate him and said, "I wish I could have played center for you."

Howe acknowledged he was glad to reach the milestone, saying, "It should help the club." He already had promised the puck to Jack Adams, who Howe credited for discovering him; the stick would go to his oldest sons, Marty, nine, and Mark, eight.

Howe's 544th goal came in his 1,126[th] game, near the start of his 18th season. Richard needed 978 games over 18 seasons to get to 544.

It wasn't scripted but could have been: Howe was quiet the next five games. On November 10, again against the Canadiens, he bagged the elusive 545th goal, earning a headline that blared "Howe Now Greatest Scorer of 'Em All." Howe set the record in spectacular fashion, scoring while the Wings were shorthanded and coinciding with Terry Sawchuk tying George Hainsworth for the most shutouts in regular season play at 94. It was a bonus achievement to cheer for the 15,027 fans that had packed into Olympia, who also witnessed a 3–0 victory over the Habs. Howe scored at 15:06 of the second period while Alex Faulkner served a penalty for high-sticking Ralph Backstrom. Manager-coach Sid Abel (Howe's former Production Line center) said before the game he had a premonition that Howe would score and said he would work him heavily to try and get it over with—hence, why Howe was on the ice to kill the penalty will Billy McNeill. McNeill got the puck deep in Detroit territory at the boards and broke out with Howe on his left and Gadsby on the far side. McNeill carried the puck down the right side, cut toward the middle and over the Canadiens' blue line and slid the puck over to Howe. Howe whipped a wrist shot from inside the faceoff circle that sailed by goaltender Charlie Hodge, who was subbing for an injured Worsley. Howe raised his right arm in celebration, holding his stick high.

The ovation lasted seven minutes, overwhelming the sound of Hodge banging disgustedly at the goal post. Faulkner was the first to congratulate Howe, jumping out of the penalty box and rushing to embrace him.

It was huge deal in the world of hockey and resonated around the city of Detroit. Local police officers on duty that

Sunday night learned of the historic shot at Olympia almost immediately thanks to their radios, which carried the following alert: "Attention all cars. Gordie Howe's new record is 545."

* * *

Game 1 of the 1936 semifinal between the Red Wings and Montreal Maroons began on March 24 and ended on March 25. Modere Fernand Bruneteau, whose fancy first name begat the nickname "Mud," scored the winning goal that ended the longest game in NHL history, putting the puck in Montreal's net at 16:30 of the sixth overtime, ending the game after 116 minutes and 30 seconds of play. It was the only goal of the game.

Bruneteau, recently brought up to the Wings from the Detroit Olympics, took a pass from Hec Kilrea and fired the puck past Lorne Chabot at 2:25 A.M. Shots on net weren't recorded back then, but Detroit goaltender Normie Smith is generally credited with making around 90 saves. In a 1986 interview, he recalled that "near the end, the pads and equipment were getting heavy from being soaked with sweat and water. When I saw the red light go on to end the game, I thought, *School's out!* I was very happy it finally ended."

Pete Kelly, who had almost scored in the eighth period, remembered Bruneteau's goal. "In those days, they didn't make ice between periods like they do now with the Zamboni," he said decades later. "They only swept the ice, so it was quite rough with a lot of skate marks. The longer the game went, the more difficult the puck was to control. Hec carried the play to the goal area and had made a play on the goal. A rebound resulted, and Bruneteau banged it in on a scramble. There was a fair crowd in the net."

The Wings went on to sweep the Maroons in three games and beat the Toronto Maple Leafs in the Stanley Cup Finals.

Bruneteau won the Cup with the Wings again in 1937 and 1943.

* * *

On May 16, 1996, the Red Wings played a game that ended with another goal memorable for the ages. It was a Game 7—by itself, a thrill—between the Wings and the St. Louis Blues. In the second round of the playoffs, the Wings had seemed in control of the series when they followed up a 3–2 Game 1 victory by routing the Blues 8–3 in the next game, but St. Louis won the next two games, at home, by one-goal margins to tie the best-of-seven series.

Then the Blues delivered a huge blow, winning 3–2 at Joe Louis Arena to push the Wings to the brink of elimination. The Wings responded by going into Kiel Center and winning 4–2.

That was on May 14. Two nights later, the game was back at the Joe. The Wings outshot the Blues 14–4 in the first period and 32–21 at the end of regulation. The first overtime was fairly evenly played with Chris Osgood and Jon Casey matching one another nearly save for save.

Double overtime began. Steve Yzerman—The Captain—shook off Wayne Gretzky and faked out Blues defender Murray Baron and took the puck to the net, but Casey made a highlight reel save on Sergei Fedorov's attempt to poke the pass into the net.

Instead, it was the most unremarkable of plays that led to a most memorable goal. Slava Fetisov gathered the puck behind St. Louis' net and played it to his defense partner, Vladimir Konstantinov. Konstantinov's attempt to get the puck to his forwards went awry, he didn't get enough on the shot, and the puck was picked off by Gretzky. Gretzky lost the puck to Yzerman, who did what he had done hundreds of times before and after—fire the puck toward the net from the blue line. It was an innocuous shot with immense ramifications, sending the Wings on to the Western Conference Finals. His lark of a 55-foot slapper hit the crossbar and bounced into the net, ending the game at 1–0 at 1:15 of double overtime.

"I don't score a whole lot from the blue line, so I was definitely surprised," Yzerman said afterward. "I shot it and looked up and heard the clang against the bar and I was like, *No way. It went in.*"

Wings owner Mike Ilitch was among the jubilant crowd that witnessed the memorable goal.

"As far as a captain, he's a total captain," Ilitch said. "He does it all. You take your Mark Messier. We've got Steve Yzerman."

33

Terry Sawchuk, Roger Crozier, Chris Osgood

TERRY SAWCHUK WAS A BRILLIANT GOALTENDER WHOSE LIFE and career were undermined by addiction before there was much understanding of the disease.

At the time of his death in 1970, he was only 40 years old and had played 971 games in 21 seasons in the NHL. He was the first goaltender in the league to record 100 shutouts, and half a century after his death, his 103 shutouts still ranked second all-time in league history.

Born December 28, 1929, in Winnipeg, Manitoba, Terrance Gordon Sawchuk went by Terry and, among teammates, "Ukey," or "The Uke," a nod to his Ukrainian heritage. Sawchuk played hockey, baseball, and rugby as a teenager. It was while playing the latter, at age 12, that he severely injured his right elbow, but fearful of telling his parents, kept it to himself. The joint never healed properly, leaving Sawchuk's right arm shorter than his left, a malady that gave him lifelong discomfort.

His was a short, spectacular life. By the time he was 14, Sawchuk had drawn interest from NHL scouts. The Wings signed him to a professional contract in 1947. Sawchuk's career took off immediately, as he was named rookie of the year in the United States Hockey League in 1948 and in the American Hockey League in 1949.

He debuted with the Wings on January 8, 1950, the first of seven games he played that season while filling in for injured goaltender Harry Lumley. Sawchuk's performance—he posted a 4–3 record with a 2.29 goals-against average—convinced general manager Jack Adams he could handle the job, and as a result, Adams traded Lumley to the Chicago Black Hawks shortly after Lumley had recorded three shutouts and a 1.85 goals-against average in the 14 games it took the Wings to win the Stanley Cup in 1950.

Lumley was good; Sawchuk was great. From 1950–51 through 1954–55, he led all NHL goaltenders with 195 victories (Gerry McNeil, in second place, had 112). Sawchuk's 1.93 goals-against average was the only one below 2.00 among goaltenders who appeared in at least 100 games. His 56 shutouts were 20 more than Lumley, who ranked second with 36. Sawchuk backstopped the Wings to the Stanley Cup in 1952, '54, and '55, and was named an All-Star consecutively from 1950 to 1956 (and four more times later in his career). Sawchuk went 28–15 in 43 playoff games, posting a 1.87 goals-against average. He was spectacular in the 1952 playoffs, going 8–0 with a .63 goals-against average.

Sawchuk played at a time before backup goaltenders were common. From 1950–51 to 1954–55, the Wings played 350 games. Sawchuk played 338 of them.

His tolerance for pain was legendary. During his career he endured multiple operations on his right elbow (the one he had injured as a teenager and never received proper treatment for), an appendectomy, influenza, a broken foot, a collapsed lung, ruptured discs, and severed tendons. He was 5'11" but would crouch so low he could see through the legs of skaters, leading to permanent back damage. He didn't wear a face mask until 1962. When *Life Magazine* commissioned a portrait of Sawchuk in 1966, a makeup artist ran out of room to demonstrate all the scars and cuts Sawchuk had sustained just to his face.

It was Bruce Norris' ouster of his sister, Marguerite, in 1955 that upended Sawchuk's career. Jack Adams, untethered from the control exerted by Marguerite, broke apart the roster that had just won the Stanley Cup.

One of the victims was Sawchuk, who was traded to the Boston Bruins in a nine-player swap. Adams was secure in the belief that the Wings had their next goaltender in Glenn Hall. There was also concern about Sawchuk's elbow—by then it was described in local newspapers as "crippled," and his 45-pound weight loss. (His playing weight swung all the way from 166 to 216 during his career.)

Two years later, Sawchuk was back with the Wings. He had retired during his second season with the Bruins; depressed over the trade, he struggled mentally and physically. He spent two weeks hospitalized with a blood disorder, leading him into self-imposed exile. Still under contract with the Bruins, the Wings ended up sending forward Johnny Bucyk to Boston.

Sawchuk was just short of his 28th birthday when he began his second stint with the Wings. In his first five years, he had been voted rookie of the year, earned the Vezina Trophy three times, and backstopped the Wings to five straight NHL titles.

Adams' meddling with the roster after the 1955 championship season had weakened the Wings. Sawchuk had posted a goals-against average below 2.00 five straight seasons in his first stint, but in his comeback, his goals-against average hovered closer to the 3.00 mark. He spent seven seasons in his second go-around with the Wings, until the arrival of another elite young goaltender, Roger Crozier, rendered Sawchuk's presence obsolete. He was left unprotected in the 1964 intra-league draft and claimed by the Toronto Maple Leafs. There he found success in a tandem with Johnny Bower, leading to the Stanley Cup title in 1967. Sawchuk made 40 saves in Game 6 to lead the Leafs to a 3–1 victory, clinching the championship. Still the Leafs cut ties with Sawchuk, leaving him unprotected in the 1967 expansion draft. Sawchuk played for the Los Angeles Kings in 1967–68, then returned for a third stint with the Wings. That only lasted a season, and Sawchuk played what would turn out to be the final season of his career in 1969–70 with the New York Rangers.

Sawchuk struggled with alcohol abuse throughout his life, and it led to his divorce in 1969. In April 1970 he went out drinking with Rangers teammate Ron Stewart, who was also a housemate. The two returned to their home, where a disagreement led to a wrestling match on the lawn. Police reports described the incident as "horseplay." Sawchuk was hospitalized at Long Beach, New York, Memorial Hospital on April 29 suffering from an abdominal injury. He underwent surgery for removal of his gall bladder, and a second operation for complications. He was transferred to New York Hospital, where he underwent a third operation. He died May 31 at age 40. Clarence Campbell, president of the NHL, issued a statement: "It's a terrible tragedy. I'm so sorry."

Sawchuk was inducted into the Hockey Hall of Fame a year after his death. In 1994 the Wings retired his No. 1.

Sawchuk holds the all-time franchise record with 350 victories during his time with the Wings. The goaltender in second place won 317 for the team.

* * *

Just as Sawchuk had won the job when he filled in for an injured Harry Lumley, Roger Crozier emerged as the Wings' goaltender when he filled in for an injured Sawchuk in 1963.

"Regardless of how well Terry is playing, Crozier will go in as soon as he's ready," general manager/coach Sid Abel said in December of that year. The Wings had acquired Crozier, born March 16, 1942, in Bracebridge, Ontario, from the Chicago Black Hawks earlier that year. Crozier earned rave reviews in his debut on November 30, 1963, when he made 36 saves on the 37 shots he faced against the Toronto Maple Leafs. Crozier was injured by a flying puck in the second period; doctors needed about 15 minutes to tend to Crozier after he was nicked on the left cheekbone. Crozier, then 21 years old, had a shutout bid ruined when Toronto's Bob Pulford took a pass from Tim Horton and scored.

Still, it was enough to convince Abel that the Wings had their new net minder.

"The players played better with him in there than anyone we've had in goal," Abel said. "He fires them up, he's in the game every second, and he's got quick hands. He's got really quick hands."

Crozier evoked memories of Glenn Hall thanks to a quick, sweeping glove and the ability to slide side-to-side. To amend for his 5'8", 160-pound stature, Crozier employed a butterfly style of goaltending.

The injury to his left cheekbone forced Crozier to wear a mask, which he had not done before. A picture in the *Detroit Free Press* on December 10, 1963, showed Crozier in bed, his face being swathed in bandages by trainer Lefty Wilson for the purpose of making a plaster of Paris cast of Crozier's face.

By the age of 22, Crozier was the Wings' No. 1 man in net. He already had an impressive résumé, having won the Hap Holmes Memorial Award for giving up the fewest goals while playing for Detroit's AHL affiliate. The Wings were so convinced Crozier was their best goaltender that they left Sawchuk unprotected in the intra-league waiver draft in 1964.

Crozier played all 70 games in his rookie season, 1964–65, the only goalie to do so. He paced the league with 40 victories (14 more than second-place Charlie Hodge of the Canadiens) and six shutouts. Crozier only just lost out on the Vezina Trophy when his 2.42 goals-against average was edged out by Toronto's Johnny Bower but instead celebrated taking home the Calder Trophy. The announcement came a week after Crozier also was named to the All-Star team, the first rookie to make that honor roll since Sawchuk in 1951.

Crozier was beloved by teammates. "You never hear the boy complain about anything," Ted Lindsay said in 1966. "I've seen some goalies who blame everyone else for the goals. But you never hear Roger say a word. Not a word."

During the 1966 playoffs, when the Wings faced the Canadiens in the Stanley Cup Finals, Crozier played with his left leg taped from the instep to the thigh to ameliorate a sprained knee and twisted ankle suffered in the fourth game of the series. Crozier's gutsy effort was lauded by Abel, but the Wings went on to drop the next two games, losing the series four games to two. Crozier, however, was recognized with the Conn Smythe Trophy, which came with a $1,000 bonus from the NHL and a car from Ford Motor Company, a telecast sponsor. Crozier was the first goaltender to be named the most outstanding player of the playoffs and the first player to win it from the losing side.

Crozier battled health issues including pancreatitis throughout his life. In early November 1967, he shocked the Wings by telling them he was quitting. "Roger said he had lost all confidence in his ability and that he felt like he had forgotten everything he knew about playing goal," Abel said.

Crozier was only 25 years old and in the second year of a four-year, $100,000 contract, lucrative by that day's standard. His decision was made to offset Abel's decision to send Crozier to the Fort Worth farm team. "He said he decided to quit and asked me not to try to talk him out of it," Abel said. "He said he'd be happy to play anywhere, Fort Worth, San Diego, wherever we'd want to send him, if he felt he could play. But he said he felt if he continued to play, his health would fail him."

No less than Sawchuk, who had been displaced by Crozier's arrival, offered to help. "Terry said that if it would do any good, he would talk to Roger," Abel said. "Terry said he had been through the same thing when he was in Boston, and he thought it was the end." (Sawchuk was playing for the Los Angeles Kings, who had just walloped the Wings in Detroit the day before).

A week later, Crozier held fast on his decision.

"We're packing up and probably will leave the latter part of the week," Crozier said in a *Detroit Free Press* interview that ran on November 13. That was after days and days of nearly everyone trying to get him to change his mind, including Jacques Plante, the retired Montreal goalie and one of the game's all-time greats, who asked Crozier to return during a telecast.

It wasn't just his physical health that concerned Crozier. He had set such incredibly high expectations at a young age that he felt compelled to perform to that level every game—and back then, it was every game. Crozier said that if the NHL had a relief system for goaltenders like baseball had for starting pitchers, things might have gone differently. "I talked to Glenn Hall about it one day, and he agrees," Crozier said.

Crozier returned to his cottage in Bracebridge for about two months.

In early January he reappeared at Olympia Stadium. It was the first time he had been on the ice since November 5, when he had peeled off the 40 pounds of goalie equipment from his 145-pound frame and announced he was done.

"I had to come back sooner or later," the 25-year-old said. "Every day in some little way hockey would come up at home. Kids in my wife's class would ask her, 'When is Mr. Crozier going to play hockey again?' Or we'd be skating on the lake in front of our house, and it would seem so funny not to have a stick in my hand. And even when I'd be curling and a stone would be coming at me, I'd think about making a save on it. I guess hockey is really a great part of my life without my realizing it. That's why I thought I'd come back to see if I was still a part of hockey."

On January 21, 1967, Crozier returned to the lineup, resuming the hectic pace that was the life of an NHL goaltender in those days. He ended up playing 34 games in 1967–68, posting a 3.30 goals-against average and .890 save percentage. The Wings missed the playoffs for a second straight year that spring.

Crozier played parts of two more seasons with the Wings. In June 1970 he was traded to the Buffalo Sabres for forward Tom Webster. Crozier spent six seasons with the Sabres, finishing his playing career with the Washington Capitals in 1976–77.

Crozier died of cancer on January 11, 1996, at the age of 53. "He was just a kid who wanted to play hockey," Abel said. "He came to our club and he was like a son. He loved to play."

* * *

Chris Osgood is the most successful goaltender drafted by the Wings, who plucked him from the third round in 1991, at 54th. Then-general manager Ken Holland had scouted Osgood more than a dozen times, developing a friendship along the way. Playing for Medicine Hat in the Western Hockey League, Osgood stood out for his competitive drive and mental toughness.

The Wings had nothing in their farm system as far as goaltending when they drafted Osgood. He began his professional career in the organization with the Adirondack Red Wings in 1992–93 and made his NHL debut October 15, 1993, at the age of 20.

He lasted half the game, pulled after allowing four goals on 12 shots. The mental toughness kicked in with Osgood refusing to let a bad performance undermine all the good work he had done. Two starts later, he celebrated his first NHL victory, making 23 saves and bringing fans to their feet with a diving glove save on Los Angeles Kings forward Alexei Zhitnik. Osgood followed that up with two consecutive victories.

Osgood's steadiness helped convince higher ups in the Wings organization—it was Scotty Bowman's first year behind the bench—that Tim Cheveldae was expendable, and he was traded in March 1994 to the Winnipeg Jets for goaltender Bob Essensa, viewed as a better option for the expected long playoff run. When Essensa was benched after a mediocre performance in the opening game of the first-round series against the San Jose Sharks, Osgood slid into the spotlight.

On April 20, Osgood made 22 saves in a 4–0 victory in Game 2, becoming the first Wings rookie since Terry Sawchuk to deliver a shutout in a Stanley Cup game.

That he was still only 21 years of age showed a week later, when Osgood wept openly in front of his locker after he mishandled an attempted clearing pass late in the third period of Game 7, instead sending the puck right to San Jose forward Jamie Baker, who turned the gift into the series-winning goal.

"If I would have made the play, we'd still be playing," Osgood said as tears streamed down his face. Nearby, captain Steve Yzerman put the event into perspective.

"He's a great young goalie and he's going to have a lot of time in this league," Yzerman said. "That last goal, I wouldn't call it a mistake on his part. He's got to hold his head up high. We're pretty proud of the way he played."

The Wings did believe in Osgood, but considering his age and lack of experience, they brought in veteran Mike Vernon during the offseason. By the mid-1990s, there was tremendous pressure on the Wings to win the Cup. Osgood outplayed Vernon during the 1994–95 season, but Vernon had won the Cup with the Calgary Flames in 1989 and got the nod when the playoffs began.

Osgood and Vernon shared the William M. Jennings Trophy (goaltending duo with fewest goals against) in 1995–96, the season the Wings won a record 62 games.

In 1997 Vernon backstopped the Wings to the Stanley Cup. By that offseason the Wings were sold on Osgood as their No. 1 goalie and traded Vernon.

Osgood won 34 of the 63 games he started in 1997–98. The loudest cheers from the home crowd during the regular season, though, came on April 1 when Osgood fought Colorado goalie

Patrick Roy, just as Vernon had done during the famous March 26, 1997, game.

"He had no choice," Bowman said afterward. "There was nothing else he could do. I didn't like the idea of goalies fighting—I didn't like the idea of him being vulnerable to injuries. But Chris is a tough kid."

Kris Draper added his opinion: "It was Roy trying to show up Ozzy. I think he underestimated Ozzy, wondering if he was going to come out and fight him. Ozzy stood up for himself and did a great job, but he was also standing up for our team."

Two and a half months later, Osgood left his net again—this time, to celebrate winning the Stanley Cup. He made 30 saves in Game 4 in Washington against the Capitals as the Wings swept their way to repeating. Yzerman, the captain, was the first to get the Cup, and he placed it in the lap of Vladimir Konstantinov, who had suffered life-altering injuries a week after the Wings won the Cup in '97.

The next guy to get the Cup was Osgood, in recognition of how much weight he had carried as the starting goaltender.

Osgood loved being a Wing, but when the Buffalo Sabres called Holland in the summer of 2001 needing to move out Dominik Hašek for financial reasons, Holland could not say no to acquiring one of the all-time greatest goaltenders. It was the business side of hockey, but that did not lessen the blow when Osgood was dumped on waivers and picked up by the New York Islanders.

Osgood, by then 28, spent a season and a half with the Islanders, then was traded to the St. Louis Blues.

In August 2005 the Wings brought Osgood back on a one-year deal, in need of a veteran presence in net. A two-year deal followed the next summer. By then Hašek was back, too, for another stint with the Wings. The two largely worked well together and shared the duties.

Hašek got the nod to start the 2008 playoffs, but when he performed poorly in Game 3 and looked shaky again as Game 4 got underway, Osgood replaced Hašek in net. By Game 5 Osgood was the starter.

Osgood began the Stanley Cup Finals against the Pittsburgh Penguins with back-to-back shutouts. In Game 6, in the waning seconds, Osgood made a save on Marian Hossa that preserved a 3–2 victory and a series victory. For the third time in his career, second time as starter, Osgood was a Stanley Cup champion.

"He's always been able to bounce back," teammate Kirk Maltby said. "As an athlete, that's the greatest strength that anybody could have: being able to move on from whatever good or bad happens."

The day after the game, Osgood spoke about how special the 2008 Cup was for him. "I wasn't supposed to play," he said. "But I never doubted myself, I never looked on myself as the backup because I knew behind the scenes what I was doing to get better. I'll never give up until I'm done with my last game in Detroit. I'll always give it my all."

Osgood finished his career with the Wings, retiring in 2011. He played 744 games in the NHL, winning 401 of them.

34

Bruce Martyn, Budd Lynch, Mickey Redmond

WHEN HE RETIRED AFTER 31 YEARS OF BEING THE VOICE of the Red Wings, Bruce Martyn joked it was because radio partner Paul Woods' gin-rummy game "has gone to hell in a handbasket. It's just no fun anymore, so I'm gone."

The truth was that Martyn was 65 and had spent nearly half his life calling Wings games. His legacy had been recognized in 1991 when he was presented with the Foster Hewitt Memorial Award for broadcasting by the Hockey Hall of Fame. Martyn was ready for the joys of retirement at his and his wife, Donna's, new home in Venice, Florida.

"It would be nice to just have a winter to go out and do things, to see the family and all," Martyn said in a 1995 interview in the *Detroit Free Press*. "I wouldn't call it sadness at all; I'm kind of looking forward to it."

Born June 24, 1929 (making him one year younger than Gordie Howe), Martyn began his broadcasting career in his hometown of Sault Ste. Marie, Michigan, doing play-by-play for the Sault Ste. Marie Indians of the Northern Ontario Hockey Association. It was there that he met Howe, Lindsay, and Sid Abel—the famed Production Line—when the Wings were in town to train. Young and nervous, Martyn let the three stars do the talking, thrilling at the experience. Abel would later become a broadcasting partner, as was Budd Lynch.

Martyn's work in Sault Ste. Marie became a springboard for a move to Pontiac in 1953 and a chance to announce games for a variety of teams, including the Detroit Lions, Detroit Pistons, and Michigan State sports. But hockey remained at the forefront of Martyn's career ambitions, and he jumped at the chance when the Wings offered him a job broadcasting home and away games. Modern announcers memorize opposing rosters' names and numbers to facilitate calling games, but when Martyn began, players didn't wear helmets, and there were only six teams.

Martyn was known for his great inflection and for how his voice would rise an octave when he was describing a dangerous play in the offensive zone.

"I would consider Bruce among the best at those who did his trade," Mickey Redmond, the former player turned TV color commentator, said in 2023. "Radio is, I think, harder to do than TV because you really have to bring the picture to the audience, whereas on TV you don't. Bruce painted a picture that was very vivid in your mind when he was doing radio."

Martyn's tenure with the Wings spanned calling the performances of luminaries including Gordie Howe and Ted

Lindsay, Steve Yzerman and Sergei Fedorov. After he had retired, Martyn's only regret was that he had never gotten to call the Wings winning the last game of the playoffs.

"You get to the point where you feel you're a real part of the hockey team," Martyn said in 1995, "and leaving that behind will hurt."

Martyn did call two Stanley Cup Finals: in 1966 the Wings won the first two games of the Stanley Cup Finals against the Montreal Canadiens, stoking hope of another championship. But the Habs were too good and won the next four games.

In his final season, Martyn delighted fans on the radio as the Wings worked their way through the first round, the second round, the third round, and onto a Finals series opposite the New Jersey Devils. Martyn could appreciate better than many what it meant, having voiced the Wings through the misery that was the "Dead Wings" era in the 1970s and the hope that came with the change in ownership when Mike Ilitch bought the team from Bruce Norris in 1982. But again, it wasn't to be: the next four games were losses, the Wings once again denied the Stanley Cup.

It was a special day, therefore, when he returned to call a Wings game two years later at the invitation of Ken Kal, who had taken over the play-by-play duties when Martyn retired.

"I felt so bad for Bruce because I think he thought that the Wings were going to win the Cup against the Devils, and he wanted to retire on top," Kal said in a 2023 interview. "Well, the Red Wings got swept. So, when the Red Wings got into the Finals, and that was my second year after taking over for Bruce, I thought, *He's got to call a Stanley Cup, period.* I called him and asked him if he would like to come in and he goes, 'Yes, that would be really nice.' By then, I knew we were going to win the Cup, we were up three games to nothing.

"Wouldn't you know it, this is how fate works. He calls the Darren McCarty Cup-winning goal. It was a beautiful call, too. I believe Bruce got a Stanley Cup ring, too. Not only was it a privilege and an honor to work with Bruce, but to have him call the Cup-winning goal was amazing."

It was one last, historic chance for Martyn to give his trademark call, "He shoots, he scores."

* * *

Budd Lynch had already worked for the Wings for 15 years when he helped break in Martyn. Lynch began his own lengthy association with the Wings in 1949 when the team needed a new play-by-play sportscaster. Lynch had been working with the Windsor Spitfires, returning to his hometown after World War II. Part of the third wave at Juno Beach during his service in the Canadian Army, Lynch lost his right arm and shoulder when a German shell exploded while his outfit was near Caen, France, three weeks later. His body lacerated by shell fragments, Lynch dragged a fellow soldier to safety. Years later, players would kid him about how he wound his watch.

Lynch was close to the players, but he was never their cheerleader, even as they won the Stanley Cup four times during his first five years calling games. Originally starting out on the radio, Lynch segued into calling games on the nascent industry that was television in the 1950s.

Lynch was in his late 50s when he toyed with retirement in 1975, but Alex Delvecchio, who was the general manager, talked him into a stint as the team's public relations director instead. A decade later it was Marian Ilitch who persuaded Lynch to keep working, this time as the public address announcer at Joe Louis Arena. He managed to make the announcement "last minute of play in this period" sound both matter of fact and melodious.

That same year, he received the Foster Hewitt Memorial Award, recognizing his contributions to hockey broadcasting. He was a beloved sight in the press box at the Joe, where his favorite prank was to tap reporters on their shoulders and then sneak by before they could turn around and see him. After his death on October 9, 2012, at the age of 95, the Wings continued to use his last-minute recording at the Joe until the building closed in 2017.

* * *

Mickey Redmond already had a legendary career as a player when he joined the Wings as a broadcaster in 1985. He won the Stanley Cup with the Montreal Canadiens in 1968 and 1969 and then landed in Detroit when he was traded to the Wings during the 1970–71 season. The Wings were dreadful in the 1970s but Redmond was a bright spark. In 1972–73 he scored 52 goals, breaking Gordie Howe's single-season franchise record of 49 goals. Redmond starred on a line first with Alex Delvecchio, and later with Marcel Dionne, producing a second 50-goal season in 1973–74. His career was cut short by a back injury that forced him to retire in 1976 at the age of 28.

Searching for a job to stay in hockey, Redmond took the suggestion of a friend and explored broadcasting, where his gregarious nature was a perfect fit. He spent five years broadcasting NHL games on CBC's *Hockey Night in Canada* alongside such luminaries as Bob Cole and Dick Irvin Jr.

"It has worked out very well for me," Redmond said in a 2023 interview. "I enjoy the entertainment part of what we do. Our job has become much more entertainment wise than it was 20 years ago. It was more cut-and-dry, stick to the facts. But the world today is a different world, and I've tried to adapt to that, and I enjoy that. I feel like I'm a voice for the fans, like I'm one of them. I really enjoy it."

In 1985 Mike Ilitch was three years into his ownership of the Wings and casting about for ways to generate more excitement. The solution was to bring in Redmond, who was paired with Dave Strader to broadcast Wings games on television, while Martyn and Sid Abel would broadcast over the radio. Previously, the two had been simulcast.

Redmond's first season was the Wings' worst as a franchise, when they won just 17 games in 1985–86. Less than a decade later, they were in the Stanley Cup Finals in 1995, and two years after that, they won the Cup. Through it all, Redmond entertained viewers with his country-boy charm and colorful descriptions. "Bingo-bango," "holy mackerel," and "holy jumpin'" became a regular part of the Wings' broadcasts.

"I think it's because of my enjoyment and humor, I like to keep things light," Redmond said. "I try to keep the seriousness out of it—I like to keep it relaxed. If the humor is there, then I'm going to take it. But sometimes I wonder where some of the things I say come from myself, frankly. People still quote me on 'No place for a nervous person,' because it's always there. It was there in the '60s, it was there in the '70s and '80s, and it's there today. If you're nervous, you're not going to be very good. You've got to relax."

35

Olympia Stadium, Joe Louis Arena, Little Caesars Arena

GORDIE HOWE SHOWED UP TO SAY GOODBYE AND COLLECT a few mementos. So did Alex Delvecchio, Marcel Pronovost, Johnny Wilson, Billy Dee, and Budd Lynch.

It was a chilly afternoon in May 1986 when former players and longtime fans gathered on the corner of Grand River Avenue and McGraw Street in Detroit to take one last look around what was left of the hockey shrine the franchise called home from 1927 to 1979. Olympia Stadium was earmarked to be demolished, cast into the past by the newer, though hardly prettier, Joe Louis Arena.

Howe was among many who picked up a couple of bricks as keepsakes.

Detroit Olympia, most commonly referred to as Olympia Stadium and affectionally referred to as "The Old Red Barn," was originally planned to cost $600,000, but city leaders urged the businessmen who owned the hockey club and had planned the arena to think bigger, and the price tag grew to $2.5 million. The rectangular red brick edifice with was designed by C. Howard Crane, an internationally known theater architect based in Detroit and the man who designed the Fox Theatre.

A blurb from a publicity brochure heralded the arena: "At Grand River and McGraw Avenues, there is being erected a magnificent building of steel and concrete, which, through the years to come, will be recognized as one of the city's most useful assets. This splendid edifice, located within half a mile of the center of population of Detroit, is, to state the matter briefly, another Madison Square Garden...Any thinking and conservative person will doubtless be assured by reading these few words that Olympia, with its vast diversity of appeal, can pay its way. Olympia will earn its way. No believer in Detroit can doubt that."

On Olympia stationery dated June 16, 1927, team president Charles A. Hughes wrote John Townsend, an investor who was part of owner of the hockey team and new arena, to tell him that the next meeting of the Olympia salesmen would be at the DAC soon in Private Dining Room No. 7: "Quite a few subscriptions have been secured lately, and we hope for a favorable day. Mr. Henry Ford's subscription came in today for a sizeable amount."

From 1920 to 1930—the decade that the Cougars arrived and Olympia was built—Detroit's population increased from 993,678 to 1,568,662, making it the fourth-largest city in the United States. Many landmark buildings in Detroit were erected during the decade: the GM Building in 1922, the *Free Press* building in 1923, the Buhl Building in 1925, the Fisher Building and Masonic Temple in 1928.

Olympia's opening event was a rodeo, which ran for a week. Then came a polo match for high society. Olympia finally hosted a hockey game on November 22, 1927, when the Detroit Cougars lost to the Ottawa Senators 2–1.

The opening festivities included Detroit mayor John C. Lodge presenting a floral wreath to general manager Jack Adams, a "fancy skating" exhibition by Gladys Lamb and Norval Baptie, and the University of Michigan band parading across the ice. The next day, the *Detroit Free Press* account of the game started like this: "Ottawa's collection of systematic hockey players provided the only wet blanket on the hockey inaugural at the new Olympia last night."

Five years later, the Cougars would be renamed the Detroit Red Wings, and with their success came fame for the Olympia.

It was where Jake LaMotta knocked out Sugar Ray Robinson on February 5, 1943, the only time in their fabled, six-bout rivalry that LaMotta won. It was where fans twisted and shouted and sang along as The Beatles performed on September 6, 1964. (Tickets were $3 for the show that year and had risen to $3.50 when they played at Olympia again on August 13, 1966.) Norwegian figure skater and three-time Olympic champion Sonja Henie took her Hollywood Ice Revue show to Detroit to perform at Olympia. Dorothy Hamill skated there, too. Elvis Presley played at Olympia on March 31, 1957, performing in two 40-minute segments. Elvis returned to Olympia in 1970 (his single 45-minute show drew nearly 17,000 "screaming, jumping and almost hysterical fans," according to Tom DeLisle's article in the *Detroit Free Press).*

Olympia was a hockey mecca. Its ice was considered the league's fastest and its boards, the trickiest. The seats were close to the action, the balconies were a treat, and players ambled to and from their dressing rooms in the lower concourse amid fans visiting concession stands, separated only by wooden barriers. In the days before Plexiglas was added to the top of the boards to form a shield, the rink's ends were minimally protected by wire fencing, the type that would be used to fence in a yard. There's a famous picture from 1954 that shows goaltender Terry Sawchuk crawling over the fencing to have a go at a fan who had heckled one too many times. (Back then, goalies didn't have the Michelin Man-level of equipment they have now.) Glen Skov, a teammate, has his gloves on the fencing, ready to follow Sawchuk.

Olympia was an intimate setting. The sight lines were awesome and the acoustics, tremendous. It was a deafening roar when fans chanted "We want Howe" on April 23, 1950, during Game 7 against the New York Rangers, clamoring for their injured star, who had suffered a scary head injury in the first game of the playoffs.

The Cougars played their first playoff game at Olympia on March 19, 1929, losing 3–1 to the Toronto Maple Leafs. The franchise didn't qualify for the playoffs again until 1932, by which time it was known as the Detroit Falcons. They played the Montreal Maroons on March 27 in a 1–1 tie, losing the quarterfinal series.

It wasn't until they were known as the Red Wings that playoff games at Olympia ended in victory. In 1933 the Wings won their quarterfinal series against the Maroons with a 3–2 victory on March 28.

On April 7, 1936, fans watched the Wings rout the Toronto Maple Leafs 9–4 in the second game of the Stanley Cup Final. The cheers were even louder the next spring when on April 15,

1937, the Wings defeated the New York Rangers 3–0 to claim a second straight Stanley Cup championship.

Howe's first playoff game at Olympia was April 1, 1947, in a 4–1 loss to the Maple Leafs. Back then, Howe wore No. 17 because Roy Conacher had the No. 9 on his sweater. It was Conacher's only season with the Wings, and by 1947–48, Howe wore the number he would wear for the rest of his career.

Olympia hosted another Stanley Cup clinching victory on April 15, 1952, when Metro Prystai's two goals helped the Wings defeat the Canadiens 3–0. Two years and one day later, Tony Leswick's goal at 4:29 of overtime clinched a 2–1 victory over the Canadiens at Olympia, giving the Wings another Stanley Cup title. Another followed on April 14, 1955, when the Wings again battled the Canadiens in the Final, winning the series 4–3. Howe scored the clinching goal, and Pronovost drew the assist in the 3–1 victory in Game 7. Delvecchio had the other two goals for the Wings.

When Olympia opened, the seating capacity was 11,563, but over the years, renovations expanded seating to 15,000. Padded seats were added in the late 1950s. That was also when the Wings shared the arena with the National Basketball Association Detroit Pistons, who used it as their home arena from 1957 to 1961.

The Wings went into a decline after Bruce Norris ousted his sister, Marguerite, in 1955 to establish control of the team. The deadly riots that shook Detroit in the summer of 1967 ravaged the neighborhood around Olympia. By the 1970s the arena was in as sad shape as the franchise, which fans had taken to calling the "Dead Wings" and "the worst team money can buy." As the decade wore on, talk of a new home intensified. There was chatter about moving to Pontiac, where the Detroit Lions had just moved into the state-of-the-art Silverdome. That was scuttled when an agreement was reached to build a new arena along the riverfront, keeping the franchise in Detroit.

The Wings played their last game at Olympia Stadium on December 15, 1979. Paul Woods, who would go on to a career as the team's radio color commentator, assisted on the last goal the Wings recorded at the stadium. Václav Nedomanský, the future Hockey Hall of Fame inductee, had a goal and an assist in the 4–4 tie against the Quebec Nordiques. The Wings played their next four games on the road before returning home on December 27 to host the St. Louis Blues at the brand-new Joe Louis Arena.

In 1980 the Detroit City Council bought the vacant stadium for $373,000. In December 1985 the council voted to demolish it and deed the property to the state Department of Military Affairs. The state and the city were to share the $500,000 cost of demolition. At that time, the 58-year-old building had been vacant since February 21, 1980, when more than 14,000 people came to see what was billed as the Old Red Barn's last hockey game: an exhibition game between what was then the current team vs. Wings old timers. The younger team won 6–2, but fans pulled for the older ones, giving Howe and Lindsay standing ovations again and again. It was, appropriately enough, Howe who scored the game's, and Olympia's, last goal.

"It was a fitting way to see the Old Barn close," Howe said.

Olympia was demolished in September 1987, almost 50 years to the day it opened. The Michigan National Guard took over the site, using it for an armory.

When the old-timers gathered that afternoon in May 1986, they had to pick their way through debris in the darkness of the abandoned building. There had been a fire at the old concession counter near the Hooker Street doors, causing the ceiling to fall in. Broken plaster, peeled paint, rusty pipes, and old wiring littered the ground.

Some of the players found where their old locker room used to be. Pronovost pointed to a spot where defensemen dressed. "That was our spot," he said.

Olympia was the franchise's spot for more than five decades, carrying the club from its beginnings to seven Stanley Cups, five of them clinched on home ice.

* * *

Soon after Mike Ilitch bought the Wings in 1982, he came to a realization. "I thought as soon as I stepped in, things were going to turn around," he said six years later. "Most of your life you think you have a little bit of a touch, and you notice results right away because you get personally involved. Then I was exposed to realism—I couldn't skate and I couldn't shoot."

What he could do, then son-in-law Jim Lites said, "was change the environment."

Joe Louis Arena was completed in 1979 at a cost of $57 million, heralded as the exciting new home for the Red Wings and built as a counter to then-owner Bruce Norris' threat to move the team to Pontiac.

Named after boxer Joe Louis, who grew up in Detroit, the Wings played their first game there on December 27, 1979, losing 3–2 to the St. Louis Blues.

When Ilitch bought the Wings, Norris' Olympia Stadium Corporation still managed the Joe. It was too confusing to have a new tenant working under an old landlord, so in December 1982, six months after he bought the team, Ilitch bought the operating contract and renamed the Corporation, Olympias Arenas (it changed to Olympia Entertainment in 1996).

Ilitch set about updating the building. The locker rooms were the first to be renovated. Next, the concourse was transformed from what was described as a concrete bunker into a colorful ring of concession and novelty stands. Ilitch spent $1 million on replacing fluorescent bulbs with mercury vapor lights, and cinder block walls were transformed into billboards for products including Coca-Cola, Budweiser, and Kowalski sausages. Rosanne Kozerski Brown, a company vice president, said that "when Mike took over, he brought in the resources of Little Caesars. They have a staff of designers and architects who are tops in the business. Before, the walls were a perfect place for graffiti. Now, graffiti is down to nothing. Give anyone a nice environment, and they don't destroy it."

Ever the savvy businessman, one of Ilitch's innovations was the "Bud Hut"—a self-serve concession where patrons paid for a cup and drew their own beer from a tap. "I get frustrated when I know there's a lot of people who won't get out of their seats to get concessions because it's so hard to serve them," Ilitch said.

The Joe was an improvement over Olympia as far as offering nearby parking structures and being easily accessible from freeways. Its first major event was the 1980 NHL All-Star Game: a then-NHL record 21,002 fans showed up to watch Gordie Howe play during what was his farewell season. When his name was announced, fans gave Howe a deafening standing ovation.

It was 1984 before the arena hosted its first playoff games, and then it was for both the Wings and the Pistons, who played Game 5 of first-round series against the New York Knicks there because of a scheduling conflict at the Pontiac Silverdome.

As the Wings improved, so did the atmosphere at the Joe. Built at a steep incline, it felt like fans were right on top of the ice. "It was a great place to play," Kirk Maltby said in 2023. "You could really feel the fans, whether they were cheering your or booing you, it felt like they were right next to you. It was definitely something you noticed."

The Wings won the Stanley Cup at the Joe on June 7, 1997, and won another Cup on home ice in 2002. By then the building already seemed dated, lacking the mid-level suites and luxury suites that bedazzled newer arenas. There was talk of expanding and renovating into neighboring Cobo Hall, but by 2012, plans were announced for a new arena.

On April 9, 2017, the Wings played their final game at the Joe (it was the same year their 25-season playoff streak ended). Steve Yzerman, who had left in 2010 to become general manager of the Tampa Bay Lightning, dropped the last ceremonial puck. Dani Probert, wife of Bob Probert, the bruising icon of the team in the '80s, scattered some of Probert's ashes in the home penalty box. Bruce Martyn, the former broadcaster, also attended.

The arena was gutted with select memorabilia saved. Demolition began in 2019, 40 years after it had opened.

* * *

When the Wings opened their third home, Little Caesars Arena, in 2017, the original Olympia Stadium marquee letters were displayed in recognition of where it all began.

LCA set a standard for arenas, built at a cost of $863 million (Joe Louis Arena, 40 years earlier, had cost $57 million) and situated along historic Woodward Avenue not far from the Fox Theatre, Comerica Park, and Ford Field. The new home of the Wings—and NBA's Detroit Pistons—featured the best of everything. Taking inspiration both from the Joe and from the Bell Centre in Montreal, the stands were constructed at an incline that would make it feel like fans were right on top of the players.

That intimacy was offset by a spacious concourse that featured a handful of restaurants and more food stalls. A transparent roof on the southwest side added atmosphere. So did murals of Joe Louis, Isiah Thomas, and Aretha Franklin. Manhole covers along the concourse commemorate players past and present.

Statues of Gordie Howe and Ted Lindsay on the concourse became unofficial gathering places. Photo opportunities abounded, including posing on a make-believe bench featuring four of the captains in team history: Steve Yzerman, Nicklas Lidström, Henrik Zetterberg, and Dylan Larkin.

On the third floor, facing Woodward Avenue, the men charged with running the Wings, a group that as of April 2019 was spearheaded by Yzerman, have their offices. (Management at the Joe was stuck in windowless rooms in the bowels of the arena.)

The mega-structure, designed by HOK architects, doesn't overwhelm its surroundings because of a sleight-of-hand effect. The playing surface of the arena sits about 40 feet below street level, lowering the arena's profile. The building also houses a below-ground practice facility attached to a locker-room area that spans some 20,000 square feet and includes a kitchen with a chef.

The Wings inaugurated their new home with a game against the Minnesota Wild on October 5, 2017, celebrating with a victory for the franchise.